If you're thinking of sending your child to college one day, you have a lot of decisions to make. Decisions regarding how to save money for college, which colleges may be a good fit, whether an alternative to a four-year college may be a better option, plus seeking financial aid, scholarships, and grants. *Paying For College For Dummies* can help you make the most of your money and guide you through the decisions of choosing which post–high school path is right for your child.

Saving and Schooling Options: Tips to Guide You through College Decisions

- » The prices at four-year colleges and universities, especially private ones, are daunting to most people. So, you should absolutely, positively look around, inspect, and compare to see what you're getting for all that money.

- » Increasing numbers of alternatives to traditional four-year colleges offer students lower-cost and shorter-term programs. Take some time to find out and consider what's out there and compare those options to the best traditional colleges you're considering.

- » Raising children is a long-term and costly endeavor. So, get your personal finances in top shape to run this financial marathon. You should also understand how colleges set prices based upon your financial situation, as that may impact how you save and invest your money.

- » As your kids grow up, be sure to expose them to important money lessons, including helping them to make the connection between working and earning money.

- » A challenging and rewarding part of raising kids is helping them recognize and develop their talents and abilities. Be careful not to steer them in a particular way thinking that may make them more attractive to certain colleges. More often than not, such perceptions aren't correct. Teach your kids the value of hard work, integrity, and developing their strengths and interests.

- » There's no substitute for visiting and investigating colleges and other programs of interest. Set aside time with your teen to discuss a process for checking out schools and what factors — including the cost and expected benefits — will influence the final selection.

D0947514

- Where appropriate and cost-effective, enlist experts to help with evaluating and applying to colleges. Understand the strengths and limitations of school-based counselors and outside experts. Spending lots of money won't necessarily lead to better outcomes.

- Understand how colleges collect and evaluate your personal and financial information to decide how much to charge you.

- Four-year colleges are certainly one of the most popular options for high school graduates. But there are others including community colleges, trade schools, apprenticeships, boot camps, last-mile programs, and more. Visit schools, take tours, ask lots of questions, and do your homework on each.

- Generally speaking, parents will be better off regarding financial aid applications and college pricing if they save and invest in their own names (as opposed to their kid's) and take advantage of retirement savings plans.

- Financial aid forms can be intimidating and tedious to complete. Understand how to complete those forms accurately and to your best advantage.

- Colleges are the biggest purveyors of grants and scholarships — which are really a reduced price offered to those deemed in need of financial aid or displaying academic or some other merit (for example, sports). While some outside scholarships are significant, most are relatively small in amount and often reduce the amount of aid a given school will provide your family.

- Ideally, your teenager will gain acceptance to multiple schools, which enables comparing the value (price and quality) offered by each to one another. You should also realize that you may be able to improve upon the financial aid offered by a given college.

- Conduct more due diligence before making your final decision, which should include more campus visits.

- Federal and state tax codes include numerous tax breaks for college expenditures. Find out what's out there so you can take advantage of what you're eligible for.

- Getting through college in a timely fashion can greatly reduce your costs of attendance. Be sure you understand how to evaluate your likelihood of completing a given college program in four years.

- As your teenagers enter young adulthood, be sure you're sending them off with the financial skills and knowledge they can use and benefit from for the rest of their lives.

- Know how to best deal with student loans. In addition to keeping track of them, be sure you're aware of the myriad programs that help reduce your interest costs and repayment.

Praise for Eric Tyson

Eric Tyson is doing something important — namely, helping people at all income levels to take control of their financial futures. This book is a natural outgrowth of Tyson's vision that he has nurtured for years. Like Henry Ford, he wants to make something that was previously accessible only to the wealthy accessible to middle-income Americans."

> — James C. Collins, coauthor of the national bestsellers
> *Built to Last* and *Good to Great*

"*Personal Finance For Dummies* is the perfect book for people who feel guilty about inadequately managing their money but are intimidated by all of the publications out there. It's a painless way to learn how to take control."

> — Karen Tofte, producer, National Public Radio's *Sound Money*

"Eric Tyson . . . seems the perfect writer for a . . .*For Dummies* book. He doesn't tell you what to do or consider doing without explaining the why's and how's — and the booby traps to avoid — in plain English. . . . It will lead you through the thickets of your own finances as painlessly as I can imagine."

> — *Chicago Tribune*

"This book provides easy-to-understand personal financial information and advice for those without great wealth or knowledge in this area. Practitioners like Eric Tyson, who care about the well-being of middle-income people, are rare in today's society."

> — Joel Hyatt, founder of Hyatt Legal Services, one of the nation's
> largest general-practice personal legal service firms

"Worth getting. Scores of all-purpose money-management books reach bookstores every year, but only once every couple of years does a standout personal finance primer come along. *Personal Finance For Dummies,* by financial counselor and columnist Eric Tyson, provides detailed, action-oriented advice on everyday financial questions. . . . Tyson's style is readable and unintimidating."

> — Kristin Davis, *Kiplinger's Personal Finance* magazine

"This is a great book. It's understandable. Other financial books are too technical and this one really is different."

> — Business Radio Network

More Bestselling For Dummies Titles by Eric Tyson

Investing For Dummies®

A *Wall Street Journal* bestseller, this book walks you through how to build wealth in stocks, real estate, and small business as well as other investments. Also check out the recently released *Investing in Your 20s and 30s For Dummies*.

Mutual Funds For Dummies®

This best-selling guide is now updated to include current fund and portfolio recommendations. Using the practical tips and techniques, you'll design a mutual fund investment plan suited to your income, lifestyle, and risk preferences.

Personal Finance in Your 20s For Dummies®

This hands-on, friendly guide provides you with the targeted financial advice you need to establish firm financial footing in your 20s and to secure your finances for years to come. When it comes to protecting your financial future, starting sooner rather than later is the smartest thing you can do.

Home Buying For Dummies®

America's #1 real-estate book includes coverage of online resources in addition to sound financial advice from Eric Tyson and frontline real-estate insights from industry veteran Ray Brown. Also available from America's best-selling real-estate team of Tyson and Brown — *House Selling For Dummies* and *Mortgages For Dummies* (with Robert Griswold).

Real Estate Investing For Dummies®

Real estate is a proven wealth-building investment, but many people don't know how to go about making and managing rental property investments. Real-estate and property management expert Robert Griswold and Eric Tyson cover the gamut of property investment options, strategies, and techniques.

Small Business For Dummies®

This practical, no-nonsense guide gives expert advice on everything from generating ideas and locating start-up money to hiring the right people, balancing the books, and planning for growth. You'll get plenty of help ramping up your management skills, developing a marketing strategy, keeping your customers loyal, and much more. And, find out to use the latest technology to improve your business's performance at every level. Also available from co-authors Eric Tyson and Jim Schell, *Small Business Taxes For Dummies*.

Paying
For College

by Eric Tyson, MBA

Paying For College For Dummies®

Published by: **John Wiley & Sons, Inc.**, 111 River Street, Hoboken, NJ 07030-5774, www.wiley.com

Copyright © 2020 by John Wiley & Sons, Inc., Hoboken, New Jersey

Published simultaneously in Canada

For general information on our other products and services, please contact our Customer Care Department within the U.S. at 877-762-2974, outside the U.S. at 317-572-3993, or fax 317-572-4002. For technical support, please visit https://hub.wiley.com/community/support/dummies.

Wiley publishes in a variety of print and electronic formats and by print-on-demand. Some material included with standard print versions of this book may not be included in e-books or in print-on-demand. If this book refers to media such as a CD or DVD that is not included in the version you purchased, you may download this material at http://booksupport.wiley.com. For more information about Wiley products, visit www.wiley.com.

Library of Congress Control Number: 2020904217

ISBN 978-1-119-65147-5; 978-1-119-65148-2 (ebk); 978-1-119-65149-9 (ebk)

Manufactured in the United States of America

V10018202_032320

Contents at a Glance

Table of Contents

CHAPTER 8: **The Best College Alternatives to Consider** 115

PART 4: GETTING THE BEST EDUCATION AT THE BEST PRICE 127

CHAPTER 9: **Financial Steps You Should Take While Your Kids Grow Up** 129

CHAPTER 10: **Filling Out the Common Financial Aid Forms to Your Best Advantage**. 143

Introduction

Welcome to *Paying for College For Dummies!* I know this may be a stressful and challenging topic. But, not to worry! You've come to the right place — this book will help you to lower your anxiety, increase your knowledge, and take control of the process.

In this book, I emphasize these important topics:

>> Making the most of your finances and developing your children's potential without breaking the bank.

>> Getting the best education at an affordable price. Spending more doesn't equate to getting a better education or better employment prospects. You should look for value — meaning seek out service providers that deliver quality at a reasonable, or in some cases even an attractive, price.

>> Understanding proven alternatives to traditional and costly college education. Increasingly, high-cost, four-year colleges are seeing their enrollment squeezed while far lower cost and faster alternatives to college are seeing enrollment growth.

>> Navigating and making best use of financial aid. After baring your financial soul to colleges, they will tell you how much they will charge you. They aren't actually giving you money when they award aid so much as they charge different customers widely differing prices based upon the college's assessment of your ability to pay. I help steer you through understanding the various ways to get better pricing as well as filling out all those forms.

About This Book

College price increases, for too many years and decades, outstripped the general rate of inflation. While particular degrees from leading schools do still seem to provide a ticket to some well-paying jobs and careers, now more than ever families are questioning the value of a college degree. A recent Wall Street Journal poll found that 47 percent of Americans no longer believe that having a college degree will lead to a good job and higher lifetime earnings. Among Millennials, only 39 percent continue to believe in college.

Paying For College For Dummies helps you to sort through the range of post-high school options, including attending a traditional four-year college. If you think buying a car or a home was complicated, just wait until you begin to understand the intricacies of how colleges set their prices. Colleges charge each of their customers different prices based upon their own (hidden) analysis of your supposed ability to pay. I will explain how various colleges determine what to charge you and how you can best complete college financial aid forms and position your finances to receive more favorable pricing.

As a former financial counselor, I have counseled thousands of clients on a variety of personal finance, investment, and spending decisions, including higher education and college. With four years at the "best" private colleges having broached $300,000, and the best public college educations costing well into the six figures, more and more people who aren't wealthy are questioning the value that such an experience will provide. And increasingly, folks are wanting to evaluate and consider the alternatives, which this unique guide will also help you to do.

Foolish Assumptions

Whenever I approach writing a book, I consider a particular audience for that book. Because of this, I must make some assumptions about who the readers are and what those readers are looking for. Here are a few assumptions I've made about you:

>> You want the best for your kids and would like to understand the pros and cons of different options before making an informed choice. (**Note:** While the vast majority of readers of this book are parents, I expect that some inquisitive teens are readers too — that's great! For simplicity, please accept my apologies for choosing to write as if parents are the readers so that sentences like the one before this aside aren't more complicated.) Because money doesn't grow on trees and you're not super-wealthy, you want value for your money and need to contain costs.

>> You have some understanding about the reputation of particular colleges but don't know how that translates into post-graduation job and career prospects.

>> You've heard some rumblings from young adults and perhaps even your own teenagers about alternatives to college, and you'd like to know more about those options and whether they may make sense for your offspring. It's not unusual these days for parents and teenagers to have different aspirations

and expectations. I hope and expect my book to get both sides to see the other's point of view and bring you closer to a happy agreement or compromise!

>> You'd like a more detailed understanding of how college financial aid, scholarships, student loans, and such works.

If any of these descriptions hit home for you, you've come to the right place.

Icons Used in This Book

Throughout this book, you can find friendly and useful icons to enhance your reading pleasure and to note specific types of information. Here's what each icon means:

TIP

This icon points out something that can save you time, headaches, money, or all of the above!

WARNING

Here we're trying to direct you away from blunders and boo-boos that others have made when making college and other post–high school decisions.

TECHNICAL STUFF

Here we point out potentially interesting but nonessential stuff.

TRUE STORY

Look for this icon to find real-life examples of college decisions to help exemplify a point.

INVESTIGATE

We use this icon to highlight when you should look into something on your own or with the assistance of a local professional.

REMEMBER

This icon flags concepts and facts that we want to ensure you remember as you make your college and other post–high school decisions.

Beyond This Book

In addition to the content of this book, you can access some related material online. Head to www.dummies.com and type in "Paying For College For Dummies Cheat Sheet" in the search box to find additional tips.

Where to Go from Here

If you have the time and desire, we encourage you to read this book in its entirety. It provides you with a detailed picture of how to best make post–high school decisions to maximize your returns while minimizing your costs. But you may also choose to read selected portions. That's one of the great things (among many) about *For Dummies* books. You can readily pick and choose the information you read based on your individual needs. Just scan the table of contents or index for the topics that interest you the most.

1

Understanding Paying for College

Check out college prices, the job market, and the value of higher education.

Find out how to save and invest for college and other goals while your kids are young.

Get your kids on board with making a connection between working and earning money.

IN THIS CHAPTER

» Scrutinizing the steep sticker price of many traditional colleges

» Understanding the employment reality upon graduation

» Getting the best pricing by understanding how colleges see your situation

» Seeing the disconnect between college academics and what some employers are seeking in graduates

» Comprehending how the college landscape is changing and evolving

Chapter **1**

Confronting High College Prices and the Modern Job Market

Planning ahead. When you have kids, even if you've been a live-in-the-moment, what's-up-today kind of person, it's hard and could be costly not to do some thinking about your children's future.

Think ahead to an important and often bittersweet milestone - high school graduation. Many parents look back at the prior 18 or so years and wonder where all that time went and how fast it flew by. When your child graduates from high school, you may breathe a sigh of relief and feel a sense of accomplishment. But, what will Johnny do next and how will he (along with you) make that difficult decision?

Most parents envision their kids heading off post-high school graduation to a hopefully "good" college for four years. If that's what you did and had a mostly positive experience, of course it's natural to want the same for your own kids. Maybe you didn't attend college and have felt that you missed out on particular career options or some needed time to grow up and explore what's out there.

You may have concerns about the path you did or didn't choose or have spoken with others who do. A recent Wall Street Journal poll found that 47 percent of Americans no longer believe that having a college degree will lead to a good job and higher lifetime earnings. Among Millennials, only 39 percent continue to believe in college. And for some good reasons — high and rapidly escalating costs, increasingly specialized jobs which most college educations don't prepare you for and the political climate on many college campuses that may not match what you want for your children's formative young adult years.

REMEMBER

My goal throughout this book is to present you with the facts and the pros and cons of alternatives. While I understand that many people reading this book will end up at a traditional four-year college, I know from the statistics that increasing numbers of families are choosing alternatives to that route. Despite the fact that I attended a four-year college, I truly want what is best for your kids. Your children are unique and the post-high school options best suited to them should reflect what fits them. Choosing a particular college because it's on someone else's "best" list won't be a good idea if it's not what's best for your child's situation.

In this chapter, we confront the high prices at many colleges and universities, look ahead to the employment reality students face upon graduation and discuss how the college and post high school landscape is evolving to address these important trends.

Confronting the High Prices of Higher Education

Okay, let's get the bad news out of the way. Yes, college is expensive. Consider the supposedly "best" private colleges which on most lists includes colleges and universities like Brown University, Carnegie Mellon University, Colgate University, Columbia University, Cornell University, Dartmouth College, Duke University, Georgetown University, Harvard University, Johns Hopkins University, Lehigh University, MIT, Northwestern University, Princeton University, Rice University, Stanford University, Tufts University, University of Chicago, University of Notre Dame, University of Pennsylvania, University of Southern California, Vanderbilt University, Washington & Lee University, Washington University, and Yale University.

Tuition, room, board, books, and other fees will run you $250K to $300K or more over four years! Stop and think about that high cost for a moment.

If that's not daunting enough, getting into these schools is ridiculously difficult and competitive to do. High school students are packing their schedules with Advanced Placement and honors courses, burning the midnight oil to get that elevated grade point average, playing sports, running for student government, playing in the band, volunteering regularly and jumping through other hoops.

In the hopes of making their future college applications tempt admissions officers, students must also often seek other ways to stand out and be different. Being from a small state, rural or non-wealthy area certainly helps. Living in a non-wealthy area and attending a not so great public school may help your case also.

While quite a bit less expensive if you qualify for in state tuition rates, public colleges are getting more and more expensive and can easily set you back for well over $100K for a four-year education. If you attend a top public college as an out of state resident, expect to pay upwards of $200K for the four years — about the same freight as those going to a typical private college.

Looking back over the past 50 years, after adjusting for increases in the general cost of living, tuition and fees at four-year colleges have jumped in real terms (that is, above and beyond the general rise in the cost of living) by more than 240 percent at private colleges and 340 percent at public colleges according to data from the National Center for Education Statistics. This trend obviously can't continue because few families can afford to pay the already big dollar amounts today.

A brief historical overview of colleges and who completes it

High-priced four-year college degrees are a relatively recent and not entirely attractive phenomenon. After World War II, with the GI bill (designed to help servicemen returning to society) and massive investments at the state public university systems and federal levels with the availability and promotion of Pell Grants and student loans, adults with college degrees mushroomed from just 5 percent of the adult population to more than 30 percent.

The most recent figures show that about 35 percent of U.S. adults age 25 and older have completed a four-year college degree. 48 percent of 25 to 34-year olds have a college degree. About 13 percent of all adults have completed an advanced degree — that is a master's degree, professional degree, or a doctorate degree.

That said, here's another and truly shocking and important to know statistic: only about 55 percent of those who enroll in a four-year college degree program actually complete it. Think about that for a moment — this means that a whopping 45 percent of those who head down that costly road end up with no credential and therefore have probably wasted their time and money. In case you're wondering, community college is no better in that regard (although it's a lot cheaper) as 81 percent of students who start at community college believe they will eventually earn a bachelor's degree but in fact only 12 percent do.

INVESTIGATE

These college graduation percentages highlight an important topic. Whenever you're examining specific colleges, you should always evaluate the school's graduation rate. Higher percentages are better, of course. If a college you're considering has a relatively lower graduation percentage, inquire and investigate why. Is it because of a lack of on-campus housing and nearby affordable rentals? Is it because the college accepts students who are having trouble staying on track? Is it because students are uninspired by the overall education and experience they are having once on campus for a period of time?

According to a Chronicle of Higher Education analysis of U.S. Department of Education graduation rate data, overall private nonprofit colleges have a six-year graduation rate of 66 percent, public colleges graduated about 59 percent while for-profit colleges lagged far behind, graduating just 21 percent of their first-time, full-time students within six years. As another point of reference, Table 1-1 gives a short list of the ten private (non-profit), public, and for-profit colleges with the highest six-year graduation rates.

TABLE 1-1

Colleges with best six-year graduation rates

Four-year private colleges		
1.	Yale U.	97.4%
2.	Princeton U.	97.3%
3.	Harvard U.	96.4%
4.	Dartmouth College	95.9%
5.	Harvey Mudd College	95.9%
6.	U. of Pennsylvania	95.7%
7.	Duke U.	95.4%
8.	Bowdoin College	95.2%
9.	U. of Notre Dame	95.2%
10.	Amherst College	95.2%

Four-year public colleges		
1.	U. of Virginia	94.6%
2.	College of William & Mary	92.1%
3.	U. of Michigan at Ann Arbor	91.6%
4.	U. of California at Berkeley	91.1%
5.	U. of North Carolina at Chapel Hill	90.9%
6.	U. of California at Los Angeles	90.9%
7.	U. of Florida	88.0%
8.	U. of Wisconsin at Madison	87.2%
9.	College of New Jersey	86.6%
10.	U. of Maryland at College Park	85.4%
Four-year for-profit colleges		
1.	Los Angeles Film School	78.6%
2.	Monroe College (N.Y.)	73.6%
3.	Pima Medical Institute at Tucson	73.0%
4.	Santa Fe U. of Art and Design	69.6%
5.	New York Film Academy at Los Angeles	69.4%
6.	SAE Expression College	68.9%
7.	Bob Jones U.	65.6%
8.	School of Visual Arts	64.1%
9.	International Business College at Fort Wayne (Ind.)	59.3%
10.	Neumont College of Computer Science	58.8%

Now, I must point out here something that may seem obvious. These high graduation rates, especially at the traditional non-profit colleges, shouldn't be viewed in isolation and don't, in and of themselves, necessarily tell you much about the educational quality of the school. Or stated another way, the schools on these lists don't deserve all the credit for these high graduation rates! After all, these schools (at least the non-profit ones) are some of the most selective in the country so there's a so-called selection bias going on here. These colleges only take well-prepared, high achieving students and the vast majority of these students come from families that highly value this type of educational experience. And, because these more selective colleges have so many applicants, they generally have plenty of more affluent families that can afford the high-ticket price and can afford to keep their kids in college for the duration of the four years. So, of course these students are more likely to succeed at completing college and graduating in a timely fashion.

By contrast, colleges that have more open enrollment, that take more risks on less prepared students are naturally going to have a lower graduation rate. But that doesn't mean that some of those schools with less impressive graduation rates necessarily provide an inferior quality of education or an inability to graduate your child on time.

Don't college grads make more money?

There are plenty of studies and analyses that show that those who have more education generally enjoy lower rates of unemployment and higher employment income. The graphic in Figure 1-1 clearly shows that those with higher levels of education reap considerably higher wages from work and lower unemployment rates.

Unemployment rates and earnings by educational attainment, 2018

	Unemployment rate (%)	Median usual weekly earnings ($)
Doctoral degree	1.6	1,825
Professional degree	1.5	1,884
Master's degree	2.1	1,434
Bachelor's degree	2.2	1,198
Associate's degree	2.8	862
Some college, no degree	3.7	802
High school diploma	4.1	730
Less than a high school diploma	5.6	553
	Total: 3.2%	All workers: $932

FIGURE 1-1: What higher education means for earning higher wages and having lower unemployment.

Note: Data are for persons age 25 and over. Earnings are for full-time wage and salary workers.

Source: U.S. Bureau of Labor Statistics

There's no question that education is a good thing and can develop your brain, critical thinking skills, interpersonal skills, etc. What jumps out at me from the graphic is that it looks like there's value in completing high school, completing college if you're going to attend and possibly considering an advanced degree. But that doesn't mean that all education, or formal education, is worthwhile regardless of the cost. You should always consider the expected cost versus benefit or the return on the investment since attaining a college degree takes a good deal of time and money.

Another important point about Figure 1-1 — the "income premium" associated with college (compared with a high school degree) peaked in the year 2000 and declined about 10 percent over the next 15 years. College costs of course continued rising rapidly over this period further undermining the potential value of a college degree.

Parents and families should also be aware of the research report entitled, "Is College Still Worth It? The New Calculus of Falling Returns" by William R. Emmons, Ana H. Kent, and Lowell R. Ricketts, published by the Federal Reserve Bank of St. Louis Review, Fourth Quarter 2019. That report found:

"The college income premium is the extra income earned by a family whose head has a college degree over the income earned by an otherwise similar family whose head does not have a college degree. This premium remains positive but has declined for recent graduates. The college wealth premium (extra net worth) has declined more noticeably among all cohorts born after 1940. Among families whose head is White and born in the 1980s, the college wealth premium of a terminal four-year bachelor's degree is at a historic low; among families whose head is any other race and ethnicity born in that decade, the premium is statistically indistinguishable from zero. Among families whose head is of any race or ethnicity born in the 1980s and holding a postgraduate degree, the wealth premium is also indistinguishable from zero. Our results suggest that college and postgraduate education may be failing some recent graduates as a financial investment."

You can read this study at: https://files.stlouisfed.org/files/htdocs/publications/review/2019/10/15/is-college-still-worth-it-the-new-calculus-of-falling-returns.pdf.

SUCCESSFUL PEOPLE WHO NEVER GOT A COLLEGE DEGREE

You've surely heard of a number of "successful" people who accomplished significantly without a college degree. This would include folks like Michael Dell founder of Dell Computers, Steve Jobs founder of Apple, Bill Gates founder of Microsoft, John Mackey founder of Whole Foods Markets, Travis Kalanick founder of Uber, Larry Ellison founder of Oracle, performers Russell Simmons and Ellen DeGeneres, fashion designer Anna Wintour, and food guru Rachel Ray to name a few. These folks obviously are outliers in terms of their high level of professional success and associated financial earnings.

And there are plenty of lower profile people who have done quite well for themselves without a college degree including some plumbers, landscapers, dental hygienists, MRI technologists, commercial pilots, physical therapist assistants, respiratory therapists, air traffic controllers, transportation inspectors, diagnostic medical sonographers, electricians, construction managers, licensed practical nurses, web developers, elevator installers, radiation therapists, massage therapists, medical assistants, firemen and police officers. I chose to highlight some of these occupations because they are populated with relatively high numbers of people without a college degree.

Now, this is not in any way to suggest that the majority of people or your kids should bypass college! Each person's situation is unique and different. But the point is that there are many paths to career success and some of those paths include going to college whereas others do not.

Clearly, there's likely to be value in completing a college degree and getting a degree from a program with a good reputation and track record for graduates with that type of degree. Conversely, those who don't complete their degree or who get a degree from a program with a subpar or mediocre track record will probably get a poor return on their invested education dollars.

TIP

In Part 3 and especially in Chapter 8, I discuss the increasing numbers of shorter term and lower cost alternatives to traditional four-year colleges such as bootcamps, apprenticeships, trade schools, last mile programs, etc. The best of those programs have well-documented and impressive track records for the employment and compensation of their graduates.

Mushrooming student debt and its underlying causes

Why does college cost so darn much?

Don't plenty of schools pack a few hundred students into a lecture hall? That can't be too expensive, right?

Well, not so fast! Look at the course offerings at most schools and you will be surprised at how many courses they do offer and the fact that most don't have a large number of students enrolled. Also, only $0.21 out of every college tuition dollar is actually spent on teaching.

So where are colleges and universities spending their money? On administrators, the number of whom has grown twice as fast as the number of students, on facilities and athletics, and schools prioritizing research over teaching.

Colleges and universities have increased tuition prices at twice the rate of inflation while jacking up room, board, and student fees at four times the rate of overall inflation. Ouch!

Student debt is a major problem for many college students. The total amount of student loans outstanding in the U.S. has surpassed $1.5 trillion, making it the second largest form of debt outstanding by consumers, exceeded only by mortgage debt. And, more than one million student loan borrowers default annually on their loans and only 57 percent are current on their payments.

According to LendEDU's analysis of student loan debt figures at nearly 1,000 four-year private and public higher education institutions across the United States, the average graduating borrower received their diploma and left campus with $28,565 in student loan debt. That's a pretty hefty number.

According to the National Association of Colleges and Employers (NACE), the average starting annual salary for college graduates is about $50,000. These averages can be deceiving and not super relevant to individual situations. For example, some college grads complete their degree with more debt than the amount of their starting annual salary. Conversely, some have little to no debt and a salary a good deal higher than average.

Looking at How College Pricing Works

Now, time for some better news. Despite having dropped a bunch of respected college names on you earlier in this chapter that most people believe are "top" or "premier" colleges, I'm *not* suggesting that you need to attend a brand-name college and spend hundreds of thousands of dollars for your child to get a great higher education. You and they don't have to do that in order to find a fulfilling job or career with good compensation.

Even if you do aspire to a costly private college for your offspring, you should know that the average price that colleges typically charge and collect from each family equals about half of the stated full cost of attendance. So, for example, with private colleges charging around $60K per year the average family is actually paying about half of that or $30K. This happens due to "financial aid," which is another way of saying that a college or university will charge you and your family less the less able they deem you to pay the full retail price. High-income and affluent families generally pay full price or near full price unless their son or daughter qualifies for some sort of athletic or merit-type scholarship (price reduction). Some colleges, for example, Ivy League colleges, don't offer these types of scholarships and only offer so-called need-based scholarships (price reductions). Check out Chapter 11 for more on scholarships.

How colleges see you

Of course, first and foremost, colleges will evaluate your child's academic record including high school grades, standardized test scores, and so on. College applications also ask students to document what they've done outside of the classroom.

Parents, students, and even some well-intentioned high school personnel have all sorts of misconceptions and misperceptions as to how colleges evaluate applicants. Chapters 4 and 5 pull back the curtain on that process and provide you with the information you need to know.

College pricing and associated "financial aid" is even more poorly understood and for good reason. You will have to answer scores of questions about your financial and family situation and then submit that information in order for the college, through their own black box process, to tell you the price they will charge your family. See Chapter 6 for a thorough overview of that process.

Saving now and later

You should be in the habit of saving money towards your financial and personal goals. Helping to pay college or other higher education expenses is likely one of your goals.

You need to be careful, though, as to how and where you save your money if you plan to apply for financial aid, get favorable pricing, and want to minimize your income tax bills. Chapters 2 and 9 will help get you off on the right foot financially.

Somebody give me some money!

Financial aid is a misnomer. When your kids apply to college, you will need to complete various financial aid forms. The information you provide on those forms will be used by colleges to determine how much to charge you. I explain in Chapter 10 how to best complete that process.

Borrowing money and seeking grants and scholarships helps close the gap between what a family can afford and a college's full sticker price. Chapter 11 covers how those things work.

Employment Reality and What Students Say They Want from College

Increasingly, surveys show that students' biggest objective for their college education is not surprisingly for their job, career and income prospects. And for good reason — a four-year college degree is time consuming and costly and parents and students rightfully want to see a return on that huge investment.

REMEMBER

Unfortunately, many existing degree programs are not well aligned to graduate's first jobs and only 16 percent of students believe college is preparing them for their first jobs. I've known plenty of students who end up at a particular college because they or their parents thought the name and image it carried was good. I can't emphasize enough and it's a point which will recur throughout this book that you should take the time and effort to explore what it is you're actually signing up for at a given school that on the surface seems appealing.

With regards to college not actually prepping students for their first jobs, in his book, "A New U: Faster + Cheaper Alternatives to College" (BenBella), Ryan Craig cites the former Computer Science chairperson at Yale (where both Craig and I graduated from) Roger Schank, as saying that the faculty in that department are mostly theoreticians who don't now do programming anymore and instead are interested in teaching about new ideas and their latest theories. Schank was hearing increasing numbers of complaints from Yale undergrads who were being snubbed in hiring by Google. Schank also cites how the head of Columbia University's economics department told him that calculus is required for the major simply to reduce the volume of students who want to work in finance and seek out the major.

> "Many faculty members resist the idea that teaching should be aligned to employment opportunities," says Craig.

He provides numerous examples of colleges failing to ever solicit input from employers as to what they should consider teaching undergraduates.

> "The implication — one that is absolutely in the mainstream of faculty thinking — is that updating curriculum to reflect current labor market needs may not be a worthwhile pursuit because such needs will change in five to ten years. Can you imagine similar thinking in any other sector of the economy?"

This is, of course, ridiculous. Even though colleges like my alma mater Yale charge big bucks to families for the educational services they are providing, they don't think enough of the students and their parents who are paying the bills as their customers. Hence, the disconnect about best preparing their graduates for the modern job market.

Career services is another area where colleges and universities too often fail to meet the employment imperative. I frequently hear this complaint from parents and college students alike including from top name schools. With increasing recruiting and hiring being done online, fewer employers are finding the need to recruit on campus and go through career services.

What students actually do in college

After running the gauntlet of various honors and advanced placement courses in high school and participating in after school activities and doing endless homework assignments nightly, some students find college to be dare I say a tad easier. This is generally true for students who graduated from a demanding high school that offered lots of Advanced Placement and other challenging college level courses. Many students find that they have more free time, in part because they don't actually spend much time in class in college compared with high school.

Numerous studies raise questions about the critical thinking skills of college graduates which isn't surprising given how most students spend their time in college and given what some schools and courses actually require of them. According to the Heritage Foundation, the average college student spends only about 2.8 hours per day on education-related activities. By contrast, college students are averaging 4.4 hours per day on leisure activities (e.g. playing video games, working out at the gym, perusing social media, etc.) which doesn't include shopping, grooming, personal care, housework, cooking and eating.

Of course, different students have different schedules. Those college students who must work a fair number of hours to afford their college education are particularly busy. So too are those who have a demanding major and courses (e.g. pre-meds, engineering majors), participate in time intensive extras like a varsity sport, performing arts, etc.

Hiring and jobs

In generations past, employers advertised job openings and applicants submitted paper-based resumes usually by mailing it (through the US Postal Service, that is). My how times have changed! Today, the hiring process is dramatically different as job openings are generally posted online which makes it easy for hundreds (or even thousands) of applicants to quickly and efficiently apply for a desired job. That creates a different type of sorting problem for employers which is why the vast majority of them utilize applicant tracking systems to screen resumes and manage the hiring process. To do well with those systems, job applicants should understand how to match desired keywords in their resume from the job description. It can also help to have a personal contact or recommendation at an employer an applicant desires to work for. Networking with alums of your college can help and that can be part of the "value" that is derived by graduating from a particular college.

According to CompTIA, an information technology industry association, the most significant technology skill gaps are in areas like artificial intelligence, automation, integration of apps, data and platforms, cloud infrastructure and apps, digital business transformation, cybersecurity, software or app development, and data management and data analytics.

Ryan Craig notes that increasing numbers of students who recognize the disconnect between impractical course offerings that don't connect to real world jobs are double majoring. They are doings so as a way of hedging their risks and hopefully increasing their future employment chances and options.

What does Craig see that employers are looking for? "Most experts agree that a combination of technical skills and soft skills is the sweet spot in the labor market. . .By soft or noncognitive skills, I'm referring to fundamental capabilities such as teamwork, communication, organization, creativity, adaptability, and punctuality. In a LinkedIn study of hiring managers, 59 percent said soft skills were difficult to find and this skill gap was limiting their productivity."

So, what are employers doing about this unhappiness? Several things according to Craig:

>> Refraining at times from hiring. Higher skill jobs may go unfilled.

>> Degree inflation. Requiring master's degrees when a bachelors would do before or requiring a college degree when only a high school diploma was previously required.

>> Experience inflation. Requiring more work experience.

>> Jettisoning degree requirements. Some employers (e.g. Google, IBM) have removed degree requirements from some entry level positions or evaluate candidates regardless of whether they have particular degrees. Some employers are instead looking for micro-credentials from providers like Credly or e-Portfolios from Portfolium.

TIP

As you and your teenager evaluate colleges (and other post-high school options), it's well worth keeping in mind the total package of what employers are looking for. Remember the soft skills that employers say they are looking for — teamwork, communication, organization, creativity, adaptability, and punctuality, and so on. Consider how well potential colleges and other programs hone those attributes in your son or daughter.

Looking at How the Higher Education Landscape is Changing

Those who have spent time on college campuses either as students or as a place of employment know that they are places where change is generally slow to happen. A good part of this is because unlike companies operating in the private sector, colleges are insulated from many (but by no means all) the forces of competition.

Change is happening and will continue and the good news for you the college consumer is that these changes should provide more and better choices. And by better I mean those that don't cost so darn much and take so darn much time!

In this section, I highlight changes that are happening now and likely to continue in the years ahead.

College enrollment is declining

In fact, college enrollment has now declined for eight straight years and has dropped nearly 10 percent. This has pressured some of less-selective colleges financially and actually led to some closing their doors (see next section).

Beyond the most highly selective colleges, increasingly, colleges are having to compete more for students and that's a good trend for you. It's leading to pressure on college pricing and better overall pricing at some colleges.

Of course, enrollment isn't down at all schools and certainly isn't at the most selective schools out there. Some of those schools, which have seen greatly increased numbers of applications over the years and decades, especially with increases in U.S. population as well as more overseas applicants, have expanded their enrollment a bit. Yale recently added two new residential colleges, which enabled the college to boost undergraduate enrollment from 5,400 to 6,200. Princeton increased their enrollment from 4,700 to 5,700. In recent years, a number of other leading colleges including Babson College and Johns Hopkins University have similarly expanded their enrollment.

Some colleges are failing and closing

Unless it's a school near you or that you have some personal connection with, you likely haven't noticed the significant increase in colleges closing their doors and colleges cutting their prices.

Colleges are competing for a shrinking pool of students. There are more spots available on college campuses than there are students available and willing to pay the high price of attendance. Thus, some schools are struggling financially, and some are going under and closing their operations and campuses. The following table lists private non-profit colleges that have closed just in the past several years.

Private non-profit colleges that have closed just since 2016:

College Name	Location	Prior Enrollment
Atlantic Union College	Lancaster, MA	500
Burlington College	Burlington, VT	245
College of New Rochelle	New Rochelle, NY	2900
Concordia College (Alabama)	Selma, AL	600
Crossroads College	Rochester, MN	185
Dowling College	Oakdale, NY	6750
Grace University	Omaha, NE	480
Marylhurst University	Marylhurst, OR	1900
Green Mountain College	Poultney, VT	775
Marygrove College	Detroit, MI	1850
Memphis College of Art	Memphis, TN	380
Morthland College	West Frankfort, IL	400
Mount Ida College	Newton, MA	1500
Newbury College	Brookline, MA	1280
Oregon College of Art and Craft	Portland, OR	140
St. Catharine College (Kentucky)	Springfield, KY	750
Saint Joseph's College (Indiana)	Rensselaer, IN	1100
St. Gregory's University	Shawnee, OK	690
Southern Vermont College	Bennington, VT	360
Trinity Lutheran College	Everett, WA	300

INVESTIGATE

Of course, you wouldn't want your child to choose a college only to see that school shutter especially while your kid is in attendance. So, you should investigate the financial health of colleges you're considering. Historically, this was difficult and time consuming to do. But, no longer thanks to Forbes. You can find their most recent "College Financial Health Grades" at

https://www.forbes.com/sites/cartercoudriet/2019/11/27/how-fit-is-your-school-the-methodology-behind-forbes-2019-college-financial-health-grades/#2532733261c4

Colleges are under pressure to contain their prices

Another trend that has picked up steam in recent years are colleges cutting their advertised prices. This may sound contradictory to the long-term fast rising prices I covered earlier in the chapter. What's happening here is after so many years of raising prices much faster than the overall rate of inflation and many of their peers, some private colleges found that they weren't even being considered by some families that were suffering sticker price shock and set limits on the price of schools they would consider.

As I explain in detail in Part 4, what matters is the net price that a school charges your child — that is the list price less any scholarships or grants (discounts) they may offer to your family. Colleges that have decided to do overall one-time reductions in their prices also reduce the amount of grants that they offer so that net, the school is still effectively collecting the same amount of money annually. Doing these resets helps these schools get their pricing back down to a more reasonable level.

Lower cost and faster alternatives to colleges are growing

Trade schools and apprenticeship programs are hardly new. But coding boot camps started in 2012 and will have 29K graduates in 2019. These programs originated because entry level software developer jobs were going unfilled due to the inadequate training that college graduates were receiving. These were the first so-called "last mile training programs" according to industry observer and venture capitalist Ryan Craig. Now these programs encompass a wide range of IT related disciplines and other fields with a technology component.

The early coding boot camps were tuition-based — meaning that the enrolled students paid for the training they got. The coding boot camps were quickly able to show the hiring statistics for their graduates and began to shift over to income-share programs whereby their students agree to pay a modest percentage of their future income for a set period of time instead of having to pay up-front for the training. Most but not all coding camps use this income-share approach which shows an alignment of interests of the school and the students.

Craig recounts speaking before hundreds of college administrators and asking those in attendance to raise their hand if they provided any training on the widely used Salesforce platform and not a single hand went up. "There is the myth of the digital native. College administrators seem to believe that since their students know how to use an iPhone, Netflix and computers they are digitally competent and savvy," says Craig. But of course that doesn't mean they have the required technological training for entry level jobs which Craig points out in most companies is on a SaaS (software as a service) platform.

According to the website Alternatives To College, which Craig was instrumental in founding (https://www.alternativestocollege.com/), at last check the site lists more than 420 alternatives to college, nearly 20K open jobs not requiring a college degree, and over 800K open jobs requiring some type of certification.

REMEMBER

Programs that provide an employment path for those who don't go to college are on the rise so that also means that more employers are hiring people without a college degree.

Bottom line is good for you, the college and higher education consumer

Competition and increased choices are generally a good thing for you the consumer. That's what has produced amazing technological products like smartphones, powerful personal computers, safer and more fuel-efficient cars, fast casual restaurants of a mind-boggling variety, ultra-safe jet airplanes, and so forth.

Thanks to the increasing numbers of alternatives to college that are doing a good job meeting their customers' needs, colleges are under far more pressure now to contain their costs and better meet the needs of their students. Some of the worst and most inefficient colleges are shuttering their doors.

It is precisely because colleges weren't doing enough to meet their customers' needs — by providing cost effective education that met the needs to what employers and students wanted — that these college alternatives are multiplying and expanding. And the better colleges that are open to change and what their customers want are improving what they offer and trying to contain their costs. That's the beauty of competition. Enjoy it and reap the rewards from it!

Chapter **2**

Financial Planning Steps When Your Kids are Young

Life changes are often a wake-up call as to the value and importance of making the most of your money and money decisions. Generally speaking, the sooner you make and implement a sound financial plan when you have kids, the better off you will be. The more years your plan has to work on your behalf, the better your future financial position should be.

In the likely event that your children will apply to and possibly attend college, it is imperative that you plan ahead so 'you can be ready for those upcoming costs. *Note:* If your kids end up selecting an alternative to college (see Chapter 8 for options) that is likely less costly, the good news is that you may have some extra money you weren't counting on!

Kids Are Costly! Getting Your Finances in Order

I have mixed feelings about citing the costs of raising a child for 18 years and getting them to adulthood. I don't want to come across as a Scrooge and detract from what should be one of the joys of your life. But I don't want you to be financially clueless and end up in trouble years down the road because you didn't fully understand the financial stresses and strains kids can cause for many household budgets.

I don't think it's helpful to examine the total estimated costs of raising a child from birth to high school graduation as a six-figure lump sum. Examining your monthly spending and being sure that you're able to save regularly to meet your personal and financial goals are what should matter. And that's the subject matter for the rest of this section.

Building the pillars of personal finance

While there are many tasks and strategies to make the most of your money, there are basically three important pillars of sound personal financial management. They are

» **Spend less than you earn.** Put another way, this is the same as saying save money regularly. Saving is especially challenging when you're younger and' earning a lower wage from work and may have student loans of your own to pay back. Adding children and housing expenses to the equation as you get older doesn't make it any easier. The amount of your gross (pretax) employment income that you "should" be saving depends upon your goals. Saving 10 percent is a good starting point, but you may need to save more than that to hit your goals (see the next section). And plenty of folks who aren't saving at a rate to accomplish their goals either need to revise their goals and/or review their spending and find a way to reduce that.

» **Invest wisely.** When you save money, you should put it to good use. Investments that provide higher potential rates of long-term return such as stocks, real estate, and small business ownership also tend to carry more short-term risk compared with less volatile investments like a savings account or bonds with high credit ratings. Rest assured — I give you some specific suggestions for the best places to consider investing money earmarked for your kid's higher educational expenses (check out Chapter 9).

>> **Secure insurance coverage to protect against potentially catastrophic losses.** There are several compelling reasons to carry insurance coverage. You need insurance coverage to protect your assets, such as your home and personal property. You also buy insurance to protect your income, for example, disability insurance and possibly life insurance if you have dependents. Finally, you carry insurance to protect against potential liability, which can arise from an auto accident or accident on your property.

Developing and hitting savings goals

From a planning perspective, one of the most important things you can do is to spend some time and energy contemplating what your personal and financial goals are. Common financial goals include saving for a home purchase, retiring or scaling back on work, or launching your own small business.

Most people want to be able to scale back on or cease work for pay completely as they get older. There are numerous ways to crunch some numbers to see how much you should be saving monthly to hit a particular goal. Among web-based calculators that I like for this purpose can be found at:

>> **Schwab's website:** `https://www.schwab.com/public/schwab/investing/retirement_and_planning/retirement_planning_tools`

>> **T. Rowe Price's website:** `https://www.troweprice.com/personal-investing/advice-and-planning/tools.html`

>> **Vanguard's website:** `https://investor.vanguard.com/investing/investment-calculator`

The challenge that numerous people face is that they may have champagne tastes and beer budgets. Or simply put, they have limited funds and more desires than the money to accomplish those wishes. That's why you need to prioritize your goals and possibly moderate them to have savings targets that you can succeed in meeting.

If you have children and they may apply to college, you should understand how colleges set their prices and use your financial situation to determine how much to charge you. We begin the process of delving into that important topic in the next section.

Finding Saving Methods Given How College Financial Aid Works

This chapter is about how to whip your finances into shape and make the most of your money when you have children. I would be remiss not to begin explaining the often confusing (and some say unfair) method by which many colleges charge different families differing prices based upon their analysis of each family's finances.

What financial aid penalizes

With all the things competing for money and attention, it's no surprise that the vast majority of families are able to save a relatively small/limited portion of what they earn. Where and how they direct those savings can have a big impact on financial aid and prices various colleges may charge them.

In a nutshell, the way colleges typically vary their pricing based upon each family's individual financial situation suggests that you're best off keeping money invested in your own name and ideally in tax-sheltered retirement accounts where possible. This is because the college financial aid process generally ignores money inside retirement accounts because it's earmarked for your retirement and generally not accessible before you turn age 59½ without penalty. And even past the age of 59½, you owe current federal and state income taxes on money withdrawn from your retirement accounts that has not previously been taxed.

REMEMBER

So, presuming that one of your longer-term goals is financial security and independence, and to have the financial wherewithal to be able to cut back on full-time work and perhaps not work at all, saving money in a tax-advantaged retirement account is somewhat of a necessity.

Now, because of the early withdrawal penalties, if you literally put all of your savings into retirement accounts, that will likely pose some problems. With regards to paying for college, if you're forced to withdraw money inside retirement accounts to help pay some of those costs, you will owe current federal and state income taxes and probably penalties.

WARNING

Saving and investing money in your children's names in nonretirement accounts is generally the worst thing you can do if you're hoping to get some discount (financial aid) from a college's full sticker price. If you plan to apply for financial aid and a reduced price from colleges, save money only in your name, not in the names of your children.

Equity in your home is more of a wild card as different schools count that differently. Some colleges ignore home equity, others generally count up to a certain amount of it, and some may even consider all or nearly all of it as an asset that you can supposedly use toward your children's college costs.

Another perk or benefit of contributing money to retirement savings accounts like 401(k)s and SEP-IRAs if you're self-employed is that doing so reduces your taxable employment income for the year. This immediately reduces your federal and state income taxes. Also, the money invested inside retirement accounts can compound and grow without taxation year after year.

Recognizing that financial aid rules change

In Parts 2 and 3, I delve into far more detail about how colleges determine what they will charge you and how "financial aid" works. If you think the federal income tax system is mysterious and complicated, unfortunately the various financial aid forms and process can be equally, if not more, cumbersome and confusing. Every year, families have to complete a federal income tax return. You will complete the financial aid forms when you have a kid about to enter college and before each additional year they are to be enrolled.

Both the federal income tax system and the financial aid system have something in common — the involvement of the federal government! With colleges and universities, though, you have institution-specific quirks and requirements to navigate.

TIP

With all the moving parts and parties involved in college financial aid forms and rules, like the federal income tax system, you can rest assured that the system will change in the years ahead. I raise this point because when you make decisions with your finances when your children are young, it may be 10, 15, or more years until they are of an age to apply to college. So, you do your best with the rules as they are laid out today, but you need to keep an eye on changes as you may benefit from making some tweaks and adjustments in the future. This is not to suggest that rules change frequently or change dramatically when they do change, but over a number of years, there will surely be changes.

Spending on Your Kids without Breaking the Bank

Temptations abound for spending on your children. In their infant and preschool years, there are plenty of toys, premium foods, and clothing vying for your dollars. As they enter their elementary school years, there will be all sorts of technology gadgets and devices along with myriad activities from music lessons to sports teams and instructions, academic and sports camps, and more. I've seen plenty of situations where families spend all the money they are making as quickly as they are making it!

It is imperative that you and your spouse communicate regularly about setting limits both in time and money for your kids' activities and that you also provide a unified front to your kids on the topic. I explain how and why in the next sections and also provide an example with youth sports activities, teams, and spending to close out this section.

Setting limits, guidelines, and goals with your spouse

It is easy for children's activities and spending on those activities to get out of control over time. When your kids are young, they have more time, and most parents naturally sign up their children for things that are of interest or seem to provide some redeeming value. Schedules can fill up quickly, and most people don't tally up the total amount they are spending on such activities.

TIP

In many households, the parent who is at home more or who has more direct involvement with the kids may be the one to make most or even all of these decisions. Even so, both parents should set aside time to discuss their thinking about what their young kids will participate in. While some spouses are on the same page, 'differences are fairly typical. Both parties should respectfully state their desires and concerns and really listen to the other person's perspective. Compromise is key.

Ultimately, these discussions should involve financial considerations and the family's overall money situation and desire for family time. The spending for children's activities needs to fit in with your household's budget and other spending and savings goals.

Setting limits with your kids

TIP

Once you and your spouse agree upon activities and spending limits, especially as your kids get older, you need to communicate clearly with your children as to what you are and are not willing to provide and allow. Present a unified front and never allow your kids to pit you and your spouse against each other as they may whine and complain to overturn your decisions.

As your kids get older, you will surely involve them more in discussing possible activity options before making final decisions. Just be careful about you and your spouse disagreeing in front of them as that can cause a variety of problems, especially if the two of you aren't on the same page.

Keeping Spending in Line: Using Youth Sports as an Example

One area where increasing numbers of parents are experiencing stress and pressure to spend more money is with youth sports. Besides the long-shot hope of your child growing into a future professional athlete, plenty of parents hope for a college athletic scholarship.

Everyone with children wants to see their kids succeed and do their best. But with that admirable desire, unfortunately, come behavior and attitudes that lead us astray. And, parents of youth athletes are sometimes led off course by the worst of self-serving paid coaches and instructors.

A lot can be learned from sports in relation to raising kids and making wise saving decisions. To protect your family and your wallet, the following sections highlight the key insights and tips I have to offer.

Focusing on the lifelong benefits of sports

For most kids, playing on youth sports teams teaches positive physical fitness and health habits that can last a lifetime. It's also a great way to make friends. Your kids don't have to be on an elite travel team to derive these perks!

Just as they can with academic disciplines like algebra or a foreign language, kids derive happiness mastering sports skills and individual and team accomplishments, says Dr. Edward Hallowell, author of *The Childhood Roots of Adult Happiness* (Ballantine).

Young athletes also discover that different people have different strengths and weaknesses and see the value in being a contributing member of a team — something larger than just themselves. And, many young athletes, having experienced the good feelings that come with exercise and fitness, continue to remain active into adulthood. As adults, former youth sports participants often find enjoyment following professional sports teams and leagues, especially for sports that they have enjoyed playing themselves.

Being mindful of expenses and set budgets

Spending on youth sports can quickly escalate out of control, especially if you have multiple children who play on travel sports teams throughout much, if not all, of the year. "One of the biggest reasons why the current generation of sport's parents find themselves in this situation is if the kid shows some talent at a young age, they could be asked to join an elite travel team. Parents of younger kids don't realize the costs involved," says Rick Wolff, long-time host of the *Sports Edge* radio show and author of numerous youth sports books, including *Coaching Kids For Dummies* (Wiley).

Wolff gave me an example of a seven-year-old youth hockey program that runs from Labor Day through the end of March and costs $3,000 to $5,000, which doesn't include the cost of driving (and even sometimes flying) kids everywhere and staying in hotels during out-of-state tournaments. In high cost of living areas, I've seen and heard about a travel sport not covering nearly as many months (for example, spring/summer baseball) costing $5,000!

TIP

Recreational sports programs don't cost anywhere near that much and often cost around $100 to $200 for a season. Travel sport program costs vary tremendously, so it pays to shop around. Some travel programs can cost just a few hundred dollars. Be sure to review your overall spending and goals with an eye towards how much you should be saving monthly to reach your goals and making adjustments to your spending as needed.

Being aware of the agendas of "professional" (also known as paid) coaches

The biggest driver behind the explosion of travel sports and teams as well as their escalating costs are paid/"professional" youth sports coaches. Often these coaches played the sport through high school and college and perhaps beyond. Wolff hears lots of complaints about travel team coaches. "Anyone can hang out a shingle and be a professional coach; there is no credentialing. Parents must perform due diligence . . . go discretely and talk to parents of kids on the team from last year. Ask if the coach is a yeller/screamer and how playing time is handled. On many travel teams, only the best players play. Make sure it's a good fit for your child. It's not that important that the coach played at a high level of the game. The coach may not be able to teach or have sensitivity to work with kids," says Wolff. I can emphatically say from my own experiences and from having spoken with many parents over the years that Wolff is correct.

No doubt, just as a tutor can help a child academically, hired sports instructors or coaches may be able to do the same with your kids and sports. But hired coaches have an agenda to push kids to train more and play a sport year-round. I saw this repeatedly with hired soccer coaches. Some of the coaches push kids to play year-round because that's what they grew up with, for example, in Europe. But one coach simply said to me that he's got to make money year-round off of soccer and can't exist simply with his earnings from coaching fall soccer teams.

Realizing good parents can make good coaches

"I do urge parents to do it yourself or be an assistant coach," says Wolff. Of course, other parents may be concerned about a parent coach favoring his own child(ren) on the team, and a parent coach needs to be clear with everyone, including his own kid(s), that everyone must abide by the same team rules and guidelines.

Involving parents to help with coaching also has a financial benefit — it can dramatically lower the cost of a travel sports program. Some money can be spent bringing in instructors from time to time to work with the team on particular skills.

Coaches who make their living from coaching may disparage parent coaches as being clueless or coaching for the wrong reasons (for example, to favor their own kids) and sometimes some of these criticisms have validity. But, often they do not.

Letting kids simply play — the value of pick-up games

Just a few decades ago, there weren't anywhere near as many travel sports programs as there are today. And, you know what? The best athletes were able to find their way. How did they do that? The answer can be found in reading Derek Jeter's life story in his book, co-written by Jack Curry, *The Life You Imagine: Life Lessons for Achieving Your Dreams* (Broadway Books). Jeter, the now retired all-star New York Yankees shortstop talks extensively about playing pick-up baseball with friends. Of course, he played on organized baseball teams, but he played other sports too (e.g. basketball) in addition to a lot of pick up baseball games with friends and neighbors.

Hall of Famer Cal Ripken Jr., co-author along with Rick Wolff of *Parenting Young Athletes the Ripken Way: Ensuring the Best Experience for Your Kids in Any Sport* (Gotham) also talks about the importance of letting kids experiment, which they can do without adult interference when playing pick-up games and playing different sports. Like Jeter, Ripken played multiple sports growing up and points to the complementary skills kids acquire playing different sports rather than just one, which can lead to other problems: injuries (and my next point).

Understanding the increased risk of overuse and serious injuries

Orthopedic doctors and physical therapists' offices are booming in business with young athletes who have overuse injuries from excessive training and playing the same sport year-round. In the worst cases, kids end up needing costly surgery to repair damage (for example, pitchers having surgery on their throwing arms) and having long-term recovery time along with extensive rehabilitation and costs.

While all sports come with risk of injuries, understand the specific risks and dangers you child's chosen sport has and what you can do to minimize those risks. The National Center for Catastrophic Injury Research at the University of North Carolina at Chapel Hill found, for example, that by far, cheerleading was statistically the most dangerous sport for girls due to the increasingly dangerous tosses and associated head and neck injuries and fatalities.

Discovering the facts about scholarships

Some parents believe that an accomplished youth athlete will have better college options and access to full athletic scholarships. The facts show otherwise.

"Most schools only give a handful of scholarships, and these get sliced and diced," says Wolff. He gave me an example of a nice, private Division I university in the northeast where with baseball, they might give two scholarships a year (the school costs $50,000 per year). The team's coach recruits players and gives one-half and one-quarter scholarships to the best players. Some are getting much less. "This scenario happens everywhere. The chance of getting a full scholarship is close to zero . . . parents are dreaming if they think that's what their child will get," says Wolff.

College sports without big attendance simply don't have that much money to spread around. "Football and men's basketball are about the only sports generating revenue for some colleges," says Wolff. There are exceptions, of course, such as hockey at the University of Vermont. Wolff also says most parents aren't aware of the NCAA statistics showing that less than 5 percent of today's high school varsity athletes ever make a team in college (Divisions I through III). And the odds of playing professionally are that less than 1 percent of college players go on to the professional level.

If a youth athlete does get a scholarship, Wolff warns that the sport's program generally dictates the kid's schedule and academics take a back seat. (There are no athletic scholarships at Ivy League schools.) To maintain eligibility, athletes end up in easy majors that don't prepare them for the post-graduation world or desired careers, according to a *USA Today* study. Also, sports scholarships are only offered one year at a time, and there's no guarantee your student athlete will get it for four years. Athletic scholarships are only a possibility at Division I and II schools. Division III schools are prohibited by NCAA regulations from offering athletic scholarships.

Considering the opportunity cost of sports' time and expenses

Youth travel sports not only can cost a lot of money, but they can also take an enormous amount of time. This can create strains and stress on an entire family.

As discussed earlier, there clearly are benefits for young athletes to playing sports, but the impact of those programs on the rest of a family's members should be considered before committing to any team.

Being wary of the winning addiction

We all want to be winners and be on the winning side. Competition can challenge and develop many good values in kids, but it can go too far. Some youth sports teams get addicted to and obsessed with winning, which can bring out the worst behavior and reinforce excessive spending by parents.

"When a parent shells out thousands of dollars, the parent feels emotionally and financially invested. If a kid isn't a star or doing as well as expected, emotions can really bubble over," says Wolff.

TIP

Teams that recruit players from a wide area and attend a lot of tournaments are more likely to be too focused on winning at any cost as opposed to developing all the players and teaching good values and life lessons. Be especially wary of teams claiming undefeated status or those that win excessively.

Also, don't buy into the nonsense when teams crow about winning a "national championship." In many cases, teams simply qualify to play in a larger tournament after winning a smaller local one. One middle-school-age football team I was familiar with went to a Florida tournament that was attended by just three other teams in their age group and got "national champion" status by winning. And, the kids had to miss a full week of school because the tournament was held on weekdays. The winning team simply won against the few other teams whose parents were willing to spend the money to fly to an out-of-state tournament, live in a hotel for a week, and have their kids miss school. What kind of message is that sending to the kids?

REMEMBER

Sports can be a wonderful experience for children. But even the best athletes should be putting their education first. Every sport has extraordinary athletes who flamed out in college or early in their professional career. Without a solid education and career to fall back upon, young athletes who have made sports their first priority will be poorly positioned for their adult working lives. And, even those lucky few who "make it" professionally can tell you that a good education benefits them in managing their careers and money, including after their playing careers come to an end.

Completing the Personal Finance Olympics of Childrearing

Raising children and accomplishing the rest of the things you desire within your household and family is challenging, especially if, like most families, you don't earn high incomes or have a lot of money saved already. It takes balance, planning, sacrifice, and prioritization.

If you remember Olympic competitions, perhaps you'll recall the decathlon. Athletes compete in ten different events over two days. On the first day, there is the 100-meter sprint, long jump, shot put, high jump, and 400-meter run. This is followed by the 110-meter hurdles, discus throw, pole vault, javelin throw, and 1,500-meter run on day two. Managing your family's finances well has something in common with the decathlon because there are numerous moving parts that you want to do well in order to achieve a solid overall result.

That said, managing your money and accumulating savings and investments isn't a competition. Set your own goals and live your own life. Don't worry about what other people are doing or thinking.

TIP

Here are some key things to do both before and after you begin your family:

>> **Set your priorities.** As with many other financial decisions, starting or expanding a family requires that you plan ahead. Set your priorities and structure your finances and living situation accordingly. Is having a bigger home in a particular community important, or would you rather feel less pressure to work hard, giving you more time to spend with your family? Keep in mind that a less hectic work life not only gives you more free time but also often reduces your cost of living by decreasing meals out, dry-cleaning costs, day-care expenses, and so on.

>> **Take a hard look at your budget.** Having kids requires you to increase your spending. At a minimum, expenditures for food and clothing will increase. But you're also likely to spend more on housing, insurance, day care, and education. On top of that, if you want to play an active role in raising your children, working at some full-time jobs may not be possible. So, while you consider the added expenses, you may also need to factor in a decrease in income.

No simple rules exist for estimating how kids will affect your household's income and expenses. On the income side, figure out how much you want to cut back on work. On the expense side, government statistics show that the average household with school-age children spends about 20 percent more than a household without children. Going through your budget category by category and estimating how kids will change your spending is a more scientific approach.

>> **Boost insurance coverage before getting pregnant.** Make sure you have health insurance in place if you're going to try to get pregnant. Even though the Affordable Care Act mandated maternity benefits in all health plans, if you lack coverage and then get pregnant, you won't be able to enroll outside of the small portion of the year designated for open enrollment. With disability insurance, pregnancy is considered a preexisting condition, so women should secure this coverage before getting pregnant. And most families-to-be should buy life insurance. Buying life insurance *after* the bundle of joy comes home from the hospital is a risky proposition — if one of the parents develops a health problem, he or she may be denied coverage. You should also consider buying life insurance for a stay-at-home parent. Even though the stay-at-home parent is not bringing in income, if he or she were to pass away, hiring assistance could cripple the family budget.

>> **Check maternity leave with your employers.** Many of the larger employers offer some maternity leave for women and, in rare but thankfully increasing cases, for men. Some employers offer paid leaves, while others may offer unpaid leaves. Understand the options and the financial ramifications before you consider the leave and, ideally, before you get pregnant. Also, check laws within your state for mandated maternity and paternity leave.

>> **Update your will.** If you have a will, update it; if you don't have a will, make one now. With children in the picture, you need to name a guardian who will be responsible for raising your children should you and your spouse both pass away.

>> **Understand child-care tax benefits.** You may be eligible for a $2,000 tax credit for each child under the age of 17. That should certainly motivate you to apply for your kid's Social Security number! If you and your spouse both work and you have children under the age of 13 or a disabled dependent of any age, you can also claim a tax credit for child-care expenses. The tax credit may be for up to 35 percent of $3,000 in qualifying expenses for one child or

dependent, or up to $6,000 for two or more children or dependents. Or you may work for an employer who offers a flexible benefit or spending plan. These plans allow you to put away up to $5,000 per year on a pretax basis for child-care expenses. For many parents, especially those in higher income tax brackets, these plans can save a lot in taxes. Keep in mind, however, that if you use one of these plans, you can't claim the child-care tax credit. Also, if you don't deplete the account every tax year, you forfeit any money left over.

>> **Skip saving in custodial accounts.** If you start saving for future college and other educational expenses in your child's name in a so-called custodial account, you may harm your family's future ability to qualify for financial aid (reduced college pricing) and miss out on the tax benefits that come with investing elsewhere.

>> **Don't (over)indulge your children.** Toys, art classes, music lessons, travel sports and associated lessons, smartphones, field trips, and the like can rack up big bills, especially if you don't control your spending. Some parents fail to set guidelines or limits when spending on children's programs. Others mindlessly follow the examples set by the families of their children's peers. Introspective parents have told me that they feel some insecurity about providing the best for their children. The parents (and kids) who seem the happiest and most financially successful are the ones who clearly distinguish between material luxuries and family necessities.

As children get older and become indoctrinated into the world of shopping, all sorts of other purchases come into play. Consider giving your kids a weekly allowance and letting them discover how to spend and manage it. And when they're old enough, having your kids get a part-time job can help teach financial responsibility.

Chapter **3**

Exposing Your Kids to Work, Finances, and the "Real World"

When you raise kids today, you may rightfully want to keep them in a protective cocoon or bubble, insulated from the harsh realities and downsides of the adult world. A good parent naturally wants to protect their kids, especially until they accumulate sufficient knowledge, life experiences, and judgment.

Part of the adult world, of course, is working and making and managing your money. The education that kids receive growing up, both in and outside the classroom, contributes to preparing them to someday enter the working world. And, for many (but by no means all) teenagers, that post–high-school education includes going to college. In the subsequent parts of this book, I explore those alternatives and how to pay for them.

There are many money lessons and concepts to master in order to make good financial decisions and to make the most of your money as an adult. Much of the groundwork for sound money decisions can and should be laid in childhood. So, no matter whether your children attend college after high school or choose some other path, you can and should provide them with an excellent foundation in the form of a solid personal financial education. That's what this chapter is all about.

Laying the Foundation for Raising Money-Smart Kids in the Early Years

According to a survey conducted by the National Bureau for Economic Research, children who get personal-finance education in high school save 5 percent more of their future employment incomes than kids who aren't exposed to such education. Five percent may not sound like a lot, but when you consider that most adults should be saving about 10 percent annually to accomplish their financial goals and actually save less, saving 5 percent more is a huge difference.

TIP

While high school is a terrific time to teach kids key personal financial concepts before they're nudged out of the family nest, you can and should begin to teach kids about money much sooner. The latter preschool and elementary school years, when kids are learning math concepts and getting comfortable with numbers, are an excellent time to lay a solid knowledge base.

When you welcome a new baby into your family, he needs you to do everything for him. You must feed him, clothe him, change his diaper, and so on. Slowly and gradually over time, your baby learns to do some simple things like beginning to crawl and then walk. That creates a whole new set of hazards as the more he is able to move on his own, the more trouble he can get into!

In the early years, you will need to make all the choices for your children with regard to spending money. Eventually, as they go through the preschool years, they will begin to understand that you buy them things and they can have some influence over those purchases and decisions.

Educating when shopping

One of your child's first money lessons is likely to come by accompanying you shopping. Take her grocery shopping so she can see all the items available for purchase and the price on each of them. You can explain to your child how you pay for food and how the money is earned in the first place. She can also learn how to comparison shop and live within a budget. (*Note:* I don't generally think you should share personal financial information like your salary with your children. This is highly personal information, and kids don't have a context for understanding it nor can you be sure that they won't share it with others.)

Kids obviously get much more out of shopping when they've been introduced to counting and basic math. This typically happens late in the preschool years and early in elementary school.

Of course, you don't have to visit a physical store to teach your kids these concepts. You can plop them down at your side while you shop online, but when you do that, you lose something, I think. But online shopping is certainly more convenient, especially for time-pressed families.

TIP

Being a smart consumer requires doing your homework, especially when buying more costly products. Teach your kids the value of product research (including using sources like Consumer Reports for product reviews) and comparison shopping. Demonstrate how to identify overpriced and shoddy merchandise. Finally, show them how to voice a complaint when returning defective products and go to bat for better treatment in service environments, two additional tasks that are part of being a savvy consumer.

Taking your kid to work

Even better, I think, than taking your kid shopping and focusing on the consumer and spending side of money, how about talking to them about your work? After all, this is the reality that most people deal with for most of their adult years.

I'm not suggesting that you need to tell your kids everything about work, but when your children are young, you can certainly explain the basics of your work and job. You can begin by describing what your job entails and who your employer is and what, broadly speaking, your employer does. Importantly, you can explain how you get paid money to perform your job and that money helps provide and pay for the things that your family needs and wants like your home, food, clothing, car, medical and dental care, vacations, and so on.

Dealing with What Kids Are Exposed To

Listen in to school-age children talking today, and you will find that money often comes up. Time is spent discussing the latest consumer products and clothing and what things cost. Kids are also surprisingly aware of what the snazziest sports cars sell for and how much pro athletes make and spend on homes and other things. This actually should be no great surprise, given the extent to which such topics are covered in the media and online, and the amount of that many kids are exposed to these days.

Although most of the parents I know want their children to have the best education possible and give reasonable thought and effort to teaching their kids various real-world skills, many parents neglect to educate their kids about personal financial matters. I don't think this is a conscious decision. In the rush of day-to-day life, most folks probably don't even think about the issue. In addition, many parents may not understand or know how to teach personal finance, or they may have their own problems and issues with the topic.

Some parents assume that personal-finance skills are covered in school, but that assumption is usually wrong. While schools are increasingly incorporating money issues into the existing curriculum (such as math lessons), the broader concepts of personal financial management still aren't taught in most schools.

Looking at the effects of advertising

In the absence of financial education, kids are still "learning" about scores of product-buying opportunities on a daily basis from the many marketers and purveyors of popular culture. Advertising generally is only going to "teach" children to value companies' specific products. Without parental involvement, children rarely learn how to thoughtfully spend, save, and invest money.

Companies spend lots of money promoting their products and brands to kids for one simple reason: It works. Kids can hum and sing along with commercial jingles at startlingly early ages. Surprisingly, young children see, understand, and remember advertising. By first grade, children easily recognize many companies' advertising logos and brand names. Kids' preferences drive billions of dollars of spending, both their own purchases, and more importantly, their parents' buying decisions.

According to a survey commissioned by New Dream (formerly the Center for a New American Dream), American teens ask their parents an average of nine times for a particular item they have seen advertised before the parents give in to the purchase. Kids are developing bad habits by nagging their parents, and they're also getting their parents to spend more money.

And, consider this impact of advertising: Children's health is being harmed through the marketing of junk food. Obesity and childhood diabetes are on the rise. When children are bombarded with ads from fast food outlets, soda companies, and candy bar companies, not surprisingly, they end up eating a lot of fast food, drinking too much soda, and eating more candy. Parents can step in and make their voices heard over the advertisers.

Surrounded by constant advertising messages, it's no wonder, then, that coupled with the lack of school-based and parent-initiated personal financial education for children, kids know all too well how to borrow and spend but know little about investing and saving. According to a survey by the JumpStart Coalition for Personal Financial Literacy, only 14 percent of high school seniors knew that stocks provide better long-term returns than bonds or savings accounts.

CREDIT CARDS AND COLLEGE STUDENTS

Prior to the Credit Card Act of 2009, amazingly, one in seven of those seeking credit-counseling help were college students. This figure is less shocking and more under-standable when you consider that one in three college students had four or more credit cards and that many colleges and universities received hundreds of thousands of dollars annually from credit card companies for on-campus promotion access.

A more recent survey by EVERFI and AIG of over 30,000 college students from more than 440 institutions located across the country found that 45 percent of college students with credit cards juggle charging to two or more credit cards. And, only 51 percent plan to pay their credit card bill in full. Overall, I don't think that college students are seeing fewer credit card promotions and ads. On-campus promotions of credit cards are still allowed today; the Credit Card Act simply ended the practice of credit card companies using giveaways like free pizza, key chains, and so on to lure students to sign up.

Unless a student has a source of income or a willing cosigner like a parent, card companies don't generally offer regular credit cards to students until the age of 21. This has led more parents to provide their college students with a credit card or to cosign for the student to have a card. I'm not a fan of either of these approaches because students can easily run up a larger balance than they can pay off when the next monthly bill comes due. And, I've seen and heard of too many cases where kids are going out to eat at restaurants, buying concert tickets, and hitting local bars or buying alcohol at mom and dad's expense. These things are hardly necessities, and I think teenagers and young adults should learn to pay for these sorts of expenses themselves and learn to live within a budget.

Debit cards, which are connected to a checking account and don't allow you to spend money that you don't have, are an alternative to credit cards. Please see the section, "Introducing the right and wrong ways to use credit and debit cards," later in this chapter.

Here are some steps you can take to combat all those ads:

>> **Reduce your kids' exposure to ads.** The primary path to reduced exposure to ads is to cut down on TV time. When kids are in front of a screen, have them watch prerecorded material. Also make use of digital video recorders (DVRs) so you can easily zip past ads.

>> **Teach your kids about the realities of advertising and marketing.** Invest the necessary time to teach and explain to your kids that the point of advertising is to motivate consumers to buy the product by making it sound more wonderful or necessary than it really is. Also explain that advertising is costly and that the most heavily promoted and popular products include the cost of all that advertising, so they're paying for it when they buy those items.

Understanding habit development and setting limits

While working with clients and answering questions from many readers, it became clear to me that personal financial habits are largely formed during childhood, and those habits that we adopt often mirror the financial practices of our parents. Although some children reject the examples that their parents provide, far more often, kids mirror the personal financial habits they observe at home. Adults who live it up now, borrow on credit cards and auto loans, and don't save for the future tend to raise children who are accomplished spenders and poor savers.

Children, of course, learn from the example set by their parents (and others), both in words and actions. While it's bad enough that kids are bombarded with promotions and temptations to spend their money, some parents exacerbate that problem by acquiescing to too many requests and demands that their children make. This reinforces a mindset focused on spending and consumption to the detriment of saving and investing.

William Damon, professor of education and director of the Center on Adolescence at Stanford University, has reviewed and compiled the results of many studies that examined indulging children. These studies tracked kids into adulthood. Damon found that, when given too much too soon, indulged kids grow up into adults who have difficulty coping with life's disappointments and end up with a distorted sense of entitlement that gets in the way of success at work and personal relationships. He also found that indulging children causes them to grow up into adults with a more egocentric, self-centered perspective, which raises mental health risks for depression, anxiety, and greater risks for alcohol and substance abuse.

One of the great challenges in raising kids among our country's relative economic abundance is fulfilling the natural parental desire to provide children with opportunities for personal growth and development without spoiling them into dependency. Regularly overindulging kids can result in long-term damage to their well-being, but you surely don't want to deprive them either.

Suppose your daughter seems to have a talent and passion for music. Should you not enroll her in music classes or get her private lessons outside of school simply because doing so may seem extravagant — especially if you didn't grow up with such opportunities? And, where do you draw the line with such expenditures, especially when money is tight, or you and your spouse have different philosophies and beliefs about such spending?

Of course, you should provide for your kids. The great danger, especially in more affluent families or in less affluent families willing to spend beyond their means, is engaging in continuous and excessive spending on our kids with the implicit belief that more is always better. Being a good parent requires some hard work.

Although saying "yes" is more fun and makes you more popular, especially in the short term, psychologists universally agree on the importance of setting limits and saying "no." Explaining and enforcing limits creates feelings of security for children and actually demonstrates to them that you care. And, it teaches them that, indeed, money doesn't grow on trees or come in unlimited supplies from credit cards.

Parents who buy too much for their kids, in my observations, have difficulty changing that habit. The key is to find new ways to show that you love and care for your children rather than buying so much. Here are some suggestions:

>> **Rededicate yourself to hugs.** The busier we get, the less affection we tend to give our kids. Like work, raising children can become a series of tasks to accomplish, activities to complete, and deadlines to meet. We can all benefit by slowing down and giving affection to our kids.

>> **Play a game together.** Here's a warning: After you make the decision to spend some time playing games with your kids, you may have to free up their time and, quite honestly, provide some encouragement to win them over to the idea. Try doing an activity or sport outdoors to get some fresh air and exercise.

To facilitate the process, it helps to have electronic-free days in your home. In our family, we set aside two weekdays each week where there's no television, computer, or video games. (On other days, we had time-usage restrictions in place.) We imposed this digital moratorium to make time for other things that were increasingly being crowded out.

>> **Go for a walk and talk.** Although many kids will resist, taking a walk with one of your kids can be a great way to enjoy the outdoors and exercise while taking a few minutes to connect and have fun. Just try not to have unrealistic expectations for lengthy, deep, and profound conversations. Just take a walk and see what happens.

>> **Catch them doing something good.** In many parents' efforts to teach their children good habits and extinguish poor practices, too much focus can be placed on correcting the negative. Praise and compliments increasingly get crowded out and overlooked. Don't let that happen in your family — catch your child doing something well several times every day!

>> **Get involved in their world.** Whether you build something, do an art project, or play catch in the yard, don't always be a spectator. Get down and dirty, have some fun, and enjoy being a kid again! All those to-do lists around the house and at work that keep you from lending a hand or joining the fun more often will always be there waiting for you, but, before you know it, your kids will be grown and out of the house.

>> **Go out for a meal with one child.** Okay, so this one does involve some spending. However, many parents find that, when they think about it, they don't have much one-on-one time with individual kids, especially in families with multiple children. Make it a habit to grab lunch or dinner with one of the kids on a regular basis. Try restaurants without table service to minimize the cost, interruptions, and time involved.

Developing the Work-Money Connection

Kids benefit immensely from learning to work for things — saving, making choices, sacrificing, and contributing to their families and households. Usually the first work that kids do is in their own home and is called "chores." During their teenage years, you want to encourage them to do some work outside of your household.

Regarding allowances and chores

An allowance is a terrific way to introduce children to a whole host of personal-finance lessons. In fact, a well-implemented allowance program can mimic many money matters that adults face every day throughout their lives. From recognizing the need to earn money to understanding how to responsibly and intelligently spend, save, and invest their allowance, children can gain a solid financial footing from a young age.

Deciding on amounts

Consider beginning a regular allowance when your kids enter elementary school, which is around the time that a child is learning to read and master basic math skills like simple addition and subtraction. As for a dollar amount, consider a weekly allowance of $0.50 to $1.00 per year of age. So, for example, a six-year-old child would earn between $3 and $6 per week. Of course, the size of the allowance should depend, in part, on what sorts of expenditures and savings you expect your child to engage in and, perhaps, the amount of "work" you expect your child to perform around the house.

I believe that allowances should be earned — children shouldn't just get an allowance for "showing up." That's not to say that kids should get paid for all of their work around the house; some things should be done for being part of the family. And you don't want kids extending their hand in expectation for money every time they help in some way around the house.

Picking tasks

The tasks required of children to earn the allowance can vary. For younger children, they can be as simple as making their bed daily and carrying their dishes from the table after a meal. As kids grow older, you can assign other household chores, such as cleaning their room, taking care of the family pets, loading and unloading the dishwasher, helping with laundry, or mowing the lawn. This approach demonstrates that increased responsibilities and harder work are often accompanied by additional rewards. Also, if you have children close in age, consider rotating the various tasks to keep things interesting and avoid "fairness"-based grievances from the younger set.

Putting money away

Have kids save a significant portion (up to half) of their allowance money toward longer-term goals, such as college. The allowance system that I personally prefer is for children to reserve about one third of their weekly take for savings.

TIP

After they've earmarked their savings money, you can take the opportunity to pass along the importance of charity to your kids, perhaps by having them put a portion of their allowance into a box earmarked for charity. (This can also provide an opportunity to teach them about how to evaluate potential worthy causes.)

The amount that can be spent should by and large go toward "discretionary" purchases, especially when kids are younger. You want kids to learn how to make purchasing decisions and learn from their mistakes, including running out of money until their next allowance payment if they overspend. (I don't agree with the philosophy of giving kids a larger allowance and then having them, for example, buy their school lunches and other required purchases with that money. Do you really want your child to miss school lunch next week because he spent too much this week?)

Helping with purchases

I've long cautioned my own kids about viewing all forms of advertising with a skeptical eye, but a single purchasing decision provided a more powerful lesson for them than all my warnings and reminders combined, when they ran into some used Pokémon cards on eBay. They thought they were getting the deal of a lifetime because they'd heard of single Pokémon cards being "worth" $40, yet here they were buying dozens of cards for less than $10! As I expected, they were quite disappointed with their purchase because they ended up with a bunch of mediocre cards that were likely "worth" less than they paid.

One obvious caution when allowing kids to make their own mistakes is that you need to be involved sufficiently to keep them from buying or accessing inappropriate items and material and to keep them from committing to a transaction that is more costly than they can afford. The internet is particularly problematic in this regard.

For larger desired purchases, kids can learn to save the portion of their weekly allowance earmarked for purchases over weeks and even months. For example, a family I know has a boy who wanted a more expensive bike than his parents were willing to pay for. So, the boy saved the extra $75 he needed, and it took him nearly six months to accomplish his goal. Besides learning how to save toward a larger purchase and not getting in the bad habit of borrowing for consumption, this experience provided some additional benefits that surprised the parents. "I've never seen my son take such good care of a bike as the new one he bought partly with his own money," said his father.

Encouraging work outside your home as they get older

Your child's initial exposure to the work-for-pay world outside your home can start with something as simple as a lemonade stand. I understand that some parents are reluctant and have concerns about the dangers in the real world, and for sure, you should investigate outside endeavors. With older children, such as those in high school, you will likely provide more advice than direct oversight.

I cut lawns and did other yard work during high school and college summers. By holding down such jobs, kids can learn about working, running a small business, earning, saving, and investing money. (Beware, though, that your kid's employment income, if large enough, could lead to a smaller college financial aid package. See Chapter 6.) It also provides welcome relief for parents to not continually be the source for spending money.

There are many jobs that teenagers can perform and get paid decently to do. Here are some examples:

- >> **Yard work:** I did this for numerous high school and even early college year summers. The money is good, and you're doing work outdoors and getting exercise. Just be careful of the poison ivy, bees and wasps, and ticks!

- >> **Snow shoveling:** This kind of work is more intermittent and obviously weather dependent! Older people in particular appreciate help with shoveling as that's not a safe activity for the elderly due to the risk of falls and stress on the heart.

- >> **Helping older people with technology:** Young people today grow up with technology, but most older people struggle to master using computers, cellphones, and the like.

- >> **Youth sports refereeing:** Some training and certification are typically required. In addition to decent compensation, this kind of work teaches teenagers and young adults how to handle and work with different types of people.

- >> **Youth sports lessons and camps:** Your teen's love of a sport and years of playing it can be put to work at the large numbers of sports camps. If your son or daughter has had lots of experience and training in a sport, offering individual lessons may be a possibility.

- >> **Work at a summer camp:** Many communities have some summer camps of varying types that can be reasonable places to work so long as your teenager enjoys working with younger kids.

- >> **Work as a waiter in a restaurant or country club:** This is generally only open to teens age 16 and older. These can be great jobs for providing lots of opportunities to serve customers and find out how a business operates.

TRUE STORY

A colleague of mine recently shared his childhood work experiences with me, and I think they further highlight the value of work-related experiences for kids. "When I was young, my dad wrote up contracts for me when I wanted something, like a new baseball glove. I would be paid modest amounts for various chores, and once I had accumulated enough for the item, we would go and buy it. Once a year, the town fair came, and I would get paid a penny for every dandelion that I pulled from the yard. I usually pulled 500 to 1,000 and had 5 or 10 bucks to blow on rides and cotton candy at the fair. In about fifth grade, I realized that there was far better cash to be made outside the confines of my extortionist family. I began to hire myself out to the neighbors for shoveling snow and yard work. I took great pride in my work, and I loved being my own boss and setting my own schedule."

Teaching Your Kids About More Real-World Money Topics

As your kids move through their high school years, you will have many opportunities to share important money lessons with them. In this section, I discuss a number of additional valuable topics for you to consider.

Being mindful of your statements and attitudes about money

Kids are little sponges. They learn a lot from what you say and how you say it and your actions. Do you encourage shopping or gambling as a form of recreation and entertainment? If you're critical or judgmental of people with money, your kids may learn envy or believe that having money is somehow wrong.

As your children grow into teenagers and then finally into young adults, you will likely encounter a period where they seem to ignore much or nearly all of what you tell them. Some kids are worse than others in this regard. Try not to take it personally. I've long reasoned and said this is nature's way of easing the transition for them of moving out of your home and leading their own lives. Ultimately, that's what you should want — to raise an independent, well-adjusted young adult who can largely manage on her own. But, of course, most parents find this a bittersweet moment.

REMEMBER

In the natural process of teenagers and young adults pushing you away and tuning you out, the foundation that you laid earlier will still be in place. Also, teenagers are listening some of the time, and some of what you are saying will positively impact them even if it seems like you're being universally ignored. Pick your spots for offering advice and give them their space. Don't nag and endlessly repeat yourself!

Don't buy them a car!

Okay, this is my opinion so hear me out on my logic for this one. I understand that getting a driver's license is a rite of passage for high school students. But, getting behind the wheel of a car is the most dangerous thing your teenager will likely do. And since insurance companies know in aggregate how dangerous young drivers are, adding your teenager to your auto insurance policy will cost a small fortune. That should tell you and your teenager something very real about the dangers of young drivers. So, don't be in a rush to have them get their license!

THE FACTS ON TEENAGER DRIVING DANGERS

Annually, more than 2,300 teenagers in the United States aged 16–19 die, and about 300,000 are treated in emergency departments for injuries suffered in motor vehicle crashes. That means six teens aged 16–19 die every day due to motor vehicle crashes, and hundreds more are injured.

The risk of motor vehicle crashes is higher among teens aged 16–19 than among any other age group. In fact, per mile driven, teen drivers in this age group are nearly three times more likely than drivers aged 20 and older to be in a fatal crash.

Teens who are at especially high risk for motor vehicle crashes are

- **Male:** The motor vehicle death rate for male drivers aged 16–19 was over two times higher than the death rate for female drivers of the same age.

- **Driving with teen passengers:** The presence of teen passengers increases the crash risk of unsupervised teen drivers. This risk increases with increased numbers of teen passengers.

- **Newly licensed:** Crash risk is particularly high during the first months of licensure. Data from the National Household Travel Survey indicate that the crash rate per mile driven is 1.5 times higher for 16-year-olds than it is for 18- and 19-year-olds.

What factors put teen drivers at risk?

- **Inexperience:** Teens are more likely than older drivers to underestimate or not be able to recognize dangerous situations. Teens are also more likely than adults to make critical decision errors that lead to serious crashes.

- **Speeding:** Teens are more likely than older drivers to speed and allow shorter headways (the distance from the front of one vehicle to the front of the next).

- **Seat belt use:** Compared with other age groups, teens and young adults often have the lowest seat belt use rates. Only 59 percent of high school students always wear seat belts when riding as passengers. Among young drivers aged 15–20 who die in car crashes, almost half were unrestrained at the time of the crash.

- **Alcohol use:** Any amount of alcohol increases the risk of crashes among teens as compared with older drivers. Drinking alcohol is illegal under the age of 21; therefore, so is drinking and driving. Despite this, 15 percent of drivers aged 16–20 involved in fatal motor vehicle crashes had a blood alcohol content (BAC) of .08 percent or higher (a level that is illegal for adults aged 21 and older in all states).

(continued)

(continued)

Of drivers aged 15–20 who were killed in motor vehicle crashes after drinking and driving, 58 percent were not wearing a seat belt. Among male drivers aged 15–20 who were involved in fatal crashes, 31 percent were speeding at the time of the crash and 20 percent had been drinking.

- **Nighttime and weekend driving:** Forty percent of motor vehicle crash deaths among teen drivers and passengers aged 13–19 occurred between 9 p.m. and 6 a.m., and 51 percent occurred on Friday, Saturday, or Sunday.

(The statistics given here are from the U.S. Centers for Disease Control and Prevention.)

No matter when they get their license, I strongly recommend against buying them their own car. There are several reasons for my recommendation:

>> **The costs are high.** Buying, insuring, and maintaining another car for your household is costly. Insurers already charge a lot to insure a teen on your auto policy, and they charge even more if the teen has a car dedicated for their personal usage.

>> **It encourages more use.** If your teen has his "own car," that means that it's always available for use, which — guess what — will lead to your teen driving more!

>> **They didn't earn it.** Your teenager is young and likely earns little money — certainly nowhere near enough to afford a personal car.

When your teenager needs or wants to use a car, he can use one of yours. I like that system because it's clear who the car belongs to (you) and who is asking for the privilege of using it at a specific time (your teenager).

You may decide to ignore my advice, and please know that I fully understand and appreciate that everyone's household circumstances and situations are different. Maybe your teenager has a schedule — due to part-time work and/or after school activities — that doesn't mesh well with yours. If you feel that your teenager should have and can handle the responsibility of her own car, that's your decision. Just be sure she has a safe vehicle to use and that she understands she lives in your house with your rules! You might consider having them contribute to the costs.

Introducing the right and wrong ways to use credit and debit cards

Those plastic cards in your wallet offer a convenient way to conduct purchases in stores, by phone, and over the internet. Credit cards, unfortunately, offer temptation for overspending and carrying debt from month to month.

Teach your kids how a checking account works, explaining that debit cards are connected to your checking account and thus prevent you from overspending as you can on a credit card. While your kids are still living at home and you can closely monitor the transactions on their account, a debit card is a good way to go. These come with a Visa or MasterCard logo and are accepted anywhere merchants accept cards from those payment processors.

Cash still works too and is great for helping you set spending boundaries for your teenagers when they need money. Don't want them spending more than $20 when they are out with friends this Saturday? Then just provide them with that amount of cash. One downside if they only have cash with them and no plastic like a debit card as backup, is that then they may find themselves in a situation where they need money and don't have it. If they're with friends, those friends could serve as a backup.

WARNING

Debit cards do have their downsides. If someone fraudulently obtains the debit card information and uses it, you need to be on top of the situation to prevent your checking account balance from being drained and overdrawn. You also generally have less time, compared with a credit card, to dispute charges. Credit cards typically give you 60 days.

While credit cards can be subjected to fraud also, you have the time delay between when you get your monthly statement and several weeks later when the payment is due to review and challenge any charges that aren't yours. By contrast, when a payment is processed with your debit card, the money comes out of your checking account within one to two business days.

Talking to kids about investing

As kids accumulate more significant savings as the weeks turn into months and the months turn into years, you can introduce the concept of investing. Rather than trekking down to the boring old local bank and putting the money into a sleepy, low-interest bank account, I prefer having kids invest in mutual funds (which you can do online or through the mail).

Although stocks returning an average of 9 percent per year sounds attractive to most grown-ups, young kids may not be able to comprehend what that kind of return really means or the long-term power of compounding returns. Most kids can better understand these mathematical concepts beginning in late elementary school when they're comfortable with more complicated multiplication.

TIP

I have two useful ways to illustrate to kids how small regular investments can grow into substantial amounts over time through modest returns from sound investments. One is to work out on paper how money grows over the years. The second approach is to show kids with play money. You could use simple examples such as they invest $50 in a stock (or stock mutual fund) that doubles in value over 7 years.

Rather than investing in stocks through mutual funds, another option for kids is to buy individual stocks. I generally advocate that adults invest in funds. That said, kids can learn more about how the financial markets work and understand stocks better by sometimes picking individual stocks rather than using funds. Just be careful to keep transaction fees to a minimum and teach your kids how to evaluate a stock and its valuation and not simply buy companies that they've heard of or that make products they like. (My book *Investing For Dummies* provides advice for researching stocks and other investments.)

Another way for kids to learn about investing in stocks is through one of the online investing games like The Stock Market Game (www.stockmarketgame.org). The website explains that the game is for educators and other interested adults. So, unless your child has a teacher who is interested in getting involved with the game, you can create an account and work with your teenager on it. Simply select the "Participate by myself" option. Each participant has a virtual $100,000 to invest.

2

Finding
Acceptance

IN THIS PART . . .

Help your kids become all that they can be.

Develop a family decision-making process for higher education and utilize experts economically.

Chapter **4**

Making the Most of Your Kid's Academic and Outside Experiences

Most parents I know want the "best" for their kids. Everyone has their own definition of what that means, but for the vast majority, it generally includes raising children who are well-adjusted, self-confident, and happy, and helping them develop their talents and abilities. Of course, no one is happy all the time, and good parents understand that kids learn from failure and adversity.

There are plenty of myths and misconceptions about what it takes to develop your children's potential and for them to gain admission to the "best" colleges. And, there are lots of myths and misconceptions about what makes a particular college one of the "best."

This chapter helps you to navigate and make the most of the choices your kids have during their primary, middle, and high school education years. (*Note:* I understand that some families believe in homeschooling and what I discuss in this chapter and book apply well to those types of students as well.)

Understanding the Value of Academic Success (Good Grades)

Your kids should strive to do their best in school. Their grades do matter. Now, that's not to say they should stay up past midnight, hole up in their rooms, and toil away to get every point possible on that next test or try to write the perfect paper.

REMEMBER

Perfection isn't possible, and kids (and adults) can make themselves miserable trying to attain the impossible. Balance matters, and there's more to life than high grades, making more money, and so on.

While an imperfect measure, grades and test scores indicate mastery and achievement. Unless a student is taking easy courses or is a naturally gifted whiz at something, getting better grades and higher test scores usually takes more effort and work.

Want your kids to get more out of their pre-college education and improve their chances of getting into a desired college and other post–high school options? Here's what they can do leading up to and during high school:

>> **Strive for better grades.** All other things being equal, colleges are going to admit students with better grades (higher GPAs) and also give more merit scholarship money to students with better grades. This doesn't mean that your kids should take easier courses that enable them to get higher grades. High schools today use a weighted GPA, which gives a higher point value to grades earned in harder courses. And, more selective colleges also expect students to challenge themselves with higher level courses.

>> **Take advanced placement (AP) courses.** Not only do AP courses demonstrate that your children are taking challenging courses, but some colleges also offer credits to students who earn a good score (typically four or five on a scale of five) on AP tests, which are typically administered in May. These credits may allow your child to accelerate his college experience by a semester or even a full year, saving you some serious money. Some colleges simply use mastery of AP subjects to place a student out of a comparable introductory course in that area.

>> **Prepare for taking the SAT (Scholastic Aptitude Test) or ACT (American College Testing).** The first step for students in preparing is for them to study and do their best throughout middle school and high school. Many high schools administer a practice test in 10th or 11th grade. On their website, the College Board offers ten free practice SAT tests for students to download: https://collegereadiness.collegeboard.org/sat/practice/full-length-practice-tests. Once completed, the test is scored through your phone by simply taking a picture of your answer sheet. Or through the same link on that College Board web page, you can take entire SAT practice tests

through Khan Academy. The ACT folks charge $39.95 for their six-month online prep course with practice tests. See all of their test prep products and services at: www.act.org/content/act/en/products-and-services/the-act/test-preparation.html.

Some colleges offer a lower price (through grants and scholarships) referred to as "preferential packaging." This simply means that the college or university can choose to offer a better mix of aid (pricing) to academically stronger candidates they are trying to attract to their school. A bonus for those students who worked hard in school!

Table 4-1 shows a list compiled by *U.S. News & World Report* of the colleges that offer merit scholarships to the greatest percentage of their students. (*Note:* This list excludes athletic awards.) The list includes a real mix of schools in terms of quality. The colleges that are consistently ranked as the top colleges are absent from this list for good reason — they don't have any trouble attracting plenty of qualified applicants.

TIP

To help your kids' chances of getting merit money offers from colleges, in addition to being sure to apply to numerous colleges that make such offers, they should also apply to schools that are likely to accept (and therefore want) them. To *really* maximize their chances of getting merit money, your child should apply not just to colleges that are likely to accept them, but to schools for which they are somewhat overqualified and where they'll stand out from the crowd of applicants. (Of course, you don't want to take this to an extreme and have your offspring be the absolute biggest fish in a little pond and not have peers who are like them.)

TABLE 4-1   Merit Scholarship Percentages by School

School	Location	Percent of Students Receiving Merit-Based Aid
Hellenic College	Brookline, MA	100%
Fort Valley State University	Fort Valley, GA	94%
Oklahoma Baptist University	Shawnee, OK	94%
Vanguard University of Southern California	Costa Mesa, CA	94%
Webb Institute	Glen Cove, NY	81%
Keiser University	Ft. Lauderdale, FL	73%
Indiana Wesleyan University	Marion, IN	60%
Franklin W. Olin College of Engineering	Needham, MA	56%

(continued)

TABLE 4-1 *(continued)*

School	Location	Percent of Students Receiving Merit-Based Aid
New England Conservatory of Music	Boston, MA	53%
Fairfield University	Fairfield, CT	52%
Trinity University	San Antonio, TX	50%
Oberlin College	Oberlin, OH	49%
Samford University	Birmingham, AL	49%
Denison University	Granville, OH	48%
The New School	New York, NY	47%
Cooper Union	New York, NY	46%
Furman University	Greenville, SC	46%
Hillsdale College	Hillsdale, MI	46%
Gonzaga University	Spokane, WA	45%
San Francisco Art Institute	San Francisco, CA	45%
University of Puget Sound	Tacoma, WA	45%
Rhodes College	Memphis, TN	44%
The University of the South	Sewanee, TN	44%
Rose-Hulman Institute of Technology	Terre Haute, IN	43%
Savannah College of Art and Design	Savannah, GA	43%
University of Dayton	Dayton, OH	42%
University of Denver	Denver, CO	42%
Alcorn State University	Lorman, MS	41%
Andrews University	Berrien Springs, MI	41%
Creighton University	Omaha, NE	41%
Golden Gate University	San Francisco, CA	41%
Centre College	Danville, KY	40%
Eckerd College	St. Petersburg, FL	40%
Southern Methodist University	Dallas, TX	40%
Tulane University	New Orleans, LA	40%
Augustana University	Sioux Falls, SD	39%
DePauw University	Greencastle, IN	39%

School	Location	Percent of Students Receiving Merit-Based Aid
Truman State University	Kirksville, MO	39%
Beloit College	Beloit, WI	38%
Birmingham-Southern College	Birmingham, AL	38%
Calvin University	Grand Rapids, MI	38%
Marquette University	Milwaukee, WI	38%
University of Portland	Portland, OR	38%
Worcester Polytechnic Institute	Worcester, MA	38%
Baylor University	Waco, TX	37%
Butler University	Indianapolis, IN	37%
Landmark College	Putney, VT	37%
New College of Florida	Sarasota, FL	37%
Ave Maria University	Ave Maria, FL	36%
College of Idaho	Caldwell, ID	36%
Lawrence University	Appleton, WI	36%
University of Findlay	Findlay, OH	36%
Case Western Reserve University	Cleveland, OH	35%
Guilford College	Greensboro, NC	35%
Holy Cross College	Notre Dame, IN	35%
Mississippi College	Clinton, MS	35%
Pratt Institute	Brooklyn, NY	35%
Southwestern University	Georgetown, TX	35%
University of Texas of the Permian Basin	Odessa, TX	35%
Abilene Christian University	Abilene, TX	34%
Benedictine College	Atchison, KS	34%
The Catholic University of America	Washington, DC	34%
High Point University	High Point, NC	34%
Whitman College	Walla Walla, WA	34%
Willamette University	Salem, OR	34%
College of Wooster	Wooster, OH	33%

(continued)

TABLE 4-1 *(continued)*

School	Location	Percent of Students Receiving Merit-Based Aid
Colorado School of Mines	Golden, CO	33%
Illinois Institute of Technology	Chicago, IL	33%
Iowa State University	Ames, IA	33%
Lewis & Clark College	Portland, OR	33%
Saint Louis University	St. Louis, MO	33%
St. Lawrence University	Canton, NY	33%
St. Michael's College	Colchester, VT	33%
Stonehill College	Easton, MA	33%
University of South Carolina	Columbia, SC	33%
Carroll College	Helena, MT	32%
Drake University	Des Moines, IA	32%
Florida Polytechnic University	Lakeland, FL	32%
Florida Southern College	Lakeland, FL	32%
Gordon College	Wenham, MA	32%
Hobart and William Smith Colleges	Geneva, NY	32%
John Brown University	Siloam Springs, AR	32%
Miami University—Oxford	Oxford, OH	32%
New Mexico Institute of Mining and Technology	Socorro, NM	32%
Sacred Heart University	Fairfield, CT	32%
Suffolk University	Boston, MA	32%
Biola University	La Mirada, CA	31%
California College of the Arts	San Francisco, CA	31%
Covenant College	Lookout Mountain, GA	31%
Drexel University	Philadelphia, PA	31%
Drury University	Springfield, MO	31%
Harding University	Searcy, AR	31%
Loyola University Chicago	Chicago, IL	31%
Marist College	Poughkeepsie, NY	31%

School	Location	Percent of Students Receiving Merit-Based Aid
Pepperdine University	Malibu, CA	31%
Ringling College of Art and Design	Sarasota, FL	31%
Rollins College	Winter Park, FL	31%
Union College	Schenectady, NY	31%
University of North Alabama	Florence, AL	31%
University of Tampa	Tampa, FL	31%

Source: U.S. News & World Report

Jumping Through Hoops: Marketing of High School Students

As kids move up through middle school and then navigate the high school years, families hear about all the boxes you're supposed to check in order for prospective students to best present themselves to colleges. It's simply not enough to take challenging classes and get good grades and test scores on standardized tests. High schoolers today often juggle many of these (and other) balls:

>> Playing a sport or two, or even three

>> Joining the school band

>> Writing for the school newspaper

>> Participating in or starting a school club or two or three

>> Serving in or running for some student government role

>> Doing volunteer work.

There are many more options beyond these. This section discusses how to think about activities outside the classroom.

Quality over quantity

Many try to play the game of activity overload in the hopes of bolstering their collegiate admission's chances. But there are only so many hours in a day. And given the fact that so many high school students are playing this same game, playing it along with everyone else isn't likely to distinguish your son or daughter in the eye's of college admissions officers and committees.

It's concerning to me to see many teenagers living the lives of time-crazed adults. While I have nothing against "hard work," children should learn about balance and enjoying their lives and childhood.

Workaholism is a real concern and a bad habit that you don't want your kids to develop and carry into adulthood. Psychotherapist and author Dr. Bryan Robinson provides quantifiable proof of what should be intuitive — putting in long hours may provide financial riches, but it can leave workaholics and their families in rags emotionally. Robinson's research found that the children of workaholics suffer many of the same ills — depression, anxiety, and other emotional disorders — as do the children of alcoholics.

His study also found that spouses married to a workaholic felt more estranged in their marriages and less in control of their lives. In Robinson's study, just 45 percent of spouses married to workaholics remained married compared to 84 percent in marriages where no one was a workaholic.

When people overinvest in work, there are consequences. Kids don't get enough of their parent's time; physical, emotional, and mental health problems develop among all members of the family; and divorce (and even suicide) happens. I personally know several people who had a nervous breakdown as a result of the pressures they faced at work. And I know others whose spouse walked out after feeling that their partner's job had become more important than the marriage.

Admissions officers and evaluators at colleges and other post–high school options will not be impressed that your child is enrolled in enough activities to fill up multiple pages on their application forms. For starters, they probably won't spend more than a minute or two glancing over such information. And, they know that students sign up for lots of stuff to make their application appear better. Common sense suggests that students with scads of listed activities typically haven't invested themselves much in any of them.

'Focusing on interests and passions

High school students should be *selective* about what they sign up to do outside of their academics. Their first and primary motivation in committing to a given so-called extracurricular activity should be their interest and passion for that activity. And, the activity doesn't have to be affiliated with their school. It's important to acknowledge that time is precious and shouldn't be wasted.

Let me speak from personal experience. When I was in middle school, my dad got laid off from his job as a mechanical engineer. At that time, his company disbursed a modest amount of money to him in a retirement type account and my father struggled to figure out how to invest it.

He made a number of mistakes investing in stocks and spent a lot of time at this, and it caused him some deal of stress. This led to my interest in what caused the stock market to go up and down over time, and I ended up doing a science fair project on that topic in eighth grade. I won the top prize, which ended up being an unattractive trophy.

During high school, I spent some time continuing to learn about stocks and other investments and actually invested some of my own money earned from cutting lawns and doing other yard work for customers I found on my own. So, in addition to learning about running a small business and servicing customers, I was also gaining more knowledge about investing and personal finance.

At no point in this multi-year process was I thinking about how my interest in this area might help me to get into a college. It was the furthest thing from my mind! But, looking back, I do believe my passion and interest in this area came through in my college application essays and interviews and played a positive factor in my admission to college (I applied to Yale University early). I'm sure you can see how I ended up where I did career-wise.

Life is too short to waste your time on things you don't care about, especially living in America where you have the freedom of choice and so many options to choose from. And, life has plenty of mandatory things to do — don't unnecessarily add to that lengthy list!

Think about high school this way — there are *soooo* many required courses that students have to take. Year after year high schoolers are slogging through English and literature, math, various science courses, social studies and history, a foreign language — and that's on top of all the other stuff they have to take like health class, physical education (gym), and so on.

REMEMBER

While students have a little bit of choice as to what specific classes they take to meet various requirements, there's not much room for electives. So, what a student chooses to do outside of the classroom is one area where they can truly express themselves *and* do what they are really interested in and passionate about.

That's not to say that a student can't do something relating to his favorite classes. For example, maybe inspired by personal experiences and interest in the sciences, some kids elect to explore the medical or veterinary fields. Or perhaps some economic and history classes spur an interest in the business world. The point is to follow interests and yes, aptitude, which happens naturally. Most people normally gravitate toward things that they are comfortable and competent doing.

Helping your teenagers forge their own academic path

For sure, most high schools have plenty of course requirements. And, most kids don't enjoy being in school and being forced to take certain courses.

That said, this is all the more reason why you and your high school student should be sure to make the most of the choices that are afforded them in whatever high school they are enrolled in. Your student will likely have the most latitude to choose what they're interested in with regards to so-called electives. But, upon close examination, some families and their teens are surprised to discover some of the choices they may have regarding fulfilling particular course requirements.

Here are some suggestions to help ensure that your teenager gets the most out of his academic choices in high school:

» Review the entire course catalog for your high school. These days, most schools publish this on their website. You should be able to easily find it by visiting the home webpage for your high school. If you can't find it, call and ask someone in the guidance office where it can be found. Perusing all the courses offered in your high school takes time and effort, and some students don't want to be bothered. Encourage the effort by pointing out the benefits — chief among them is having a course schedule that gets them more excited! Consider scheduling some time to sit down with your teenager to discuss options, which will encourage them to spend some time investigating what's offered.

» Don't just simply follow the expected progression in a particular subject area without at least finding out about your options. Just because "everybody else" or your counselor tells your child that they should take a particular course next, you almost always have options. Encourage your children to check out what those options are and consider what makes the best sense for them and their interests and passions. Of course, students should keep an eye on how given course choices impact preparing them to attend a desired college. But your family should get the facts and not blindly accept conventional thinking about what courses should or shouldn't be taken.

» Research who the inspirational teachers are. This is ideally done by the student, who should speak with other students who had that teacher in the past. You have to be careful not to simply accept any one person's opinion as they surely have different concerns and values than you do. Encourage your teen to probe others as to what specifically they liked or didn't like about a given teacher.

>> Choose advanced courses selectively. Often with the best of intentions, parents (and some counselors) want their kids to be in all the various AP and honors classes available. That can be a mistake because your kids likely have strengths and weaknesses and subject areas they enjoy or even love and those that they don't. If your kid has more of an aptitude for math and science but struggles with history and literature classes, then it's probably a good idea to encourage taking advanced classes in math and science but not so much in history and literature.

>> Check out course offerings at other local schools including community colleges, colleges and universities, adult education programs, and so forth. Take courses not offered in your high school to go deeper into something of interest.

>> Take advantage of online course offerings. There are all sorts of free and low-cost online courses through websites like Codecademy, Coursera, edX, Harvard Extension, Khan Academy, MIT OpenCourseWare, Open Yale Courses, Stanford Online, and Udemy.

>> Read great books. Inspire the love of reading. Whether your son or daughter is passionate about great chefs, technology, designing clothing, or robotics and artificial intelligence, help them find great books on the topic. Now, the challenge for many high school students is having the free time to read books. This is another reason to encourage their selectivity in signing up for activities and not having them be overscheduled!

Playing sports

I love sports. Done well, there are so many benefits that kids and adults derive from them. As a kid, I have fond memories of playing youth baseball, and I still have the team photos from those teams and lots of fun recollections of various teammates.

In high school I ran track, which taught me the value of training and how good it felt to be in shape. (It was also a great way to meet girls who ran track on their team!) I would have loved to play a team sport like basketball — I tried out and got cut. That's okay. I learned that you can't just show up in the middle of high school and make a sports team. I was a decent athlete, but my basketball experience up to that point in time involved shooting baskets in my driveway and playing an occasional pick-up game with friends, who like me, were mediocre basketball players.

In college, I loved playing sports recreationally — in fact, it's one of my favorite college memories and experiences. A friend of mine taught me how to play squash;

up until that point in my life, I thought that squash was just a vegetable I didn't like. I found a group to play pick-up basketball games with weekly. For my residential college, I won the award for being the most committed to going to the gym — my award was a pair of gym socks.

Most kids today have an amazing number of sports options to choose among. However, the business aspect of travel teams presents some challenges and drawbacks. Please see Chapter 2 for the best ways to navigate youth sports teams and youth sports in general.

Getting work experience

Understanding the value of work, and making the connection between working and earning money, is an important step, I believe, in growing up and reaching adulthood. In Chapter 3, I cover this topic extensively, so I won't repeat myself here.

In high school and as post–high school alternatives approach and are considered, your children may want to work for pay, or you may want them to. Especially if they're on track to go to high cost colleges, every little bit earned and saved may help!

Work experience is valued just as much in the college admissions process as school-sponsored clubs, sports, or other extracurricular activities. In fact, in today's world, where fewer teenagers work, college counselors tell me that it's something that can help your college application stand out from the crowd. (Please, though, don't force your teenager to get a job because of what I just stated in the prior sentence!) And, it gives teenagers a taste of what they will likely do after college or whatever alternative they pursue post high school.

During high school, the main work experience that I had was doing lawn cutting and other yard work and maintenance for customers I cultivated in the town where I lived. I pursued this work after becoming disenchanted with being a dishwasher at a nearby Howard Johnson's restaurant where the pay (and food) were lousy and the work mind numbing.

I thought that I could do better and enjoy being outdoors. I had experience helping with yard work around my family's own modest home. So, I put together a marketing sheet and knocked on some doors and left it for people who knew me or seemed like they might be interested.

Soon enough, I had a couple of customers. I did good work for them and my prices were quite reasonable, so those satisfied customers referred others to me. Over time, I soon had plenty of work to keep me busy part-time in the spring while I was still in school, and I worked typically 20 hours or so per week over the summer. I remember those summers fondly — I worked in the mornings before it got too hot and headed to the town beach in the afternoon to hang out with friends.

I learned about marketing and selling, customer service, developing the ability to expand the range of things I could provide customers with, and how to deal with different types of people and customers. The vast majority of customers were great to work with and understood that I was a high school kid, so while they were getting a good price, they weren't getting a "professional landscaper" and all that that entailed! A rare customer or two could be difficult to deal with, and I certainly learned from those experiences — including that sometimes a small business is better off parting company with certain customers!

When it came time to apply to college, I had some worthwhile experience I was able to put on my list of activities and write an essay about. That was never why I started doing this work in the first place — it was simply a matter of wanting to work and have some money of my own. These were good habits that my parents encouraged and instilled in me and my siblings.

TIP

The specific type of paid work your teenager seeks isn't the most important thing so long as it's legal! As my story highlights, the work doesn't have to be anything fancy or impressive sounding. Learning to build your own business can provide a wealth of real-world education. Many entry level jobs open to teenagers provide important lessons in punctuality, listening and following directions, meeting customer needs, and so on. If your teen can find work in a field that interests or intrigues them, so much the better.

In terms of saving money toward college, the portion of those costs your son or daughter may be able to save toward paying for college costs is likely to be quite small. And, remember that the more they make and save in their names, the higher the price most colleges will generally charge them, as I explain in Chapter 6.

Finally, students should also be careful not to work so many hours that it negatively impacts their academic efforts and achievements. There should also be sufficient time to socialize and be a kid in high school!

Volunteering

College applications have a section where applicants detail their activities, including volunteer work. That in and of itself isn't the primary reason that most families value volunteering and other charitable work and giving.

You may not realize this, but many studies have shown that Americans are the most charitable givers in the world. According to one such study from the *Almanac of American Philanthropy* by Karl Zinsmeister (published by Philanthropy Roundtable), on a per-person basis, Americans donate about twice as much as Brits and Canadians and about 20 times as much as Germans and Italians.

You've likely heard about the concentration of wealth in America and wealth inequality. Most people don't know that the top 1 percent of U.S. income earners made about one-third of all donations made. "The wealthiest 1.4 percent of Americans are responsible for 86 percent of the charitable donations made at death," according to the survey.

Americans are also generous with giving their time to good causes, and since most teenagers lack money, the main way they "donate" is through their time. But you certainly hear stories about children raising money for worthy causes.

Volunteering is another area in which teenagers can choose to express themselves and select endeavors that personally interest and engage them. I strongly encourage that, especially if it's something they commit to over a period of time. I think that is vastly superior to just going through the motions by making small efforts in a variety of areas that a kid doesn't really care much about.

Chapter **5**

Guiding Your Child

t takes time, energy, and patience to work with your kids to come up with a post–high school plan for them. In many families, the expectation is that they'll pursue a four-year college degree. But there are other attractive options out there, and you should always remember that what you envision for your son or daughter is likely at least a little bit and perhaps a whole lot different than what he or she envisions.

And trust me when I say that older teenagers can be opinionated, stubborn, and oppositional to what seems to you like the right educational path. This process takes time and patience. And more time and patience. Most parents reach points of frustration along the way and wonder what happened to their sweet young little boy or girl who has morphed into a difficult and moody teenager.

You probably know this to be true, but there's no one right answer. It's counterproductive to already have a specific preordained conclusion in your mind like expecting/wanting/hoping your offspring to attend your collegiate alma mater. Or to be pre-law, pre-med, an engineer, and so on.

The reality is that there are multiple attractive options waiting out there for your son or daughter. Consider the decades of your adult life and how your career and thinking about what you wanted to do has evolved and changed over time compared with what you thought way way back in high school! Sorry, I didn't mean to emphasize how long ago that was! But, seriously, does your current life bear any resemblance to what you envisioned when you were still in high school?

Your goal should be to help your kids develop their interests, talents, and abilities and to help guide them to sensible options. This chapter helps you and yours do just that.

Agreeing to a Process for Making Decisions

Raising kids presents many challenges. Making important decisions of all stripes is one of those challenges.

It is vitally important that both parents be on the same page, because if you're not, your child is going to latch onto the parent who is most aligned with his thinking on post–high school options. This will inevitably cause friction and hurt feelings within the family and won't do good things for family harmony and relationships in the long run.

TIP

Before your kids reach high school, I strongly recommend that you and your spouse set aside time without the kiddos so that you can discuss the range of options you would like your kids to consider. Also discuss how you're going to research and explore those options as well as how you expect to work with your teenagers to reach decisions.

I do not agree with the line of thinking that children can make a final decision without parental input, oversight, and even veto power, especially when that decision involves the parent spending a large amount of money. I've seen cases where parents allow their offspring to choose completely on their own a $70,000+ per year private college.

On the other hand, I don't think parents should dictate or push a child into a specific solution that the parents want or think is best for their kid. Parents may think they know best, but kids have ways of undermining that choice or resenting a parent forcing a choice on them. A balance should be struck so that all parties feel that they have a voice in and play a major role in selecting a good choice.

You should also have a plan for handling disagreements and differences of opinion. Compromising often works, but I do realize that sometimes one party feels extra strongly about something happening or not happening, so sometimes, one parent may seemingly get more of what they want or don't want.

As your kids enter high school, that's a good time for you to sit down with them to jointly explain the process and options you'd like to explore. Explain the process that you and your spouse have already discussed and agreed to. Should your child want to revise any portion of that, I suggest that you and your spouse discuss those suggestions separately and not in front of your child, if for no other reason than you don't want to have disagreements from the beginning of the process of involving your child.

Conducting the Right Research

In Chapter 4, I discuss the importance of academics, achievement, and outside interests and allowing your kids to develop and follow their own interests, subject of course to your wise input and oversight. You and your kids shouldn't get tangled up in what you or anyone else may think is most attractive to college admissions officers. People are often wrong about what they think colleges want.

REMEMBER

College admissions people actually want authenticity and to see passion on the part of applicants. They get tired of reading and hearing the same old stuff over and over and over again. And admissions officers do generally value uniqueness and individuality. Furthermore, you may do long-term damage to your kids by forcing them to mold themselves into something that doesn't actually suit them.

Over time, try to ensure that your kids are exposed to different types of jobs and careers as well as the steps, training, and education necessary to reach such goals. This can be as simple as you periodically discussing various jobs and careers. You can also encourage your children to speak with others you can introduce them to or whom they may meet through their friends and other acquaintances. Be sure your kids understand not just what that person is doing today but also the journey — the training, education, and so forth that led them to where they are now.

Visiting colleges is surely something you and your kids will do when they are later in their high school years. You have opportunities before then to visit and spend time on some college campuses as well. Start close to home, as those will be easiest and least costly for you to visit. You can likely find some family-friendly events, like sporting or performing arts events, at local colleges. Before high school, most kids are not actively thinking about how far from home they may or may not want to live.

The purpose of these early campus visits is for all of you to get your feet wet. It gets the wheels turning regarding the variety of dimensions — size, type and quality of academic offerings, location, and so on — upon which colleges can be categorized and differentiated.

You could also visit some colleges when you visit relatives or perhaps are on a family vacation. If your kids play travel sports, you will likely have some trips away from your home area and near some other colleges. You don't need to be obsessive about it — the point is to make it easy and rack up some visits gradually over, say, the middle school years.

Working with and Hiring "Experts"

Whether or not you believe that it takes a village to raise your children, you will surely encounter and enlist the help and services of various people for aiding in post–high school decisions, including "professionals" in the education and related fields. In this section, I discuss those folks and how to have constructive relationships with them without crushing your finances for those it costs you to hire.

Interacting with teachers

Unless you homeschool your children, teachers will be a constant in your kids' education. Of course, good parents want to keep updated with what their kids are doing in school. Most teachers employ various methods to stay in touch somewhat with parents. And, of course, you can and should regularly talk with your children about their school experiences.

REMEMBER

The key is to find the right level of involvement. Parents can be too detached and miss warning signs of problems. A lack of interest in a child's schoolwork may send the signal to your child that school isn't important or doesn't matter to you. Overly involved parents, on the other hand, may undermine their kid's development of pride and self-confidence in being able to accomplish and master things themselves.

As your kids get older, they should be interacting more with their teachers, and you should encourage them to do so. Of course, you can and should discuss how that is going with your children when they are at home. Explaining to your kids how to interact with different types of adults teaches them valuable skills that will benefit them in their adulthood.

Employing tutors

As your kids get older, you will likely hear about some families choosing to hire tutors, typically to help with specific subjects. This is more prevalent, as you might expect, in higher income communities.

PARENTAL CHALLENGES AND BEING INVOLVED

You've perhaps the terms "helicopter parent" or "snowplow parent" to convey disdain toward parents who seemingly hover over or clear the way for their kids. For sure, parents can at times be too involved. But these pejorative terms are disrespectful, I think, to the important and at times difficult job of parenting. And, I've observed over the years that those who hurl these types of insults may have an agenda in that they may be threatened by parents who know too much or ask too many questions.

No one cares about your kids as much as you do, and no one knows them better. Trust your instincts and get more involved when it seems necessary. Don't let anyone else tell you how to parent your kids. That's not to say that you shouldn't take an interest in new and constructive ways of dealing with parental challenges.

I'm not against tutors, but I do have concerns. A good tutor can provide one-on-one coaching and assistance that may help a student struggling in a particularly difficult area. Tutors aren't cheap to hire, and paying for one on a regular basis can rack up big bills and can create a crutch for a student.

The first line of help that a student should utilize and exhaust is the teacher of the class in which he is struggling. Here's where keeping in touch with teachers proves helpful (see the preceding section). You're already helping to pay for that teacher through your local taxes or private school tuition payments. The teacher should be made aware of the struggles your child is experiencing because they are likely in the best position to understand what is going on and why. Maybe your child should be in a different class or have a different type of teacher. Maybe your child is struggling with something else that is affecting her in this and perhaps other classes. Maybe your child should be in a different type of school. The teacher is the best starting point to get answers as to what may be happening.

I suggest hiring a tutor as the last line of defense and doing so for the short term. Before hiring a tutor, you should discuss the goals and time frame that make sense. Thereafter, stay in touch with the tutor to be sure you're on track and understand what, if anything, may have changed during the course of the tutoring. And, it's important to come up with a plan together so that your child understands the benefits involved along with the cost and commitment needed.

Utilizing school/guidance counselors

When your children are in high school, they should be sure to access and meet regularly with their guidance counselor. The best of these people can provide advice and perspective on course options and selection, standardized testing, grades, and a whole host of other high school issues leading up to college applications. They should also be able to provide some useful advice on selecting colleges to which to apply and preparing good applications.

Now, I can tell you from firsthand experience as well as having talked with numerous people on this topic that there's a wide range of high school guidance counselors. In fairness to them, I will say that many of them have scores of students assigned to them and they don't have the time, energy, or incentive to give most students much time. In the worst cases, counselors are not well trained and not particularly helpful.

TIP

If your child and/or you aren't satisfied with the counselor assigned to your child, you have the right to ask for a different counselor. Please do so respectfully, because you don't want to harm your kid's chances of having a good relationship with that department. Remember that counselors are involved in portions of most college applications, so you don't want them on your bad side! Also, be aware of and consider a college planning service (discussed in the next section).

Working with a college planning service

There are people and companies you can hire to help your son or daughter with the college application process. A good college planning/counseling service can help with the following types of activities:

>> Brainstorming a list of colleges to visit and consider.

>> Discussing the different types of standardized tests and how to best prepare for them.

>> Finalizing a list of colleges to which to apply.

>> Assisting with preparing and completing college applications including critiquing of essays. (They aren't allowed to and won't do the actual writing of essays.)

>> Discussing financing options and costs, including the availability of merit money at various schools.

WARNING

Please note that absent from this list is any hope or guarantee that the counselor can magically get your teenager admitted to a college that she is otherwise not qualified for. I would not hire a college planning counselor or a college planning firm that promises specific results or makes claims that they can get your child admitted to colleges that you or others otherwise cannot.

HOW HIGH SCHOOL COUNSELORS AND ADMINISTRATORS REACT TO PRIVATE COLLEGE COUNSELORS

Different high schools and their counselors react differently to private, independent college counselors. Most high school guidance counselors are fine with these outside service providers as they understand that such a counselor can devote far more individual attention to a student than a high school counselor is able to provide. In some high schools, outside counselors are invited to give presentations to parents and students with tips about the college application process.

Occasionally, high school administrators may feel threatened by private college counselors. Here's what happened to a private college counselor I know (I'll call her Michelle for purposes of the story) when she was arranging a presentation at a local public library. As is often the case, the librarian communicated with the town's public high school to inform them of the upcoming talk.

In short order, the high school principal actually tried to get the librarian to not do the event, reasoning that her high school's guidance counselors had everything covered on such topics. This is, of course, a ridiculous argument, and the librarian did the right thing and held the event anyway. Unfortunately, the petty principal didn't tell parents and others about the session that could be of help to them.

The private counselor and her local firm are highly regarded in the local community, so that wasn't the issue. The unfortunate fact is that some high school personnel are petty and territorial about their domains. As a parent, I don't think you need to be concerned about this as this story simply illustrates a school administrator trying to throw his weight around in an inappropriate way.

Most college consultants are available to hire either on a straight hourly basis or for a set fee for a given package of services. Prices are not cheap — many consultants have triple-digit hourly billing rates and complete packages can set you back $5,000, $10,000 or more depending upon the range of services desired. Some firms offer lower cost packages for a subset of services such as compiling a list of recommended colleges for your teenager to which to apply, review, and critique of application essays, and so forth.

Shop around and be sure to thoroughly interview prospective counselors to inquire about their background and experience counseling teenagers and their families. Be sure to inquire specifically about their experience working in college admissions and/or financial aid offices if that's the kind of help you're seeking. The number of college planners who have no actual college admissions experience is staggering.

Most college planners offer an introductory session (typically 30 minutes) so you can get to know one another and see if there is a comfort and compatibility with each other. I encourage parents and the teenager who needs assistance to attend an intro session with the college counselor so that everyone has a chance to check each other out.

Hiring financial advisors

Most families have limited financial resources so it makes good sense to make the most of the money that you earn and the benefits you may access through your employer. Wanting to save and invest money for future educational expenses (such as college) is a normal reaction. But, please don't head down any path until you read the rest of this book, especially the chapters about how colleges determine how much to charge you (Chapter 6) and Part 4.

I've been involved in as well as written about the financial advisory profession for decades. I urge you to be careful if and when you set out to hire someone to help you. Before doing so, it's imperative that you educate yourself and find out as much as you can because otherwise it will be much harder for you to evaluate the competence and expertise of someone you may hire. My book *Personal Finance For Dummies* (Wiley) can give you a crash course and also explains how to interview and work with a financial advisor.

WARNING

Many financial advisors and brokers are woefully uneducated about how colleges set their prices for each prospective applicant based upon their personal financial circumstances. The standard schtick you may hear will be horror stories about how expensive college is (or will be) for your children and why you need to save and invest big bucks through the broker/advisor's firm.

And, many "advisors" have conflicts of interest in how they are compensated based upon their specific recommendations. They may sell investments, insurance, and other financial products that pay them commissions. It may also cause a conflict of interest when an advisor charges a percentage of assets under management because the advisor has a disincentive to recommend strategies (such as investing in your employer's 401(k) or 403(b) plan, investing in real estate, or paying down your mortgage) that take money away from them to manage.

Getting assistance with financial aid forms

As I explain in painstaking detail in Chapter 6, colleges collect an enormous amount of personal and financial information from you and then decide how much to charge you. It's a complicated, confusing, and downright mysterious process. Each college has their own unique twist on things, and they don't disclose exactly how the process works.

As with anything so complicated and with so much potential money at stake, it should come as no surprise to learn that financial aid consultants are available for hire. While they don't come cheap, a good one may be able to more than pay for themselves if they help you get a better price from a college that your child wants to attend and receives an offer of admission from.

Be aware that the longer you wait to consult such an advisor, the less they will be able to do in terms of helping you to legally position your finances to obtain better college pricing. That's not to say that they can't add value even if you wait until around the time your financial aid forms are due.

Dealing with Mental Health Issues

While most kids are happy most of the time, childhood certainly has its setbacks and unhappy episodes and stressors. Dealing with adversity can teach your children how to be resilient and how to cope with life's obstacles and down periods.

Adolescence adds even more stressors to a young person's life, and that is a period when mental health challenges may emerge. The college years are also a prevalent time for mental health illness to arise.

Some mental health experts say that certain types of mental illnesses are on the rise among young people, but there are other opinions as well. The prevalence of subjectively determined illnesses is hard to measure over time. Please consider the insights from psychologist Dr. Brian Russell:

"Statistically speaking, I don't think that mental illness per-se — kids being born with or contracting diagnosable brain/behavioral disorders — is necessarily something that parents today need to be more worried about than past generations. I think the vast majority of kids are still within the normal spectrum with respect to their brain functioning. Parents today probably need to be more worried about their normal kids being lumped into diagnostic categories like ADD/ADHD or the autism "spectrum" as a means of pathologizing normal-but-annoying behavior than about their kids being seriously mentally ill.

That said, I do think that parents today need to worry about the attitudes that their kids can develop — particularly in the absence of concerted, constructive parental attention — from exposure to a lifestyle/culture in which they're bombarded with facilitators/promoters of self-absorption, self-pity, entitlement, etc., all of which ultimately don't serve anyone well and leave people feeling empty and unfulfilled even if not clinically/diagnosable depressed/anxious."

According to the National Alliance on Mental Illness (www.nami.org), while each specific type of mental illness will have its own unique symptoms, common signs of mental illness in adolescents (and adults) may include the following:

>> Excessive worrying or fear

>> Feeling excessively sad or low

>> Confused thinking or problems concentrating and learning

>> Extreme mood changes, including uncontrollable "highs" or feelings of euphoria

>> Prolonged or strong feelings of irritability or anger

>> Avoiding friends and social activities

>> Difficulties understanding or relating to other people

>> Changes in sleeping habits or feeling tired and low energy

>> Changes in eating habits such as increased hunger or lack of appetite

>> Difficulty perceiving reality (delusions or hallucinations, in which a person experiences and senses things that don't exist in objective reality)

>> Inability to perceive changes in one's own feelings, behavior, or personality ("lack of insight" or *anosognosia*)

>> Abuse of substances like alcohol or drugs

>> Multiple physical ailments without obvious causes (such as headaches, stomach aches, vague and ongoing "aches and pains")

>> Thinking about suicide

>> Inability to carry out daily activities or handle daily problems and stress

>> An intense fear of weight gain or concern with appearance

NAMI also highlights the fact that mental health conditions can also begin to develop in young children. Because they're still learning how to identify and talk about thoughts and emotions, their most obvious symptoms are behavioral. Symptoms in younger children may include the following:

>> Changes in school performance

>> Excessive worry or anxiety, for instance fighting to avoid bed or school

>> Hyperactive behavior

>> Frequent nightmares

>> Frequent disobedience or aggression

>> Frequent temper tantrums

3

Confronting College Costs: Traditional Colleges and Alternatives

Chapter **6**

Seeing How Traditional Colleges Decide What to Charge You

Many people don't know that colleges and universities set vastly different prices for different students. In this chapter, I explain how the process works for colleges and universities to set the price that they will charge your son or daughter to attend their school.

TRUE STORY

A number of years ago when I worked as a personal financial counselor, I was contacted by a divorced mother whose son was entering his first year of college, which she was paying for 100 percent herself. She had a relatively low-paying job but had a couple hundred thousand dollars in her name in regular nonretirement accounts. She never applied for "financial aid" because she felt that with her modest home and financial assets, she would never qualify.

After reading some articles that I had written and meeting with me, she realized that her son should apply for financial aid. During his first year, she decided to invest a healthy chunk of her savings in a low-cost annuity (retirement-type) account. She did this upon realizing that she literally had not saved any of her own money toward her own retirement. The annuity provided her with the opportunity to quickly save and invest a chunk of money at once into an account that was recognized as earmarked for her retirement.

In her son's remaining three years, they saved themselves nearly $50,000 through a reduced price (grant money) that the school offered them. This happened due to the one simple investment decision she made and the fact that she finally applied for "financial aid."

She regretted not knowing this before he started college so that they could have gotten a better freshman-year price. Or maybe he could have attended a different and more preferable school if he had completed financial aid forms and applications and gotten better pricing from several schools.

There's a lot of money at stake given the total sticker price at many colleges and universities today. Better understanding the rules and strategy of the game can easily save you tens of thousands of dollars and perhaps $100,000 or more for your kids, especially if you have multiple children.

REMEMBER

I didn't have any part in making up this process nor do I implicitly or explicitly support, condone, or endorse it. Could it be improved? Absolutely! But, that's well beyond the scope of this book. Besides, that kind of change is slow in coming. In the meantime, stick with me as I explain how colleges decide what amount to charge your child for attending their school and what you can do to get the best price from colleges and universities.

Taking All Your (Financial) Clothes OFF!

If you've applied to rent an apartment or leased or bought a car or a home with a loan (mortgage), you've had to complete a bunch of forms and divulge some details of your financial life. In each of these cases, the other party wants to know and have some reasonable assurance that you can afford the financial commitment or transaction. That makes sense, right?

Colleges and universities have a different agenda and concern when your offspring apply for admission. They will ask for more personal and financial information than you have surely ever given before to any business or organization, and they use all of that for one purpose — to determine how much of their full price they will charge your family.

Higher-education institutions say that your son or daughter can apply for and possibly receive "financial aid," which is a bit of a misnomer. When schools say they are giving you money, such as through one of their grants or scholarships, what they are really doing for you is reducing their high price to a lower price.

Financial aid consultant Kal Chany says that the most financial aid goes not to the "neediest" but to those who best understand the financial aid process.

This happens for many reasons, including the myriad complexities in the financial aid system and process. Now, not everyone involved in the financial aid process agrees with Chany's perspective.

One former college financial aid officer tells me that financial aid indeed greatly benefits many lower income students who are in fact the neediest and yet barely understand the financial aid process and grasp just enough to get through it. I can see that, but I think it's unfortunate that some people who could get a better price from colleges don't because they don't apply due to misconceptions and the mysterious, complex, and hard-to-understand process involved.

Also, the current system effectively penalizes those who work hard and save and invest their money and grants better pricing to those who don't work hard and who don't save and invest. This is not in any way to suggest that all applicants fall into one of these two categories. For sure, there are hardworking folks who don't earn a lot and who struggle to make ends meet and save money.

REMEMBER

Structuring your finances to maximize aid awarded to your children entering and in college is legal and ethical, says Chany. He argues, and I concur, that just as making decisions to legally minimize taxes is ethical, so too is maximizing aid (minimizing college prices) so long as you tell the truth in aid applications.

Understanding commonly requested information

Through standardized forms, most schools ask for the following financial information:

>> Student demographic and aid eligibility questions

>> Sibling information and college cost of attendance

>> Detailed questions about parents' employment and income and other sources of income

>> Parents' and student's personal income tax information and details

>> Value of cash, and savings and checking accounts for parents and student

>> Current worth of investments for parents and student

>> Valuation of businesses and investment

Expect to spend at least several hours answering more than 100 detailed questions dealing with the preceding topics. The Department of Education's website says,

"It takes most people less than an hour to complete and submit a new Free Application for Federal Student Aid (FAFSA®). This includes gathering any documents or data needed, completing and reviewing the application, and reading the important information on the Confirmation page you'll receive after you sign and submit your FAFSA®."

To that I say "nonsense," unless you're one of those rare people who is super financially organized, and you easily understand all types of financial and other questions on a government questionnaire! I know folks who in the past spent an hour or more just completing the Federal Student Aid (FSA) ID process (see Chapter 10), which was a nightmare for many and a prerequisite for beginning the FAFSA® form!

Also, I urge you not to rush through completing the document. Especially the first year you complete the FAFSA® form, expect that you're going to have some questions about the terminology and questions. And, you're going to need to look some things up. And ponder and research others. What is your home worth? You could spend hours researching and considering that one alone!

TIP

You can save your work and return to it later. I encourage you to review your completed answers at a time later than the first time you dive into the form to be sure you understood everything and presented your information in a way that is most beneficial to you and accurate and truthful.

Lest you think that that amount of information should be sufficient and invasive enough, we're hardly done here. Many colleges and universities require that you provide them with a copy of your recent federal income tax return. Why do they do this after they ask you a blizzard of questions about the items on your income tax return? For the simple reason that they don't trust people to provide correct and accurate (in other words, truthful) answers.

TECHNICAL STUFF

It used to be the case that in addition to all the stress that families faced in completing myriad financial aid forms by their spring deadlines, they also had added pressure to get their most recent year's federal income tax return done in time to share with colleges. Now, thankfully, you are asked to provide the prior year's federal income tax return, which you should have completed in the previous calendar year, even if you got an extension of time to complete it.

Coming to terms with supplemental information requests

Now, we're still not done! Some schools also ask for the following information:

- ❯❯ Housing and other real estate ownership and expenses

- ❯❯ Average monthly living expenses broken out by category — for example, housing, food, utilities, car maintenance and gasoline, medical expenses, insurance costs, loan payments, and so on

- ❯❯ All sources of each parent's income including money received from family members (such as gifts)

- ❯❯ Details on all cars owned including date of purchase and purchase price.

I know you're quite eager to tackle all the financial aid forms and documents. I cover that in Chapter 10.

Valuing Wanting One Another

All schools go through a number-crunching process to determine how much they believe your family can "afford" to pay for college. In Part 4, I explain how to best position your finances to deal with this unpleasant reality.

In the meantime, there's another important component to all this for you to consider. You can have two different families with identical financial situations and their respective children may receive vastly different prices from a given college or university. How can that be? It's simply a matter of how much a given school wants a particular applicant.

Here are common reasons that a school may offer lower pricing (greater financial aid) to a student they desire more:

- ❯❯ **Academic stars:** No, this doesn't mean that your offspring have to be ranked first in their class academically or have a high school transcript chock-full of advanced placement courses. But it does mean that the particular school wants higher achieving students like your child, and they are willing to offer "merit" money to woo them (see Chapter 4). Schools are most likely to offer merit money to students who have higher standardized test scores and/or GPAs than the school's typical or median student.

- ❯❯ **Athletic recruits:** Colleges have all sorts of sports teams they need to fill roster spots on, so if your son or daughter fits the academic requirements for a college and a coach desires them for a particular team, an athletic scholarship may be offered. Some, but by no means all, colleges offer sports scholarships (Division III colleges can't and don't). For more details, see the next section, "Checking on Realities for Recruited Athletes."

>> **Special categories of grant money:** There are all sorts of unusual and even quirky categories of money at various schools for applicants who have certain talents or check particular boxes. Ursinus College, for example, has a "Creative Writing Award" that provides a $40,000-per-year scholarship for "creative writers of outstanding originality and potential. The award winner will have the honor of living in the dorm room once occupied by J.D. Salinger, who attended Ursinus." Some colleges offer grant money for various specific ethnic groups, minorities, and races such as Native Americans, Alaskans, or any number of other minorities. There are special grants for women, and a number of schools offer grant money for students with particular disabilities. See Chapter 11 for more information on grants and scholarships, including those provided by non-college sources.

Checking on Realities for Recruited Athletes

In Chapter 2, I provide background information on youth sports and the costs, benefits, and decisions surrounding it. In this section, I provide and discuss some numbers showing the prevalence of different types of athletes at the college level and the realities surrounding athletic scholarships and being a recruited student-athlete.

Parents and their offspring have all sorts of dreams and fantasies about their kids playing sports, getting scholarships, and perhaps even turning pro and making big money from their sport. There's nothing inherently wrong with having dreams and aspirations, but it's important that they be largely grounded in reality and tempered with solid, back-up plans.

REMEMBER

Few people are fortunate enough to have the talent, drive, and luck that is often required to actually make decent money playing a sport. And even if that does happen years down the road, I can guarantee you that the money-making period won't last long, and your son or daughter will have many more years of adult working life remaining.

TIP

Try to stay focused on the long-term benefits that sports can provide, including:

>> **Physical fitness and wellness:** This can also include understanding the value of good nutrition and not putting bad stuff (drugs, alcohol, and so on) into your body because of how it makes you feel and the damage it can do.

>> **Understanding the value of effort and focus:** To master a sport and excel at it, a student-athlete has to put in a good deal of practice. Of course, this should be done in moderation and not infringe upon having enough time to do well in school.

>> **Experiencing the value of teamwork and having a role:** I think this is one of the greatest benefits of playing sports, especially team sports. Think about it — when your son or daughter enters the workforce, those teamwork skills will come into play and be quite useful.

>> **Mastering time-management and juggling different responsibilities:** You can't take challenging courses and have a significant outside commitment like a varsity sport if you aren't good at managing your time. To that I would also add that it's an activity to keep teenagers out of trouble. It sops up free time and leads participants to be tired!

Looking at the probability of competing in college athletics

The NCAA has compiled some useful statistics that show what portion of high school athletes go on to make teams at the collegiate level for different men and women's sports. The data also show how the collegiate sports opportunities break out by the division of play.

Overall, the NCAA calculates that there are approximately 8 million high school athletes, and of those, about 480,000 of them (or 6 percent) go on to compete at the college level. Please keep in mind as you review the data in Figure 6-1 that just because someone makes a college team, doesn't mean that they get much — if any — playing time or even a roster spot on a team over four years.

Deciding on the likelihood of competing in professional sports

Another reason that some are attracted to sports and college athletics is the hope or dream of making it professionally. This is, of course, limited to a handful of sports. Figure 6-2 shows what portion of eligible collegiate athletes are drafted in a given year.

Please keep in mind that getting drafted doesn't in any way mean that these athletes are able to make a good living for any length of time on the pro circuit. The vast majority of drafted athletes never make it to the "Big Show" or equivalent and end up moving on to something else after one or a few years in the minor leagues (at low pay) for their chosen sport.

	High School Participants	NCAA Participants	Overall % HS to NCAA	% HS to NCAA Division I	% HS to NCAA Division II	% HS to NCAA Division III
Men						
Baseball	487,097	35,460	7.3%	2.2%	2.2%	2.9%
Basketball	551,373	18,816	3.4%	1.0%	1.0%	1.4%
Cross Country	270,095	14,270	5.3%	1.8%	1.4%	2.1%
Football	1,036,842	73,557	7.1%	2.8%	1.8%	2.5%
Golf	144,024	8,609	6.0%	2.0%	1.6%	2.3%
Ice Hockey	35,060	4,229	12.1%	4.8%	0.6%	6.6%
Lacrosse	113,313	14,310	12.6%	3.0%	2.4%	7.2%
Soccer	456,362	25,072	5.5%	1.3%	1.5%	2.7%
Swimming	138,935	9,697	7.0%	2.7%	1.1%	3.2%
Tennis	158,151	7,838	5.0%	1.6%	1.0%	2.3%
Track & Field	600,097	28,698	4.8%	1.9%	1.2%	1.7%
Volleyball	60,976	2,163	3.5%	0.7%	0.6%	2.2%
Water Polo	22,501	1,047	4.7%	2.7%	0.8%	1.2%
Wrestling	245,564	7,239	2.9%	1.0%	0.8%	1.2%
Women						
Basketball	412,407	16,614	4.0%	1.2%	1.2%	1.6%
Cross Country	223,518	15,632	7.0%	2.7%	1.7%	2.6%
Field Hockey	59,856	6,103	10.2%	3.0%	1.4%	5.8%
Golf	78,781	5,375	6.8%	2.8%	2.0%	2.1%
Ice Hockey	9,609	2,400	25.0%	8.9%	1.2%	14.9%
Lacrosse	96,904	12,061	12.4%	3.8%	2.7%	6.0%
Soccer	390,482	27,811	7.1%	2.4%	1.9%	2.8%
Softball	367,861	20,316	5.5%	1.7%	1.6%	2.2%
Swimming	175,594	12,848	7.3%	3.3%	1.2%	2.9%
Tennis	190,768	8,608	4.5%	1.5%	1.0%	2.0%
Track & Field	488,592	30,018	6.1%	2.7%	1.5%	1.9%
Volleyball	446,583	17,471	3.9%	1.2%	1.1%	1.6%
Water Polo	21,054	1,216	5.8%	3.6%	1.0%	1.1%

FIGURE 6-1: Percentage of high school athletes who go on to play at the collegiate level.

Source: NCAA

	NCAA Participants	Approximate # Draft Eligible	# Draft Picks	# NCAA Drafted	% NCAA to Major Pro
Baseball	35,460	7,880	1,214	775	9.8%
M Basketball	18,816	4,181	60	52	1.2%
W Basketball	16,614	3,692	36	34	0.9%
Football	73,557	16,346	256	255	1.6%
M Ice Hockey	4,229	940	217	65	6.9%

FIGURE 6-2: Percentage of collegiate athletes who subsequently play professional sports.

Source: NCAA

The numbers in Table 6-1 show a decent number of college baseball players get drafted. However, only about 17 percent of players who were drafted and signed a minor league contract ultimately made it to Major League Baseball, and many of those for a short period of time. Here's how the odds of making it to the MLB vary by the round drafted (note that there are 40 rounds in the MLB draft).

TABLE 6-1   **Drafted Baseball Players Who Make it to Major Leagues**

Draft Round	Played in MLB	Played 3+ yrs in MLB
1st round	67%	47%
2nd round	49%	31%
3rd round	40%	21%
4th round	35%	18%
5th round	33%	18%
6th round	24%	10%
10th round	17%	8%
12th–20th rounds	10%	4%

Figuring out how college athletic scholarships work

There are plenty of misperceptions and misunderstandings regarding collegiate sport scholarships. And, there's ample opportunity to be taken advantage of and end up without good college options for those who pursue being recruited as a student-athlete, whether or not a scholarship is involved. Being an educated customer is key to making sound decisions.

Full versus partial scholarships

The vast majority of athletic scholarships (99 percent in fact) are partial scholarships and are for so-called *equivalency sports*. Division 1 men equivalency sports are baseball, cross-country, fencing, golf, gymnastics, ice hockey, lacrosse, rifle, skiing, soccer, swimming, tennis, track and field, volleyball, water polo, and wrestling. For Division 1 women, equivalency sports are bowling, cross-country, fencing, field hockey, golf, ice hockey, lacrosse, rowing, skiing, track and field, soccer, softball, swimming, and water polo.

Additionally, all DII sports and National Association of Intercollegiate Athletics (NAIA) sports are equivalency sports. The NAIA is a competitor to the NCAA and is comprised primarily of smaller colleges. (NCAA Division III sports do not offer athletic scholarships.)

Some full scholarships are awarded for equivalency sport athletes for the most coveted and valued recruits. This is more likely to happen for athletes who have offers from multiple colleges to consider and/or who could play a division higher. Some student-athletes choose to play in a lower division for a better collegiate/academic fit or because of lower cost of attendance.

In contrast to equivalency sports, there are so-called *head count sports,* and scholarships from those teams are always full scholarships (in other words, 100 percent). Just 1 percent of all collegiate student-athletes enjoy full scholarships. With men's sports, such teams can include DI basketball and DI-A football (now known as Football Bowl Subdivision). For women's sports, the head count full scholarships come from DI basketball, gymnastics, tennis, and volleyball.

As you may imagine, it's the bigger name sports colleges you may have heard of that fit the bill here. These include the following collegiate athletic conferences: American Athletic Conference, Atlantic Coast Conference, Big 12 Conference, Big Ten Conference, Conference USA, Division I FBS Independents, Mid-American Conference, Mountain West Conference, Pac-12 Conference, Southeastern Conference, and Sun Belt Conference.

Dealing with recruited athlete offers

Most recruited athletes don't receive athletic scholarships. Being "recruited" means the following typically happens. College coaches try to identify promising high school student-athletes during their high school tenure. When they find a good fit (which includes academically) for their program, they may make an offer or extend an invitation for that student-athlete to visit their campus and program.

Most coaches in most programs are given a certain number of recruiting slots by the admission's office. What this typically means is that with the coach's support, most of these recruited student-athletes are admitted, typically through the early action/decision period. Coaches, in conjunction with the admission's office, will do a preliminary screening of a possible recruit early in the process to ensure that the student-athlete meets academic and other requirements important to the college.

While a student-athlete can rack up multiple offers from various schools, he needs to select just one school to which to commit and apply early. This potentially puts the student-athlete in a vulnerable spot because if the coach changes his mind or doesn't offer enthusiastic support in the admissions process or the admission's office chooses not to admit the student, the student-athlete will likely have lost the other recruited athlete offers he had at other institutions. Coaches can't wait around and will move on to other candidates when it is clear they aren't an athlete's first choice.

INVESTIGATE

Do your homework and be sure you understand what the offer and support a given coach is making to your student-athlete means and the likelihood of getting an offer of admission. Ask around to find out what the coach's and school's track records are with prior recruiting overtures. At some colleges, nearly all student-athletes who are offered a coach's support may gain admission whereas at other schools, half or less may eventually succeed.

Of course, your student-athlete should do some soul searching and be sure that the college she seeks to apply to early as a recruited athlete is really the one that she desires. A good question to ponder: If your child isn't able to play at some point due to injury, the coach cutting the player, or the player becoming disenchanted with and choosing to leave a team, how is your student going to feel about being at that college without playing her chosen sport?

WARNING

The worst that can happen, in my observation and opinion, is that chasing after playing a collegiate sport can distort the process of college applications and selection for some student-athletes. It's all about priorities and focus. Finding the right academic schools should take precedence over finding a particular sports program. A good student-athlete should be able to do both.

At a small speaking event for talented high school baseball players wanting to learn more about playing college baseball, MLB manager and player Joe Girardi advised student-athletes getting the best education that they can and said to the players that they will be found if they have talent to play beyond college. In his own case, he turned down a baseball offer from a small school with weak academics in the south and ended up getting an engineering degree and playing baseball at Northwestern and was drafted into the MLB.

TIP

Make sure your student fully understands what he is signing up for when it comes to a college sport. Some coaches put the sport ahead of academics and everything else. Be sure to explore alternatives, including playing in a lower division where you may get a better financial aid offer or have more free time to pursue academics or other interests. With baseball, for example, plenty of pitchers get drafted out of Division III play and end up making it to play Major League Baseball.

Club sports are worth considering at some schools and can be quite good, especially at larger or big sports schools. Finally, don't rule out the possibility of your son or daughter getting into a school that fits them well and then trying out (walking on) for their desired sport.

Understanding the realities of athletic scholarship offers

When a scholarship is involved, be sure that you understand the process. The first step typically is for the coach to extend what is called a *verbal scholarship offer*. As you may imagine, a verbal offer is not a legally binding offer on either party.

The next step is for the school to offer the student-athlete a *national letter of intent.* If the student-athlete accepts and signs this, the school is committing to offer an athletic scholarship for one year and the student is accepting the offer and is committing to come to that school and program. See the NCAA's website on this topic at www.nationalletter.org.

Many folks don't understand that athletic scholarships are not four-year commitments on the school's part. It's a year-to-year proposition and can be discontinued for a variety of reasons, including but not limited to breaking of program behavior or academic rules or guidelines, change of coaches, inadequate performance (judged solely by the coach), injuries, low grades, and so on.

Don't be shy about inquiring about what has happened with prior student-athlete scholarship recipients and what portion of them received that money all four years. For those who didn't last that long, find out why.

IN THIS CHAPTER

» Considering and evaluating four-year colleges

» Understanding what the U.S. military academies have to offer

» Contemplating community colleges

» Taking time to work or try something else

Chapter **7**

Surveying the Range of College Options

As I explain in Chapter 1, in recent generations, more and more people go to college after high school. Unfortunately, many colleges have gotten prohibitively expensive and are too often not preparing students for the workforce realities that await them. Furthermore, a surprisingly large percentage of students fail to complete their four-year college degrees.

By all means, most high school students should examine the range of college options available and seek out institutions that provide a quality education at a good price. That said, now more than ever, families should also explore the increasing number of and attractive alternatives to traditional colleges. This chapter and the next one should help you with jump-starting that process.

Considering Four-Year Colleges

Ryan Craig, author of *A New U: Faster + Cheaper Alternatives to College* (BenBella Books), predicts that increasing numbers of future high school graduates will realize that they have a choice with "faster + cheaper alternatives" to traditional colleges and universities. He still sees the college degree as the "default choice" for the foreseeable future.

And he argues that that route makes a good deal of sense for students who gain admission to the top 200 or so colleges (which have acceptance rates of less than 50 percent) and for whom the expense is affordable. "If you go to any prominent company or organization, you'll be hard-pressed to find anyone in a leadership role who hasn't attended one of these schools," says Craig.

What Craig is suggesting here is that those students (and their parents) who should most consider alternatives to high-priced, traditional four-year colleges are those who would struggle to afford college and who can't gain entrance to the top 200 or so colleges. He (and I) have seen too many families and their students taking on crushing levels of debt for mediocre college educations and degrees that don't prepare them for the better and higher paying jobs of today. That said, everyone should explore alternatives and weigh the pros and cons and then make an informed choice.

Understanding a liberal arts education and alternatives

When looking at colleges, a lot of students don't know quite what they want to study. Perusing the lists of the highest ranked colleges and universities, you will find in examining many of them that they tout offering a so-called "liberal arts education."

Examining what a liberal arts education can include

Allow me to borrow from my alma mater (Yale University) and how they define it:

"Yale is committed to the idea of a liberal arts education through which students think and learn across disciplines, literally liberating or freeing the mind to its fullest potential. The essence of such an education is not what you study but the result — gaining the ability to think critically and independently and to write, reason, and communicate clearly — the foundation for all professions.

There is no specific class you have to take at Yale, but you are required to learn broadly and deeply. Depth is covered in your major. Breadth is covered in three study areas (the humanities and arts, the sciences, and the social sciences) and three skill areas (writing, quantitative reasoning, and foreign language). A Yale education instills in students the values, goals, skills, and knowledge they need to pursue inspiring work, to take joy in lifetime learning, and to lead successful and meaningful lives."

That sounds all well and good, and for some people, a liberal arts education may be a good fit. Proponents of a liberal arts education argue that such an education teaches students to think critically and write and communicate well — skills valued by employers. And, as I discuss in Chapter 1, employers value soft skills (such as teamwork, communication, organization, creativity, adaptability, and punctuality), which can be learned and improved upon in college. (A four-year college, of course, isn't the only place to hone such skills.)

For others, in our increasingly competitive global economy, I think there are some potentially better alternatives to consider. I fully dive into those alternatives in the next chapter.

REMEMBER

Also, please keep in mind that many folks like me who attend the leading liberal arts colleges and universities end up going on to graduate school for advanced degrees, for example in business, law, medicine, and so forth.

Knowing when liberal arts may not fit

WARNING

For some students, a liberal arts degree can be a significant waste of time and money. One example might be a student who has a high level of interest in business and entrepreneurship and wishes to gain a solid undergraduate business education. A traditional liberal arts school lacking any business courses would probably be a poor choice for such a student.

Another example would be a student for whom a trade or technical school might be a better fit. Trade or technical schools (including community colleges) can provide specific training in particular areas such as automotive technology, carpentry, computer-aided drafting and design, computer information systems, dental technician, manufacturing technology, medical assistant, nursing, paramedic, and physical therapy.

Solid technical training has the advantage of providing skills that should lead to jobs upon graduation. The counter argument to getting technical training is that you're more limited in the range of work you can potentially be considered qualified to perform. And what if, for example, a student is trained to be an auto mechanic and then ends up disliking the actual work after not that many years of employment?

Finding where the job openings will be

For those who like to think opportunistically, consider the recent analysis done by the Conference Board that shows future labor shortages that are expected to cluster around three major occupational groups:

"Health-related occupations. The same aging of the U.S. population that will curtail working-age population growth to as low as 0.15 percent by 2030 is also driving up demand for medical workers. At the same time, high education and experience requirements limit entry into the job market. The result is a dearth in many healthcare professions, including occupational therapy assistants, physical therapists and therapist assistants, nurse practitioners and midwives, and dental hygienists. Among doctors, optometrists and podiatrists are the specialists most at risk of shortage, with the general physicians and surgeons category not far behind.

Skilled labor occupations. These jobs typically require more than a high-school education, but not a bachelor's degree. Unlike healthcare, the primary driver of shortages here is not increased demand — employment growth is expected to be low in the coming decade — but instead a rapidly shrinking supply of young people entering these fields as increasing numbers retire. Skilled labor occupations most at risk include water and wastewater treatment plant and system operators, crane and tower operators, transportation inspectors, and construction and building inspectors.

STEM occupations. U.S. policymakers have long been concerned about shortages in science, technology, engineering, and mathematics, but many of these fields rank surprisingly average in a national context. Moderating the risk of shortages is the relatively high number of young entrants compared to baby-boomer retirees, as well as the large proportion of new immigrants in STEM jobs. Moreover, strong productivity growth means that output will continue to expand in areas like information technology, telecommunications, and high-tech manufacturing even as workforces in these jobs are expected to shrink. Nevertheless, certain STEM fields—including mathematical science; information security; and civil, environmental, biomedical, and agricultural engineering — do face significant shortages."

One final point. I think that everyone can benefit from gaining background about business. It's the universal language of the workplace. Even if you want to work in a nonprofit, you should understand concepts such as revenues, customer acquisition and service, marketing, expenses, financial statements, and so on.

Creating your own business education

Because my family moved in the middle of my high school experience, I was able to attend and graduate from a reasonably well regarded public high school. And, then I attended Yale University, which is well regarded for higher education.

Despite the excellent schools I was able to attend, looking back, I was disappointed not having gotten some grounding in the world of business through the age at which I graduated from college. (I certainly got that through my own work experiences, including small businesses I ran growing up.)

WARNING

At liberal arts–focused colleges and universities, the closest you will generally get to a business-related course are economics courses. Having majored in economics in college (along with biology), I can tell you that you will learn very little about how business works in the real world from taking most economics courses. That is not only because of the arcane subject material but also because of the academic types who teach most college economics classes (there are, of course, some exceptions).

For students who attend a college that doesn't offer business courses, don't despair. There are numerous other ways you can find out about the world and language of business:

>> During your latter years of college (summers) and immediately after, go to work in business. Find the best organizations that you can, work hard, and be a sponge and soak up all that you can.

>> Read the best business books and publications, especially those on small business and entrepreneurship if that is what you are most interested in. Among books that I recommend are those written by James C. Collins, my *Small Business For Dummies* (co-authored with Jim Schell), the classic *How to Win Friends and Influence People* by Dale Carnegie, *The Greatest Salesman in the World* by Og Mandino, and *How to Win at the Sport of Business* by Mark Cuban. (Some of these books are older classics and have wisdom that has stood the test of time.) *Inc. Magazine* is a monthly publication that has lots of worthwhile content, including articles on their website at www.inc.com.

>> Take some free or very low-cost online business courses from leading colleges and universities. You can do this through Coursera (for example, Northwestern, Stanford, U Penn's Wharton, or Yale), edX, MIT's OpenCourseWare, and Udacity. Also check out the short courses/videos offered by the U.S. Small Business Administration.

>> Watch the best business television shows. Among those worth checking out are *Shark Tank* and *The Profit.*

If you're willing to spend money and want to take a course or two online, check out courses offered by some of the leading online colleges, institutes, and universities (such as Kaplan, the University of Maryland Global Campus, or the University of Phoenix). I'm not suggesting these institutions for obtaining a college degree online.

Evaluating the career placement prospects at different colleges

High school students and their parents make all sorts of trips and visits to college campuses. Many take the obligatory "campus tour" and sit through "information sessions" conducted by the college's admissions office. Families look at the buildings, check out the dining halls and some dorms, look over the athletic facilities, and so on. (And why does nearly every campus tour visit the on-campus mail facility despite the fact that most young people don't send or receive regular mail anymore?)

Rarely do these campus visits and research include a visit to the career and professional advising placement office or similarly named area. They most definitely should!

INVESTIGATE

Most colleges cost a small fortune to attend. What are you getting for that? Clearly, the outcomes and opportunities for graduates of that school should be an important part of your research. Here's what I recommend you investigate:

» Visit the college's career advisory and placement office. Do this in addition to a broader campus tour. They may have some reading material to send you home with. Ask to speak with one of the career advisors/counselors and see if they can explain what their school is doing to help most students secure worthwhile jobs upon graduation. You may also ask them about the information contained in the next two points.

» Spend some time on the career advisory and placement section of the school's website. You can usually find lots of good information there. Seek out reports that provide data on the outcomes for what recent graduating classes did after graduation. Most schools call these "outcomes reports." Check out Figure 7-1 for an example.

» Ask for access to the job postings for summer internships or full-time employment opportunities for graduating students. Most schools are unlikely to grant access to this since an online account is needed and access is generally restricted to current students and perhaps alumni. On your office visit to career services at the school, if you do meet with one of the employees in that office, you can ask them to give you a quick tour of the online account if they won't provide short-term access for you. Alternatively, maybe you can get indirect access through someone your family knows who is an alum of the college.

FIGURE 7-1:
Yale University's
Office of Career
Strategy's
Statistics and
Reports webpage.

College rankings that include useful measures of graduates' employment outcomes (most notably salaries) can also help with evaluating and comparing colleges. See the next section.

Using college rankings and ratings for finding the right match

You can easily find lots of college rankings, especially online. Website owners, publishers, and media companies love them because lots of people with money to spend are online looking for college information. Some are pretty good, others are mediocre, and some are downright useless or perhaps even greatly misleading.

WARNING

Beware of websites that purport to rank colleges and then accept all sorts of advertising and affiliate fees from website links they provide. There is simply no way that a website or publisher can objectively and independently evaluate and rank colleges if they are accepting money from them to advertise or to direct students their way.

Another problem with college rankings is that they can make parents and students crazy and unhappy. For starters, each ranking is only as good as the specific criteria used. The colleges at the tippy top of the rankings are of course ridiculously difficult to get into. They have a limited number of slots and students from around the globe are flooding them with applications and competing to gain entrance.

All the data and other information about various colleges is best used to find colleges that provide the best match for a student. A number of the better ranking surveys enable you do to just that by allowing you to decide what criteria you'd like to use and emphasize to come up with your own personalized college list.

What follows are the two college ratings and matching websites I have found to be the best. *Note:* College ranking and ratings services generally don't include the military service academies. Please see the section, "Learning and Serving in the Military," later in this chapter.

Forbes: America's Top Colleges

Long one of the United States's leading business magazines and websites, Forbes annually compiles their top college rankings (www.forbes.com/top-colleges/#d16b86519877). The Forbes rankings are based upon six categories:

>> **Alumni salary (20 percent):** Early and midcareer salaries as reported by the federal College Scorecard and PayScale data and research

>> **Student satisfaction (20 percent):** Includes results from Niche surveys on professor quality and data, and freshman retention rates from the federal Integrated Postsecondary Education Data System website

>> **Debt (20 percent):** Rewards schools for low student debt loads and default rates

>> **American leaders (15 percent):** Based on the Forbes database of successful people, including billionaires, powerful women, 30 Under 30 honorees, leaders in public service and in private enterprise, and more

>> **On-time graduation rate (12.5 percent):** Four- and six-year graduation rates

>> **Academic success (12.5 percent):** Counts alumni who win prestigious scholarships and fellowships like the Rhodes and the Fulbright or have earned PhDs

Kiplinger: Best Value Colleges

This long-time publisher of tax, economic, and financial magazines and newsletters has their Best Value Colleges, which comes out annually. The most recent list includes 400 colleges that meet its criteria plus another 100 that "just missed." (www.kiplinger.com/fronts/special-report/college-rankings/index.html).

Their website also includes a handy "College Finder" that enables users to customize their search criteria to find their own best-match schools.

How do they define their Best Value Colleges? Kiplinger's says, "All the schools on our list meet our definition of value: a high-quality education at an affordable price." This includes:

- **Academic measures:** Includes the student-to-faculty ratio, test scores of incoming freshmen, and percentage of students who return for sophomore year. "We award the most points for four-year graduation rates because graduating on time helps keep costs down." They also consider to a lesser extent five-year and six-year graduation rates. Higher scores are awarded to schools that graduate a higher percentage of students who had financial need.

- **Cost:** Emphasizes colleges with lower sticker prices, generous financial aid, and low levels of student debt at graduation.

Understanding the political climate on college campuses

Politically speaking, it's no secret that the vast majority of college campuses tilt left. When I visited and then applied to colleges in my late teenage years, I hadn't a clue about the political climate on college campuses and there wasn't near the level of discussion back then as there is today.

INVESTIGATE

When you and your kids are checking out various colleges, in addition to considering the academic reputation and offerings, on-campus housing, dining halls, athletic facilities, and so on, I urge you to understand the political climate on each campus. I think you should know what you're signing up for in going to a particular college or university.

If you're thinking that you don't care about politics and the climate won't matter to you, that's up to you. However, I would say that your offspring will have some exposure to it in their environment and likely more so than in high school.

Simply taking a campus tour or sitting through an admission's office information session isn't going to educate you on this topic. Here are some useful ways you can assess and be informed about the political climate on a given college campus:

INVESTIGATE

- Check out the "News" section (sometimes called something else like "Headlines") of the school's website for releases from the administration. Go back recent months and years and see what topics they've chosen to write about and publicize.

- Review recent copies of the school's newspaper or journal. Increasing numbers of schools are publishing online, which makes your research here easier since you can quickly peruse back issues and see what topics are being discussed or creating controversy on campus.

>> Spend some time searching on the college news websites Campus Reform (www.campusreform.org) and The College Fix (www.thecollegefix.com) for articles about schools your kids are considering or that you'd simply like to research. Campus Reform describes itself as, ". . . a conservative watchdog to the nation's higher education system, Campus Reform exposes liberal bias and abuse on the nation's college campuses." The College Fix is published by the nonprofit Student Free Press Association and was founded by John J. Miller. He is the founder and executive director of The College Fix and its parent organization, the Student Free Press Association. He is also director of the Dow Journalism Program at Hillsdale College, a national correspondent for *National Review,* and a frequent contributor to the *Wall Street Journal, Philanthropy,* and other publications.

>> Conduct some searches for colleges on The Foundation for Individual Rights in Education's (FIRE) website (www.thefire.org). "FIRE's mission is to defend and sustain individual rights at America's colleges and universities. These rights include freedom of speech, legal equality, due process, religious liberty, and sanctity of conscience — the essential qualities of individual liberty and dignity. FIRE protects the unprotected and educates the public about the threats to these rights on our campuses and about the means to preserve them." FIRE is a nonpartisan organization.

>> Review the course offerings including majors and specific classes. Doing this kind of research is always a good idea for prospective students. After all, you should understand what you have to take (graduation requirements) as a student. The specific majors and courses offered at a college shed light on how oriented the curriculum is toward students' employment futures versus faculty and the administration wanting to spread their political point of view.

A useful column that hits the highlights of the partisan leftward tilt on many college campuses is Victor Davis Hanson's, "Universities Breed Anger, Ignorance, and Ingratitude: In turning out woke and broke graduates, they have a lot to answer for" (www.nationalreview.com/2019/10/universities-breed-anger-ignorance-ingratitude). Hanson is a Senior Fellow at Stanford University's Hoover Institution.

Now, one former college administrator said the following to me:

"I've seen northern students be shocked by the conservatism on some southern campuses. Yes, more colleges lean left than right, but it's not exclusive and I don't think it's fair to imply that mistakenly sending your conservative child to a liberal campus is the only problem with political fit that could occur."

Well, okay, that makes some sense to me. If the student from the north comes from a liberal family or is used to that kind of environment, leaving that environment could produce some surprises. For me, my concern isn't about "sending a conservative child to a liberal campus." I don't think most teenagers have deep political convictions — there are exceptions, of course. What concerns me is students and their families not knowing what the political climate is like on a particular campus *before* making the important decision to attend that college.

Most families don't want to choose a college that tries to promote a partisan political ideology and instead would rather that college administrators and faculty stay away from taking partisan political positions on issues. We want our kids to get a good education and to learn critical thinking skills. And, to do that, folks need to be open-minded to hearing others, collecting facts, and not attacking others who hold a different point of view.

Deciding if traditional four-year college is the right choice

In the beginning of this chapter, I highlight Ryan Craig's excellent book, *A New U: Faster + Cheaper Alternatives to College.* He urges some caution and consideration for those for whom such an education is "unaffordable" or who can afford it but who are only admitted to less selective colleges. He suggests — and I agree — that those who really should consider noncollege alternatives are those who are admitted to nonselective schools and for whom that expense is unaffordable. But, as I say earlier in this chapter, I think everyone should test their thinking, explore and learn about a range of alternatives, and then make an informed decision.

For those on the fence in terms of affordability, Craig suggests tipping the scales toward going to college if at least three of the following characteristics apply to you:

>> You have never stopped or dropped out of college previously.

>> You have a network of family and friends to support and encourage you to finish college.

>> You live in the Northeast.

>> You're a woman or minority.

>> You're going to major in finance or accounting if you major in business.

>> You may desire to work in a field that requires a license such as medicine, law, education, and so forth.

>> You're not interested in or are "hopeless" at technology.

For those for whom not going to college is a hard decision to accept, Craig suggests doing a "gap year" to gain some life experience and perhaps doing some work to at least pay for your living costs during that year. (See the section, "Taking a Year Post–High School to Work or Volunteer," later in this chapter.) He also suggests formalized programs like Year On, which involves three phases: a 10-week overseas volunteer experience, a 12-week bootcamp-like program in San Francisco "where students collaborate on projects and develop an e-portfolio for employers," followed by a 12-week internship with an employer partner.

Please see Chapter 8 for a complete discussion of noncollege alternative programs.

Learning and Serving in the Military

There are five U.S. military service academies that provide a four-year higher education experience that offers tremendous value for those who qualify and for whom it's a good match. The academies are

>> The United States Military Academy (Army) in West Point, New York, founded in 1802

>> The United States Naval Academy (Navy) in Annapolis, Maryland, founded in 1845

>> The United States Coast Guard Academy (Coast Guard) in New London, Connecticut, founded in 1876

>> The United States Merchant Marine Academy (Marines) in Kings Point, New York, founded in 1943

>> The United States Air Force Academy (Air Force) in Colorado Springs, Colorado, founded in 1954

Benefits and required commitments

Gaining admission to the U.S. military service academies is highly competitive — only about 10 percent of applicants are accepted, and as I explain shortly, the process of even being able to apply is difficult in and of itself. These are highly sought-after spots as accepted applicants who become cadets have free tuition, free room and board, free medical and dental care, and 100 percent job placement (guaranteed and well-paying jobs) upon graduation.

REMEMBER

This is no free lunch, of course. Cadets must serve at least five years upon graduation. Air Force and Army grads are required to serve an additional three years in the reserves. Graduates who end up in certain jobs (for example, pilots) also have longer service requirements.

Why it's not for most teenagers/young adults

The military service academies are certainly not for everybody or even most students for these and other reasons:

>> **Highly structured schedule:** From 6 a.m. to typically 8 p.m., a cadet's campus life is largely scheduled with mandatory activities. In the evening, the remaining time is devoted to homework and studying. And there are specific lights-out times for bedtime.

>> **Strict behavior requirements:** This includes restrictions on alcohol and drug usage. Also, cadets may only leave campus with permission.

>> **Fitness requirements:** Cadets must either play a varsity sport or participate in intramurals. And they must attend all home football games!

>> **Limited time off:** Unlike traditional college students who typically have months off over the summer, cadets have just a few weeks off in the summer.

>> **Time-consuming and lengthy admissions process:** See the next section for the details.

INVESTIGATE

There are ways in which prospective applicants can get a decent sense of what student life is like at the military academies. You can arrange a day visit, an overnight, or a weekend visit. Want something longer? Try their weeklong summer programs. I also highly recommend speaking with current and recent military academy students.

Admissions process and requirements

Compared with traditional colleges, the application process for military service academies is much longer and more involved. It begins a year earlier — namely during a high school student's junior year — with completing questionnaires.

To be eligible to apply, a student must be nominated (except for the Coast Guard). Nominations can come from congressional representatives or military personnel. The vice president of the United States can also nominate applicants.

Candidates should be good students; transcripts, test scores, recommendations, and essays are required, just as with traditional college applications. Strength in math and sciences is also a plus given the academies' science, technology, engineering, and math (STEM) heavy curriculums.

Applicants should also be in good physical and mental health. The Candidate Fitness Assessment tests and evaluates strength and endurance.

In addition to excelling academically and athletically, candidates should demonstrate leadership traits in their high school experience and years. Finally, cadets must be U.S. citizens, single, and not have any dependents.

Considering Community Colleges

Community colleges offer a two-year associates degree program, which is a much lower cost alternative to traditional colleges. In some states like Delaware, Indiana, Louisiana, Mississippi, Missouri, Oklahoma, and Tennessee, community college is actually tuition free under a College Promise program. At schools where students pay tuition, the average tuition per year is under $4,000, and that's before any scholarships, grants, or tax breaks are considered.

With such relatively low prices, it should come as no surprise that community colleges tend to attract a generally lower-income population of students local to the area. Students often work part-time or even full-time jobs while typically taking courses part-time.

In the best cases, a good community college can save a student money on their first two years' worth of higher education and earn credits that may be accepted at a four-year college. Many community-college students attend a school local to their family's home, which enables them to live at home and further reduce their expenses.

The best community colleges also offer effective vocational programs. For example, there are dozens of community colleges that offer pilot training programs. Students who successfully complete such programs gain the certifications and log the flight hours needed to become a commercial pilot. And the cost ends up being significantly lower than an aviation degree from a four-year program.

WARNING

Community colleges are not without their shortcomings and downsides, which can be significant:

>> The vast majority of community college students don't end up completing a four-year bachelor's degree. According to the National Student Clearinghouse, only one in six students who begin coursework at a community college end up completing a bachelor's degree in six years.

>> About half of community college course credits earned are typically not honored by other colleges and universities. This is problematic since many community college students hope and plan to transfer to four-year colleges and universities to earn a bachelor's degree. Investigate whether your state offers a guarantee transfer program to ease the transition from the state's two-year to four-year schools and help mitigate this problem.

>> Most community colleges fail to prepare/train students for today's jobs and have an academic orientation. This is especially problematic since community colleges are not seen by employers as among the leading academic institutions.

INVESTIGATE

Don't blindly be lured in by the seemingly lower costs of community colleges, which look relatively attractive and cheap compared to traditional four-year colleges. Do plenty of homework and be sure to investigate the following:

>> Critically evaluate the job-placement record and potential of any community college program you may be considering.

>> Emphasize community college programs that are employer-connected and well-focused upon job placement for their graduates. Ask for and review the hard data showing the placement of the school's graduates.

>> Examine the graduation rates. Start with the graduation of the community college itself. Then, examine what happens with the graduates who proceed onto four-year colleges and how those students fare.

>> If you're wanting to transfer to a four-year college, be sure to check with those you're interested in to see if they will accept your course credits from a given community college and what you will need to do to gain admission.

Taking a Year Post–High School to Work or Volunteer

As teenagers close in on the end of their high school years, some have difficulty grasping the longer-term decisions at hand. Researching and making post–high school plans also poses some challenges while a student is full-time with their high school coursework and perhaps doing some things outside of their school-work. Parents often lead busy lives too.

And even in those families where the student completes various college applications, there's no guarantee that offers of admission will materialize. Finding the right match between students and schools isn't easy, and neither is doing a great job on those applications.

So, in some cases, it may make sense for a graduating high school student to hit the pause button and take a year to do something else before forging ahead with higher education. This section discusses some options to consider including those that are commonly considered.

REMEMBER

Taking a year or two do something different after high school is a fine thing to do so long as all family members involved (student and parents) are on the same page about the potential value and cost. This can give a student more time to grow and mature and better understand what it is that they do or don't want. Colleges will not penalize or look down upon time spent doing something different so long as it is a constructive use of time and benefits the student.

Working for a living (temporarily)

Going to work at a job for a year is worth considering. For starters, full-time work makes most young people better appreciate what options they might consider in the future. Working at a regular job can also help a teenager realize the fact that you have to work for money rather than relying on the bank of mom and dad!

Living at home during this period of short-term work can certainly help with keeping expenses, especially housing, to a minimum. If time and energy allow, doing some volunteer work locally can be a worthwhile activity to consider as well.

Volunteering/travel programs overseas

A number of organizations arrange and manage overseas volunteering programs, which actually include a lot of travel and touring. They can be as short as one week and as long as one year. Typically, they run several months.

Here's an example of a program that operates in Asia, South America, and Africa. The typical length of their program is three months.

". . . programs combine adventure, travel, community service work, intercultural exchange, and homestays to create a jam-packed and life-changing experience. Most programs run for around three months and go through multiple countries to fully immerse gap-year travelers into the travel life. Through homestays and community projects, travelers will have the chance to create meaningful and memorable relationships and experiences."

This program costs $600 to $900 per week depending upon the type of accommodations that are chosen.

WARNING

These types of programs are often recommended to students who are contemplating doing a so-called "gap year" between high school and college. I'm not super enthused about these programs generally because families are paying a lot of money for the student to take an extended overseas vacation. Beware that the websites promoting these programs profit from referring people to them, and as such, are certainly not to be viewed as objective sources of information about them.

TIP

If your student really wants to do one of these programs, you might consider asking him to work and save enough money to pay for it (or at least half of the cost). Should that proposal cause your student to quickly lose interest, that would suggest to me that he was attracted to the program for the wrong reasons!

Taking a post-grad year at a boarding/prep school

Another option sometimes considered is for a high school graduate to attend a boarding/prep school for a so-called "post-graduate" (PG) year. The two most common types of cases where this is done are as follows:

» **Student-athletes hoping to be recruited college athletes:** This may occur because the student-athlete was significantly injured late in high school and couldn't participate in recruiting events or because the student didn't have attractive options. Do-overs sometimes make sense where the student-athlete and her family made mistakes in the recruiting process and hopes and expects to better navigate the process the second time through.

» **Students in need of shoring up academics and test scores:** Some students may benefit from an additional year to get some additional classes under their belts as well as better standardized test scores. Counselors at boarding schools may also have more time and expertise to better assist with the college selection and application process.

WARNING

Boarding schools, especially the better ones, are pricey. Including tuition and room and board, the total bill can easily approach or exceed that of a year at a private college. Financial aid can help for those who qualify. Good athletes, especially from a nonwealthy family, may receive a significantly reduced price.

Is College Necessary or the Best Option for Your Children?

Increasingly, there are more and more alternatives to college that require much less time than a traditional four-year college and that cost far, far less. In some cases, you won't have to pay out of pocket at all for these alternatives.

Let's face it, as parents it's natural to have certain expectations for our kids, in part based upon what we had or wanted to have for ourselves. Especially if you're raising your kids in a more affluent and well- educated community, there are a lot of expectations and pressures for kids to graduate from high school and then move on to a four-year college. Those types of high schools like to boast about how something like 97 percent of their graduates go on to college.

But, that's not a super-informative number because I have never found these high schools track what percentage of their graduates actually complete college and do so within a reasonable number of years. Also, what portion of them transfer or go on to do something completely different? Or are satisfied with the path they've chosen and the options it has afforded them?

I encourage you and your kids to cast a broad net when investigating post–high-school options. Examine traditional four-year colleges. But also investigate the alternatives. In the next chapter, I present and discuss the best noncollege alternatives to consider.

Chapter **8**

The Best College Alternatives to Consider

I n Chapter 7, I discuss the traditional paths that high school seniors typically follow upon graduation. There are, however, increasing numbers of attractive, lower, and faster alternatives, especially compared with traditional four-year colleges.

Some of these programs aren't new. Some, in fact, have been around for generations. Others are new and emerging. Overall, the good news is that now more than ever, high school graduates have more, better, and less costly options than ever before. And, a number of the programs discussed in this chapter can be combined with college programs discussed in Chapter 7.

So, don't leap to conclusions too quickly as to which path your kids will take. Explore the options and then begin to make some fully informed choices. This chapter helps you understand and explore the alternatives to traditional colleges.

Looking at Last-Mile Programs

The concept of "last mile" comes from the telecommunications industry, where the term means the final leg of the connection to each home. "The last mile in higher education is technical training and placement," says Ryan Craig, author of *A New U: Faster + Cheaper Alternatives to College* (BenBella Books). "In terms of placement, the last mile involves building reputations and relationships with employers so that providers are able to promise candidates, implicitly and explic-itly, a good first job," adds Craig.

Last-mile programs are being offered by a new set of education/training interme-diaries. These programs share the following characteristics:

>> **Technical skills plus:** "While last-mile programs are laser focused on the technical skills employers don't typically see in new college graduates, employers also desperately want proven problem solvers who have demon-strated success working in teams," says Craig.

>> **Intensity:** Students are assigned projects with real deadlines and often work 12-hour days or more.

>> **Demonstrated competencies:** Students complete these programs with a portfolio of work products, so employers can actually see their skills.

>> **Strong connection to employers:** Last-mile programs consult employers in the development and continuous revision of their curriculum. In order to attract students, they need to provide and document their program's place-ment rates and starting salaries of their students who complete their programs.

>> **Clear pathways:** Last-mile programs are charting clear pathways to jobs in the growing industries of tomorrow — technology, biotech, fin tech, and healthcare.

>> **Credential = job:** The credential of last-mile programs is the job. And, these are not blue-collar or vocational jobs but digital/technology jobs.

Staying at boot camps

The last-mile programs that most people have heard about are known as boot camps and are usually focused on coding. Those that have generally succeeded with employers are those of at least three months in length. According to Craig, "Learning to code is like learning a language. Coding boot camps train students in various languages. Fullstack JavaScript is the most common, followed by Ruby on Rails, .NET, Python, and PHP."

Coding boot camps originated in 2012 as "top-up" programs for students who already graduated from college. According to Course Report, there are now 95 coding schools offering programs at 300 sites in 74 cities across 40 states. Upwards of 23,000 students graduate annually from coding boot camps in the United States, and you don't need to be a college graduate.

In a survey done by Indeed, a job search engine website, 80 percent of technology hiring managers reported hiring coding boot-camp graduates, and an astounding 99.8 percent of those said they'd hire more.

REMEMBER

Coding boot camps are full-time endeavors, just like a job. Classes are small, and most of the time spent is actually working in teams on projects. Some have observed that you learn a lot in these boot camps when you teach others. Students come from all walks of life.

Check out these examples of different boot camps and what they can offer:

>> **Galvanize:** Galvanize is a popular coding program that cites an 84 percent placement rate within the first six months following their program's completion at an average starting salary of $70,000. Galvanize takes only about 20 percent of applicants.

>> **PrepMD:** "While boot camps are most prevalent in coding, there are a variety of boot camps or immersives in other areas. PrepMD is a last-mile training pathway, with a tuition of $30,000, to careers in the medical device industry," says Craig. PrepMD boasts a 94 percent placement rate within three months of graduation and an average starting salary of $90,000 plus bonus.

>> **AlwaysHired:** Gabe Moncayo is the entrepreneur behind a successful San Francisco boot camp called AlwaysHired, which trains people for technology sales. "Sales associate is the most common job for new college graduates, in large part because every employer has a sales function. Moncayo noticed that technology companies seeking salespeople expect entry-level candidates to already have sales experience and particularly experience on the Salesforce CRM platform — something colleges and universities don't teach," says Craig.

One student described his experience with AlwaysHired: "I learned how to have a better online presence and how to interview. I sharpened my sales skills in managing leads, creating leads, opening and closing sales." He also said that he learned about the tech industry including the language and jargon, culture, and players.

AlwaysHired, which has a 90 percent placement rate, also has an interesting financial arrangement. Students are only on the hook for a $200 deposit. AlwaysHired only gets paid if and when their students get hired — either by receiving 6 percent of the student's first-year salary or perhaps less if the company doing the hiring is in the AlwaysHired network.

REMEMBER

Good bootcamp/last-mile programs aren't cheap — the average coding boot camp costs around $12,000. But that price is a bargain compared with the cost of traditional colleges and the amount of debt students struggling to find good jobs have taken on.

TIP

Check on financing options. Some last-mile programs — such as Flatiron School and Code Fellow — actually offer money-back guarantees if students don't get good jobs. And, some programs have partnered with private lenders like Meritize, Climb Credit, and Skills Fund to enable students to borrow needed money to pay tuition costs.

Considering college minimal viable products (MVPs)

In Silicon Valley parlance, a minimal viable product (MVP) is the ". . . simplest, smallest product that provides enough value for consumers to adopt and actually pay for it." Craig states that traditional colleges are the ". . . polar opposites of a minimum viable product."

College minimal viable product (MVP) programs combine the technical skill training and placement of traditional last-mile programs with sufficient cognitive and non-cognitive skill development that students get from a good college.

"Like General Assembly, most last-mile providers are now considering how to shift from top-up programs to full-on college MVPs. . .. All college MVPs aim to provide faster + cheaper pathways than the colleges and universities they hope to displace. But, by definition, college MVPs are slower and more expensive than last-mile programs," says Craig.

Income-share arrangements (ISAs) are a newer financing method that is gaining strength. Graduates of these programs repay money owed to the program through paying a small portion of their employment income for a short period of time.

Craig argues that ISAs protects students from poor outcomes — namely not getting a job or a decent-paying job. Students have no such protection when simply borrowing money for program costs — as with traditional four-year colleges.

He cites the example of the Holberton School, which is a San Francisco–based coding MVP program that declares itself a "college alternative." It typically takes two years, but some students get jobs after just one year. Holberton's ISA is 17 percent for the first three years of employment after leaving the program and while earning at least $40,000 per year. The program is highly competitive for admission — only 3 percent are accepted.

Appealing to apprenticeships

Historically, apprenticeships have been most prevalent in building and industrial trades such as electricians, plumbers, carpenters, and iron and steel workers. "Emerging digital apprenticeships provide pathways for exactly the same entry-level jobs in growing sectors of the economy as boot camps or income share programs or even four-year colleges," says Craig.

Many companies in Germany use apprenticeships — in fact, about half of German high school graduates go into such programs instead of going to college. In London, WhiteHat is known for creating the "Ivy League of apprenticeships."

Apprenticeships are now gaining some momentum in the United States through the cooperation of employers, nonprofits, and some state governments. In June 2017, President Trump signed an executive order that sought to have five million disconnected workers be trained through apprenticeships.

In the United States, apprenticeships are most common in South Carolina through an affiliation with the South Carolina Technical College system with apprenticeships in many industries, including advanced manufacturing, healthcare, pharmacy, and IT.

Elsewhere in the United States, Craig notes a surprising industry — insurance — where employers have taken action with digital apprenticeships. Aon launched their apprenticeships when they took note of a high level of turnover in entry-level positions among "overqualified people" in the first 18 months. This led to them getting rid of their college degree requirements and getting behind apprenticeships.

In the financial services industry, Wells Fargo has an apprenticeship program for numerous positions, as does JP Morgan. There are also pharmacy technician apprenticeships at places like CVS Health in partnership with local community colleges. Accenture and Amazon are offering some apprenticeships for technology jobs such as cloud support associates and data center technicians.

Craig also discusses apprenticeships being done on an "outsourced basis," which he sees as a promising model since employers use many outsourced services (for example, IT services, accounting, payroll, legal, insurance, real estate, sales, customer support, human resources, staffing, consulting, marketing, public relations, and design).

Techtonic Group based in Boulder, Colorado, is a software development company that also does a registered apprenticeship program. By week six of their apprenticeship, aspiring software developers shadow experienced software developers. Within a few months, according to Craig, apprentices are ". . . billing hours on meaningful client projects. A year later, Techtonic clients are invited to hire the software apprentices they've been working with and whose work they've seen, which dramatically reduces the risk of entry-level hiring."

Joining staffing firms

Staffing firms — like Manpower, Allegis, Adecco, Randstad, and Kelly Services — are firms that hire workers and then staff them out to clients. Craig states that while staffing firms, which hire about 14 percent of the nation's workforce, have been focused on college graduates, he sees them getting into last-mile training to provide faster and cheaper alternatives to college.

Revature is an example of a staffing company in the IT space that hires experienced software developers and staffs them out to clients. The founder of Revature noticed around 2011 that his client companies also had an appetite for entry-level software developers. Today, the company has partnerships with numerous colleges such as Arizona State, UNC Charlotte, UVA, Davidson, and more and offers a free 10- to 12-week advanced training program on campus. Students are actually hired before training and receive housing as part of the training.

Avenica is another staffing model company (with seven regional offices), that places students from many colleges and offers last-mile training across many industries. "Avenica matches candidates to positions and prepares and schedules them for interviews. . . . Avenica hires them and staffs them out for a four-month evaluation period. Employers love the ability to evaluate candidates on a trial basis before committing to hire. And more than 85 percent of the time, that's exactly what they do," says Craig.

Getting Oriented with Online Programs

Plenty of money and effort have been poured into online courses and programs, but they generally haven't been successful in providing an alternative to traditional college. If you're already employed and trying to chart a newer pathway, part-time online programs may have a role. I see less of a role for first-time jobs.

As discussed elsewhere in this chapter, there are many programs that provide last-mile training — but that's hard to do online. Online learning can be useful for those who are already employed and if you or your company wants you to master a specific level of skill.

There are millions of unfilled jobs in the United States now for which candidates don't have the right skills. Sales jobs, for example, now want candidates with Salesforce platform experience.

Craig points out that the one thing last-mile programs have in common is their intensity and that's a big reason that online courses haven't worked as well as last-mile programs to prepare people for their first jobs. MIT developed a Massive Online Open Course (MOOC) in partnership with edX called "Entrepreneurship 101." Tens of thousands of people enrolled in the free online course, but only a small percentage completed it.

MIT then decided to invite those who completed this online course to a one-week on-ground boot camp — ". . . a single email to students who completed the MOOC generated 500 applicants interested in paying $6,000 for the boot camp," says Craig.

The staffing company Revature has followed in this path of using online learning to qualify candidates for its immersive last-mile program.

"Beyond using online learning to screen or qualify students for last-mile programs, a few new providers have launched online-only models that are showing promise in connecting students to good jobs . . . the most important element of these programs is intensive real-time coaching sessions with an industry-connected mentor," per Craig. An example of this approach is Designlab, which provides last-mile training across a range of design professions and boasts a 94 percent placement rate among students who have completed their program. Another example is Bloc, which runs an online last-mile program for coding. Bloc also relies upon an intensive mentorship approach.

Another approach that shows promise online according to Craig has been utilized by companies like Yellowbrick, which uses an, ". . . accessible online experience to orient students to possible career paths and ensure they develop a portfolio of relevant work to showcase in their job search." Yellowbrick works in conjunction with top universities on "career discovery courses in areas millennials are passionate about." They offer online certificates in Fashion Industry Essentials with the Parsons School of Design, Sports Industry Essentials with Columbia University, and Beauty Industry Essentials from the Fashion Institute of Technology.

"Portfolium is an e-portfolio network that allows students to make their work (and the competencies demonstrated therein) visible to employers. . . .. Employers across a range of industries, not simply IT, are now utilizing Portfolium to identify and recruit talent. Portfolium is the most advanced competency marketplace for entry-level jobs," says Craig.

Another way in which students can demonstrate their competencies is through the sharing of microcredentials or badges which are earned from education and training providers. Craig states that Credly is the market leader in this space.

A last way to use technology to make employers aware of competencies is simulations or games. Justin Ling created EquitySim, a simulation trading platform for stocks, bonds, currencies, and other securities and targeted to college students. EquitySim's top performers are identified as entry-level talent for investment management firms.

Finding Out about Vocational/Trade Schools

Vocational and trade schools have been around for a long time. You won't find them on any of the lists of the supposed best colleges or institutions for higher education. Some look down their nose at such schools, which historically have been viewed as inherently blue collar.

The reality is that vocational and trade schools, which are also known broadly as Career and Technical Education (CTE), provide gateways to a wide range of jobs. Here's just a sampling:

» **Automotive industry:** Repair technician, body and paint technician, collision repair and refinishing, diesel mechanic

» **Culinary arts:** Prep cook, sous chef, pastry chef, line cook

» **Emergency services:** Firefighters, paramedics, police officers, CPR and first-aid instructors

» **Healthcare:** Nursing aides, certified nursing assistants, licensed practical nurses, vocational nurses, registered nurses, medical technicians, surgical prep technicians, dental hygienists, dental assistants, phlebotomy, sonography, radiology, pharmacy technician, mammography, laboratory technician, veterinary assisting, veterinary technician

» **Other skilled vocational jobs:** Welding, electrician, plumbing, web designer, carpentry, construction management, pipe-fitting, machining, computer-aided drafting, network administration, civil engineering technician, paralegal, court reporter

While vocational and trade schools don't get a lot of publicity and most of them are on the smaller side, they are ubiquitous. And, they exist in several different entities including:

>> **Community colleges:** The best community colleges include vocational and technical training that lead to specific types of jobs after completing the two-year program. See Chapter 7 for more information on community colleges.

>> **High schools:** Vocational or technical training may be offered within a larger traditional high school, where this training is a two-year proposition during junior and senior years. But there are also four-year technical high schools in many areas.

>> **Other area CTE centers:** Sometimes these are just for students in high school. In other cases, they can accept other adults. CTE centers may bring in students from area high schools, and those students come to campus for select (elective) courses to be combined with the courses the student is taking on their regular high school campus. The length of time commitment depends upon the type of program; it can range from six months to several years.

These types of schools are constantly evolving and need to be flexible to meet the changing economic environment and jobs that exist today and going forward.

Vocational and trade schools, like any other educational institution, carry some risks. One is the physical demands and requirements. Some jobs and occupations include physical demands that not all students may be able to meet, and that pose a problem as a worker ages.

Another risk is the impact of automation and competition. Some jobs may be at a greater risk for being displaced by automation and competitive forces.

One good thing about these types of schools is that you can likely conduct your search in your local area (up to a one-hour drive away). Look for information on your state education department's website. You can also do a web search for vocational and trade schools or career and technical education.

It's possible that if your son or daughter is interested in a particular type of program, you may have to travel outside of the immediate area. For post–high school education, your children may prefer the experience of living away from home, presuming that is affordable for your family to provide.

ARE COLLEGE ALTERNATIVES PREPPING YOUNG ADULTS FOR THE LONG TERM?

Throughout this chapter and the entire book, my goal has been to provide you with information and pros and cons of different options so that you and your kids are aware of the growing number of post–high school choices and be informed to make better choices. Just as each of your kids is different and unique (presuming you have more than one), what's best for each of them will surely be different and unique!

You will clearly find people who are advocates for traditional four-year colleges and those who are advocates for alternatives. Listen to those arguments and challenge the reasoning and assumptions. Also, make note of people's biases and possible agendas. A college counselor, for example, is probably going to talk up the benefits of a traditional college education and is likely not well informed and versed about alternatives. Ditto for most college administrators.

One college counselor said the following to me about alternatives to college versus traditional college programs:

> "Most obviously, these alternatives tend to prepare students for one specific thing, whereas a college degree provides flexibility to move into different jobs/roles/industries/careers. I think that should be acknowledged."

I think the reality is more complicated and nuanced. The best alternative programs teach their students a number of useful skills and typically prepare their graduates for a range of possible jobs. And once in those jobs, accumulated work experience opens more doors. Also, it should be noted that the best alternative programs take no more than two years and often far less time.

Part of the benefit of a four-year college is that it provides the time (four years) and space for students to hopefully mature and hone their interpersonal and other skills. The network and contacts that a college experience provides are also part of the value that students generally derive from the experience. For example, if you're a student at the University of Notre Dame, you can have access to a network of prior Notre Dame graduates who may at least be willing to spend some time-sharing information about their work and career. That doesn't mean that you're guaranteed a job offer through such networking, but it may help to open doors and differentiate you from the masses of others who are clamoring for an interview at a given company.

Now, I am hearing and seeing these same networking benefits begin to take place at the better alternatives to college. Graduates of particular programs can reach out to earlier graduates of those same programs who may now be working at companies that are of interest.

For me, the bottom line is that the growing alternatives to college is good for you, the consumer. Competition for your time and dollars is good, and it's slowly spurring some positive changes at colleges and universities, which need to be more responsive to you, their potential customers. They should earn your business and not get it by default.

Final Thoughts on Alternatives to Traditional Colleges

The alternatives to traditional colleges discussed in this chapter have been and will continue to undergo significant changes. So, if this is an area that interests you, it will require a good amount of your time to learn about and explore. In this final section, I highlight some relevant programs at traditional four-year colleges as well as some summarizing thoughts from Ryan Craig, who is a guru of this field.

College cooperative educational experiences

A number of four-year colleges offer so-called cooperative programs. The idea behind these is that during a portion of the student's college experience, the student works part-time or full-time at an employer. This work is done during what would normally be the academic part of the year, counts toward school credits, and is paid. While some employers may be local to the college, others are not.

These programs vary greatly from school to school, so you really need to do your institution-specific research to find something that is a good fit. Also be aware that at some schools, it may take five years rather than four to complete all the graduation requirements.

Here are some examples of colleges that offer co-op programs:

>> Cornell University (Ithaca, New York)

>> Drexel University (Philadelphia, Pennsylvania)

>> Georgia Institute of Technology (Atlanta, Georgia)

>> Northeastern University (Boston, Massachusetts)

>> Purdue University (West Lafayette, Indiana)

>> Rensselaer Polytechnic Institute (Troy, New York)

>> Rochester Institute of Technology (Rochester, New York)

>> Stevens Institute of Technology (Hoboken, New Jersey)

>> University of Cincinnati (Cincinnati, Ohio)

>> University of Florida (Gainesville, Florida)

Where to go for more information on alternatives to college

Ryan Craig is the go-to expert for alternatives to college.

When considering noncollege "faster + cheaper" alternative programs, Craig advises keeping the following four points in mind:

>> Taking a noncollege path doesn't mean that you're choosing a blue-collar career.

>> Alternative programs should actually get less expensive over time as ". . . tuition pay boot-camp models are likely to be crowded out by no-tuition-upfront models: either employer-pay or income share."

>> These short programs won't work unless you performed at or near the top of your high school class. The reason: The programs simply don't have enough time to work on your cognitive and noncognitive skills. Craig says longer programs — at least six months and more typically 12 to 24 months in length — are necessary.

>> Increasingly, higher education will be purchased in smaller chunks on an as-needed basis, similar to the way in which companies buy SaaS software, buying and paying for what is needed when needed. Additional functionality can later be added for an additional charge. "At the age of 18 or 19, rather than trying to anticipate all the higher education you'll need for the rest of your life, why not opt for what you need right now to get a great first job, then go from there?"

For more information, I highly recommend Ryan Craig's excellent book, *A New U: Faster + Cheaper Alternatives to College* (BenBella Books).

4

Getting the Best Education at the Best Price

IN THIS PART . . .

Optimize your finances as your kids are growing up.

Complete the common financial aid forms to your best advantage.

Scour for scholarships and find ways to borrow money.

Review and appeal offers of financial aid.

Chapter 9

Financial Steps You Should Take While Your Kids Grow Up

The principles of sound personal financial management are far from rocket science. Boiled down, the keys are to live within your means; invest wisely in low-cost, proven investments; minimize your taxes; and secure comprehensive catastrophic insurance.

How you should best save and invest your money, however, is complicated by the college financial aid process and determination formulas. Like the income tax system, you can and should understand how the financial aid system works so that you minimize your children's college expenditures.

In this chapter I discuss sensible strategies to make the most of your money during the years when you're raising your kids and for when they graduate from high school and possibly move on to college or other higher education.

Determining a College Financial Aid Package

In Chapter 6, I provide a detailed overview as to what information colleges collect and the process by which they set an individual price for your family to pay based upon their assessment of your ability to pay. If you haven't reviewed the material yet, please do so now.

Figuring the expected family contribution

The financial aid process and associated forms at colleges and universities collect a lot of information and data. The Free Application for Federal Student Aid (FAFSA®) uses a federal formula to determine the so-called *expected family contribution* (EFC). This is the amount that the family can supposedly afford to pay annually toward their son's or daughter's college costs.

Looking at income

The most important determinants in that process are the parents' and student's income and assets (outside retirement accounts). Parental income is, by far, the biggest factor in assessing a family's ability to pay. Depending upon the school and formulas used, up to approximately 47 percent of a parent's and student applicant's incomes are "assessed" in the formulas!

Assessed is an appropriate word because the financial aid system is like the federal income tax system in that it sets effective tax rates that apply to income above a certain level. The way it works is such that for most families, the relatively high assessment rate of 47 percent of income applies for income above approximately $60,000 annually. For the income up to that approximate amount, families will end up having to contribute about 16 percent of the first $60,000. Colleges allow for basic living expenses including taxes, which generally results in families with incomes below $30,000 not being expected to pay anything toward college costs.

REMEMBER

Student's income generally doesn't factor in because the vast majority of students don't earn a high enough income. The annual threshold is approximately $7,000.

Figuring in assets

After income, assets are the next big factor that colleges consider when determining what to charge an individual student and his parents. Parents' assets beyond a basic savings allowance are generally assessed at the rate of 5.65 percent. It is important to note here that this is referring to assets outside of retirement accounts, which is why parents are generally better off from the perspective of financial aid (and taxes in general) to save money inside retirement accounts.

Children's assets are assessed at a 20 percent rate. It may seem surprising that the rate is so much higher than the rate applied to parental assets. But this actually makes some sense. The logic behind this is that money saved in a child's name is essentially earmarked for their use and benefit, and college certainly is a sensible expenditure! By contrast, parents have all sorts of other things competing for their dollars — housing costs, taxes, car expenses, insurance, food, clothing, and so on. Children don't generally have these expenses while they are being raised by their parents.

Your family's assets may include equity in real estate and businesses that you own. Although the federal financial aid analysis no longer counts equity in your primary residence as an asset, many private (independent) schools ask parents for this information when making their own financial aid determinations. Therefore, depending on where your child goes to college, paying down your home mortgage more quickly instead of funding retirement accounts can harm you financially: You may end up with less financial aid and a higher tax bill.

Calculating the EFC

REMEMBER

Financial aid officers can also tweak numbers based upon how badly they want your child, or if they feel that there are extenuating circumstances. I discuss this further in Chapter 12.

Understanding the financial aid package components

The previous section explains how colleges arrive at an expected family contribution (EFC). That number is compared with and subtracted from the college's total cost of attendance — which includes tuition, room, board, books, travel, and personal expenses. If the EFC is equal to or greater than the school's cost of attendance, a family shouldn't expect any reduction in price through need-based financial aid. The family could still possibly receive a price reduction through merit scholarships.

In many cases, however, the total cost of attendance at a given college exceeds a family's EFC so the difference can be made up in the following ways:

>> **Grants and scholarships:** Awarded by the school, this is essentially cutting the proposed price by the amount of the grant or scholarship. The school isn't really "giving out money" — it's a price reduction from their full price. These

awards can be solely given based upon financial need, but they can also be for academic merit (see Chapter 4 for more information on merit scholarships). Outside organizations can also award scholarships in the form of actual money, but unfortunately this often leads colleges to reduce their awards — see Chapter 11 for more on outside scholarships.

>> **Federal work-study:** These are low-paying jobs on college campuses (such as working in the library, dining hall, gym, and so forth) that are subsidized by the federal government. The time commitment involved isn't huge, and some of the jobs have down time, which enables students to study, for example, while on the clock! (Not that it matters, but that's not why these are called federal work-study!)

>> **Student loans:** Some loans provide for subsidized interest (again at federal government expense) while the student is in school and beginning repayment is not required until six months after graduation. Getting these subsidized loans is based upon demonstrated financial need.

REMEMBER

Financial aid and college pricing are an annual process at colleges and universities. Every year, you will have to jump through all the same hoops in terms of financial aid application forms. It is generally easier and quicker after the first year because you will have some familiarity and recollection of the prior year's process. Also, some of the forms like the FAFSA® enable you to carry over the prior year's information to save you some data entry time and headaches.

Looking into Long-Term Saving and Investing Strategies

Saving is a good thing to do, but there are better and worse ways to do so from the perspective of how colleges set their pricing/financial aid awards. You may think that money is money, but the financial aid system doesn't treat all money, saving, and investments equally — not even close!

Financial aid treatment of retirement accounts

Under the current financial aid needs analysis system, the value of your retirement plans is not considered an asset. By contrast, money that you save outside retirement accounts, especially money in the child's name, is counted as an asset and reduces financial aid eligibility and increases the price colleges will charge you. Kid's assets are assessed at 20 percent, compared with just 5.65 percent for parental nonretirement account assets.

Forgoing contributions to your retirement savings plans in order to save money in a taxable account for Junior's college fund is an unwise financial move. When you do, you pay higher current income taxes both on your current income and on the investment income and growth of the college fund money. In addition to paying higher income taxes, you're expected to contribute more to your child's higher educational expenses.

Let me stress the need to get an early start on saving for your retirement. Retirement accounts limit how much you can contribute each year. See Chapter 2 for more on saving for your retirement.

Financial aid treatment of money in the kids' names

If you plan to apply for financial aid, save money in your name rather than in your children's names (such as via custodial accounts). Colleges expect a much greater percentage of the money in your children's names (20 percent) to be used annually for college costs than the money in your name (about 5.65 percent).

However, if you're affluent enough to foot your child's college bill without outside help, investing in your kid's name can potentially save you a little money in taxes. Read on to see how to do this with custodial accounts.

Parents control a custodial account until the child reaches either the age of 18 or 21, depending upon the state in which you reside. For 2020, prior to your child's reaching age 18, the first $2,200 of interest and dividend income generally isn't taxed.

Any unearned income above $2,200 is taxed federally at the relatively high rates that apply to trusts and estates (see the following bulleted list).

Over the $2,200 threshold, unearned income is taxed at these rates:

>> Up to $2,600 falls into the 10 percent bracket

>> Between $2,600 and $9,450 is in the 24 percent bracket

>> Between $9,450 and $12,950 is in the 35 percent bracket

>> Above $12,950 is in the 37 percent bracket

Upon reaching age 18 (or age 24 if your offspring are still full-time students), all income generated by investments in your child's name is taxed at your child's rate, which is presumably a lower tax rate than yours.

529 state-sponsored college savings plans

The 529 plans (named after Internal Revenue Code Section 529 and also known as qualified state tuition plans) are educational savings plans. A parent or grandparent can generally put more than $300,000 per beneficiary into one of these plans.

Up to $75,000 per donor or $150,000 per married couple may be placed in a child's college savings account immediately, and this amount counts for the next five years' worth of $15,000 annual tax-free gifts per donor allowed under current gifting laws. (Money contributed to the account is not considered part of the donor's taxable estate, and a gift tax return (IRS Form 709) must be filed for gifts above the $15,000 annual threshold. However, if the donor gives $75,000 and then dies before five years are up, a proportionate amount of that gift will be charged back to the donor's estate.)

Of course, you can contribute much smaller amounts to a 529 plan if you so desire. Though plans vary by state, some offer investment minimums as low as $25 to get you started. But before you jump into one of these plans, you should understand and weigh the overall tax and financial aid consequences of doing so.

What works with a 529 plan

The attraction of the 529 plans is that money inside the plans compounds without taxation, and if it's used upon withdrawal to pay for college tuition, room and board, and other related qualifying education expenses, the investment earnings and appreciation can be withdrawn tax-free. The Tax Cuts and Jobs Act which took effect in 2018 enables 529 plan account holders to also use their account balances for up to $10,000 annually per student in K-12 tuition expenses.

REMEMBER

Generally, no up-front tax break is provided, although some states offer a contribution tax break. You can generally invest in any state plan to pay college expenses in any state, regardless of where you live, but you may only be eligible for a state tax deduction if you invest in your home state's plan.

In addition to paying college and K-12 education costs, the money in 529 plans may be used for graduate school expenses. Some states provide additional tax benefits on contributions to their state-sanctioned plan.

Unlike the money in a custodial account, with which a child may do as she pleases when she reaches either the age of 18 or 21 (the age varies by state), these state tuition plans must be used for higher-education expenses. However, most state plans do allow you to change the beneficiary within the family. That option can be handy if you don't end up needing as much as you thought based upon that child's actual college or other higher education costs. You may also leave the money in the student's account toward possible graduate school expenses.

You can also take the money out of the plan to use for some purpose other than educational expenses, if you change your mind. (You will, however, owe tax on the withdrawn earnings plus a penalty — typically 10 percent.)

What doesn't work with 529 plans

WARNING

A potential drawback of the 529 plans — especially for families hoping for some financial aid — is that college financial aid offices treat assets in these plans as parental nonretirement assets. If your family isn't wealthy and you aren't funding your retirement accounts, you gain better tax benefits and help your financial aid profile if you instead put your extra dollars into your retirement account(s). (Of course, in that case, that money isn't generally as accessible if you want or need to use some of it to pay college bills.) Also, be aware that the assets can be considered as belonging to an older child (independent young adult) who no longer reports parental financial information for financial aid purposes. This is also a drawback for student-owned 529 accounts. Remember that student held assets are assessed at much higher rates by the financial aid system compared with parental assets. See the "Figuring in assets" section earlier in this chapter. (If a grandparent had a 529 account, those assets aren't even listed on a family's financial aid forms.)

Please also be aware that a future Congress could change the tax laws affecting these plans, diminishing the tax breaks or increasing the penalties for nonqualified withdrawals.

Researching 529 plans

With most 529 plans, you have a choice between two major types of investment options. There are traditional fixed mix funds. And then there are those that evolve over time. The farther your child is from college age, the more aggressive the investment mix. As your child approaches college age, the investment mix is tilted to more conservative investments.

WARNING

Some state plans have high investment management fees, and some plans don't allow transfers to other plans. Avoid such plans. Look for proven, low-cost, solid performing investment options from companies such as TIAA-CREF, T. Rowe Price, and Vanguard.

INVESTIGATE

Do a lot of research and homework before investing in any plan. Check out the investment track record, allocations, and fees of each plan, as well as restrictions on transferring to other plans or changing beneficiaries.

Parents who do establish a 529 plan should be careful on financial aid forms to list those assets as their own and not the child's to avoid harming your aid chances even more, as explained earlier in this chapter.

Clearly, these plans have both pros and cons. They generally make the most sense for higher income parents who don't expect their children to qualify for financial aid. However, less affluent parents may want to consider saving some money in these plans as the investment returns aren't taxed when the money is used for educational expenses. Grandparents can consider such plans as well.

WARNING

SHUN PREPAID TUITION PLANS

Eleven states have prepaid tuition plans that allow you to pay college costs at specific state colleges within the state (calculated for the age of your child). There is also a "private college" prepaid plan that includes about 300 private colleges and universities.

The allure (and marketing) of these plans is that by paying today, you eliminate the worry of not being able to afford rising costs in the future. With state-based plans, you are prepaying with money that can be used toward colleges within the state's system. The private college plan has a specific list of colleges and universities around the country that participate in the plan.

I don't recommend these plans for several reasons. First, odds are quite high that you don't have the money today to pay in advance. Second, putting money into such plans reduces your eligibility for financial aid. If you have that kind of extra dough around, you're better off using it for other purposes. You can invest your own money — that's what the school's going to do with it, anyway.

Third, no matter how you slice it, these plans have limited choices. Yes, their complicated legal agreements, which of course are written by lawyers, have ways for you to get your money back, but you won't get a decent return on it.

Besides, how do you know which college your child will want to attend and how long it may take her to finish? Coercing your child into the school you've already paid for is a sure ticket to long-term problems in your relationship.

You and your student should explore all the post–high school options. You can make the most of your money by planning ahead and using the strategies discussed in this book to get the best pricing, save on your taxes, and get the best investment returns. Prepaid tuition plans don't help you with any of those objectives.

Coverdell education savings accounts

TIP

The Coverdell Education Savings Account (ESA) is another option that, like the 529 plan, has made sense for affluent parents who don't expect to apply for or need any type of financial aid.

Subject to eligibility requirements, you can put up to $2,000 per child per year into an ESA. Single taxpayers with adjusted gross incomes (AGIs) of $110,000 or more and couples with AGIs of $220,000 or more may not contribute to an ESA (although another individual, such as a grandparent, may make the contribution to the child's account).

Although the contribution is not tax-deductible, the future investment earnings compound without taxation. Upon withdrawal, the investment earnings are not taxed (unlike a traditional retirement account) as long as the money is used for qualified education expenses. These expenses can include pre-college expenses as well, such as private K–12 school expenses.

TIP

Parents should make sure they are listed as the owners of these accounts and should be sure that continues to be the case once the student reaches the age of majority and is no longer considered a minor. Parents who have their kids apply for financial aid can be penalized by college financial aid offices for having ESA balances. These accounts are considered the student's asset if the student is listed as the account owner and is an independent student. Many investment companies are doing away with these accounts since 529 plan account holders may now use withdrawals to pay for K–12 educational expenses. Thus, there are no longer notable differences between the two types of accounts, and the 529 plan allows for saving and investing far greater balances than the ESA.

REMEMBER

When it comes to determining financial aid (college pricing), saving in retirement accounts is generally best, but that money may not be accessible for paying college bills. The worst idea generally is to save in your child's name. Remember that children's assets, which includes money in custodial accounts are assessed at a 20 percent rate versus 5.65 percent for parents' assets.

Investing strategies and vehicles

Low-cost mutual funds and exchange-traded funds (ETFs) are excellent investment vehicles when investing. When investing for a long-term goal like your retirement, which may be decades in the future, investing mostly or completely in stock-focused funds makes sense.

In my book *Investing For Dummies*, in addition to stocks, I also discuss how to invest in real estate and small business to build wealth over the long term. If you build equity in investment real estate properties or in a small business, you may be able to pay for college expenses in the future by using some of those investments' cash flow or by borrowing against the equity of those assets.

Lending type investments, which include things like bank accounts and bonds, tend to produce lower long-term returns but are generally less volatile in value in the shorter term. Having a chunk of money in those types of investments, especially as your child nears entering college, makes good financial sense.

TIP

When investing money earmarked for future college costs, when your kids are young, the investment mix should be tilted toward stocks. As they approach high school graduation and college, you may want to scale back the risk a bit away from stocks.

Strategizing to Pay for Educational Expenses

Now I get more specific about what college may cost your kids and how you're going to pay for it. I don't have just one solution, because how you help pay for your child's college costs depends on your own unique situation and personal philosophy. However, in most cases, you may have to borrow some money, even if you have some available cash that can be directed to pay the college bills as you receive them.

TIP

Ask yourself what the best way is to help pay for college and what you want/expect in the way of contributions by your children. Even parents who can afford to pay the entire costs often require their children to contribute something meaningful in terms of costs — whether from savings over summer work, loans, and so on.

At a minimum, I believe that kids should have to pay their own out-of-pocket costs for textbooks and food bought outside the campus dining service. This strategy increases the chances of the kids having more focus via some "skin in the game" and helps ensure that they don't walk away after four or five years with a degree but no appreciation, direction, or purpose.

Estimating college costs

College can cost a lot. The total costs — including tuition, fees, books, supplies, room, board, and transportation — vary substantially from school to school. The total average annual cost is running around $55,000 per year at private colleges and around $27,000 at public colleges and universities (at the in-state rate). The more expensive schools can cost up to about one-third more. Ouch!

An investment is an outlay of money for an expected return on that investment. Unlike a car, which depreciates in value, an investment in a good education generally yields monetary, social, and intellectual profits. A car is more tangible in the short term, but an investment in education (even if it means borrowing money) should give you more bang for your buck in the long run.

Of course, not all education is created equal, and you should consider the fit and quality of a given educational experience with your goals. And, keep in mind that there are increasing numbers of attractive, quicker, and lower-cost options to four-year colleges.

Colleges are slowly and increasingly finding themselves subject to the same types of competition that companies in the private sector confront. As a result, some colleges are beginning to clamp down on rising costs. As with any other product or service purchase, it pays to shop around.

You can find good values — colleges that offer competitive pricing and provide a quality education. Although you don't want your son or daughter to choose a college simply because it costs less, you also shouldn't allow a college choice without any consideration of cost.

TIP

When considering spending money on a college or other degree, do some digging regarding the value of particular colleges and degree programs. Numerous resources are available for doing this research. See Chapter 7.

Setting realistic savings goals

If you have money left over after taking advantage of retirement accounts, by all means, try to save for your children's college costs. You should save in your name unless you know you aren't going to apply for financial aid.

Be realistic about what you can afford for college expenses given your other financial goals, especially saving for retirement. Being able to personally pay 100 percent of the cost of a college education, especially at a four-year private college, is a luxury of the affluent.

If you're not a high-income earner, consider trying to save enough to pay a third or, at most, half of the cost. You can make up the balance through loans, your child's employment before and during college, and the like.

Use Table 9-1 to help get a handle on how much you should be saving for college. I've kept this table simple, and it ignores the growth in your investment balances over time. If you'd like to use an online calculator, try Vanguard's at: https://vanguard.wealthmsi.com/csp.php.

TABLE 9-1   **How Much to Save for College**

Figure Out This	Write It Here
1. *Four-year total cost of the school you think your child will attend	$_____
2. Percent of costs you'd like to pay (for example, 20% or 40%)	×_____ %
3. Line 1 times Line 2 (the amount you'll pay in today's dollars)	= $_____
4. Number of months until your child reaches college age	÷_____ months
5. **Line 3 divided by Line 4 (amount to save per month in today's dollars)	= $_____ / month

* The average cost of a four-year private college education today is about $220,000; the average cost of a four-year public college education is about $108,000. If your child has an expensive taste in schools, you may want to tack 20 to 30 percent onto the average figures.

** The amount you need to save (calculated in Line 5) "in today's dollars" does need to be increased once per year to reflect the increase in college inflation – 3 or 4 percent should do.

Determining Later-Year Savings Tactics

In an ideal world, you manage your finances with a long-term perspective and you stay on top of things. But, we don't live in an ideal world. We live in the real world, and in that world, procrastination happens. Or maybe like most parents you were busy living your lives when your kids were young and you weren't thinking a lot about managing your money with an eye on college costs and the peculiar financial aid process.

This section, which highlights things to consider doing "late in the process," serves as a useful introduction in a sense to the next chapter, which explains how to best complete college financial aid forms. Keep in mind that the financial aid system will request data from you from the tax return you completed the year before your son or daughter is applying to begin college. So, for example, if your child is looking to begin college in the fall of 2022, the financial aid data collection will gather information from your tax year 2020 return.

Here are some examples of moves you may consider making (and which are discussed in detail in the next chapter):

>> Find sensible ways to reduce your taxable income. All other things being equal, of course, you shouldn't simply accept less income, because you'll be better off generally with higher income. That said, there may be some sensible steps you can take to keep a lid on your taxable income, as doing so should help improve financial aid offers. For example, with your investments, you have some control over the timing of when you sell an investment at a profit and realize capital gains.

>> Retirement account money is generally ignored by the financial aid process. Keep in mind, however, that for the contributions made during *base years,* reported on your financial aid forms, the financial aid analysis process will add those contributions back to your taxable income. So, be sure to contribute more if you can in the years prior to those base years.

>> Reducing your cash by making planned purchases. If one of your cars needs replacing, you might do so before your kids apply to college and use up some of your cash for that purchase. You don't want to go overboard, of course, but the reduced cash should improve the pricing offers you get from college.

>> Pay off high-cost debt. If you have debt outstanding on credit cards, auto loans, and the like and you have cash to pay it off, consider doing so. Again, the reduced cash can help improve your financial aid awards. And the financial aid needs analysis ignores and doesn't make any allowance for your consumer debt.

>> Use assets in kids' names. If you put money into your kids' names in the past and now realize that wasn't a wise move, perhaps you have current expenses for their benefit that you can use up some of this money for. One obvious example would be private K–12 schooling or travel sports teams. If you have kids, you don't need me to remind you of all the things you spend money on for them!

Chapter **10**

Filling Out the Common Financial Aid Forms to Your Best Advantage

'm not going to fib to you. Filling out financial aid forms is a pain in the posterior, intimidating, and invasive. And, it's stressful. Maybe you won't feel all these negative emotions, but most people do.

But, if you want your kids to consider one of the better/more selective four-year colleges, unless you're wealthy, you likely will be applying for "financial aid," which is actually misnamed. What you're really doing is trying to get a lower price than the full inflated and bloated sticker price colleges and universities hope to charge affluent families and those who don't take the time to apply for aid.

Completing the forms isn't usually as awful as most people think when they first begin the process. And, even if you are doing the forms online, you can save your partially completed forms and come back to them as you have time and energy to complete them. Your ultimate reward will likely be a lower and more reasonable price at some colleges your son or daughter wants to attend. Most families see savings in the tens of thousands of dollars over the four years. Perhaps the total savings may break the $100,000 threshold.

Determining Whether to Apply for Financial Aid

Before jumping into completing the specific financial aid forms that you are likely to encounter, I want to cover some important topics like whether you should apply for aid, using the net price calculator to estimate what a particular college may charge your family, financial aid form deadlines, and so forth.

Should your family apply for financial aid?

REMEMBER

As a general rule, you should apply for financial aid — especially and including so-called merit aid, which isn't based upon financial need (which is called needs-based aid). Colleges provide merit money to high-achieving academic students and athletic scholarships to exceptional athletes.

Financial aid consultants say that you should assume you're eligible. Don't rule yourself out because of income or academics. And don't rule out a college because you think it's too expensive. The higher the cost, the more aid you may receive.

Some families are rightfully concerned that applying for financial aid may affect the attractiveness of their student to the college. Don't colleges prefer accepting students from families that can pay in full? This is indeed a legitimate concern, which I help to make clear in this and the following sections.

Just over 100 colleges (see Figure 10-1) state that they engage in "need-blind admissions." This denotes that the college admissions committee is making their admissions decisions regardless of a family's ability to pay. Many of the colleges on this list are those that enjoy a hefty endowment and thus have stronger finances to be able to admit students on this basis.

Now, this is not to suggest that admissions committees literally know nothing about a family's likely financial situation, because indeed they do. Consider the fact that the information a candidate's admissions application conveys to the college admissions officers includes where the candidate lives and what his parents do for a living, among other information. Knowing this information, though, may not help a candidate with admission in the way that you might imagine.

Adrian College	Harvey Mudd College	Stanford University
Amherst College	Haverford College	SUNY College of Environmental Science and Forestry
Babson College	Hiram College	Swarthmore College
Barnard College	Ithaca College	Syracuse University
Baylor University	Jewish Theological Seminary	Texas Christian University
Biola University	Johns Hopkins University	The College of New Jersey
Boston College	Julliard	Thomas Aquinas College
Boston University	Kenyon College	Trinity University
Bowdoin College	Lawrence University	Tufts University
Brandeis University	Lehigh University	Tulane University
Brown University	Lewis & Clark College	University of Chicago
Cal Poly San Luis Obispo	Marist College	University of Illinois at Chicago
California Institute of Technology	Marlboro College	University of Maryland Robert H. Smith School of Business
Carnegie Mellon University	Massachusetts Institute of Technology	University of Miami
Chapman University	Middlebury College	University of New Hampshire
Claremont McKenna College	Mills College	University of North Carolina at Chapel Hill
Columbia University	Mount St. Mary's College	University of Notre Dame
Cooper Union for the Advancement of Science and Art	New York University	University of Pennsylvania
Cornell College	North Carolina State University	University of Richmond
Cornell University	North Central College	University of Rochester
Curtis Institute of Music	Northeastern University	University of San Diego
Dartmouth College	Northwestern University	University of Southern California
Davidson College	Penn State	University of Vermont
Denison University	Pomona College	University of Virginia
DePaul University	Princeton University	University of Washington
Duke University	Providence College	Ursuline College
Elon University	Randolph College	Vanderbilt University
Emory University	Rice University	Vassar College
Fairleigh Dickinson University	Salem College	Wabash College
Florida State University	Saint Louis University	Wake Forest University School of Medicine
Fordham University	San Jose State University	Washington University in St.Louis
Franklin W. Olin College of Engineering	Santa Clara University	Wellesley College
Georgetown University	Southern Methodist University	Wesleyan University
Grinnell College	Soka University of America	Williams College
Hamilton College	St. John's College	Yale University
Harvard University	St. Olaf College	Yeshiva University

FIGURE 10-1:
Colleges and universities that admit candidates using need-blind admissions.

For example, admissions committees at the more selective and popular schools see lots of candidates applying from zip codes populated with affluent families. So, if you work at a well-paying occupation and are yourself well-educated, admissions officers will typically think that your kids grew up with advantages compared with kids raised in lower-income areas with parents engaged in lower-paying jobs. And, from an admissions perspective, especially at need-blind colleges like those listed in Figure 10-1, high-achieving students from lower socio-economic backgrounds actually have a leg up on their peers who grew up with supposed financial advantages.

Using the "net price calculator" to estimate costs

INVESTIGATE

There is a relatively simple method you can use right now to get a general idea as to what price you may pay at a given college or university (and therefore how much financial aid or discount you will receive from those institutions). Colleges are required to have a *net price calculator* (NPC) on their websites. You can usually find this in the tuition and financial aid section of a school's website or simply type "net price calculator" in the college's homepage search box.

You will be taken to the College Board's web page for that particular college and be asked a series of questions about your family's financial situation. Alternatively, you can go to the College Board's "Tools and Calculators" page: `https://bigfuture.collegeboard.org/pay-for-college/tools-calculators#`. Then select the link for "The College Board's Net Price Calculator," which provides access to each school's own such calculator.

You don't need to sign in or personally identify yourself, so rest assured the college won't be receiving any of your information at this time.

The NPC is different for each college, so while you will be asked similar questions by each college, the resulting prices can vary quite widely. One reason for this is that different colleges treat various aspects of your situation — like your home's equity (difference between market value and the mortgage on the property) quite differently. I've seen situations for a given family where the pricing among private colleges can differ by tens of thousands of dollars among schools driven by factors like how much equity a family has in their home.

Knowing if financial aid harms your chances for admission

This is a great and important question. And the answer and truth is that outside of the 100 or so colleges that use a need-blind admission policy (listed in Figure 10-1), your applying for need-based financial aid may have a negative impact on your child's admissions chances. Is this to suggest that you shouldn't apply for financial aid at so-called "need-aware" colleges, which comprise the vast majority of schools? No, not necessarily.

Here's how I would think about the situation when applying to colleges that do not use a need-blind admissions policy:

>> If you're a higher-income family and are not going to qualify for need-based aid, you may not want to apply for financial aid. The reasoning here is that at some need-aware schools, you could put your child at a disadvantage in the admissions process. If you're in this group, be sure to apply for merit-based aid.

>> Moderate- and lower-income families that see per the net price calculator that they will be eligible for a decent or large amount of financial aid should apply for such aid. Doing so will be necessary to afford college. Be sure to apply to some need-blind schools and that you have at least one safety school that appears to offer good pricing for a family like yours and is going to accept your child.

Meeting deadlines

Before getting into the nitty gritty of completing some specific financial aid forms, here's some important overarching advice about the financial aid process and deadlines:

>> Don't wait to be accepted to a college to apply for aid. The coffers may be empty by spring.

>> Get application forms as soon as possible. You'll need the latest version of the federal FAFSA® form. You may also need to complete the College Board's CSS Profile application, state aid forms, and/or forms provided by the colleges. The FAFSA® form and Profile become available for the next academic year on October 1 of the current year (meaning the soonest you can apply for financial aid for your first year of college is October 1 of senior year of high school).

>> Know the deadlines and be sure to meet each one. Many colleges have different deadlines for different forms. Some may be due as early as November, though most are due in January–March.

>> Maximize your aid eligibility. Freshman year aid awards are based in part on income for the year ending Dec. 31 of the student's sophomore year in high school. Consider also making appropriate adjustments to your assets, debts, and retirement provisions before you apply.

>> Follow instructions carefully on the application forms. Common mistakes that can disqualify your applications are forgetting to sign them, leaving lines blank, or using the wrong academic year's version of the forms.

>> Know that only the college's financial aid office will see the information provided on the financial aid forms. Admission office people aren't supposed to know you applied for aid if the school is a need-blind admission policy school; otherwise, assume they will know. Professors and any other staff at the college outside of the financial aid and admissions offices will neither see nor have access to this information.

Taking an Overview of Financial Aid Forms

The starting point for most families seeking aid is the FAFSA® (Free Application for Federal Student Aid) form. Increasing numbers of public and many private colleges also require completing the CSS/Financial Aid Profile Form. Some private schools also have you complete their own designed financial aid data collection form.

Financial aid consultant Kal Chany accurately describes the questions as "invasive and prying." The forms capture financial data regarding parental income and assets and student income and assets. Completion of the FAFSA® form leads to determining what's called the expected family contribution (EFC). The difference between this number (for example, $24,000 for a year) and the total cost of a college (for example, $55,000) is labeled the family's financial need for college (in this example, $55,000 − $24,000 = $31,000).

REMEMBER

The EFC should in theory be the same for a given family across many schools. "This is why families should not initially rule out any school as being too expensive. The sticker price doesn't necessarily matter; it's the portion of the sticker price that you have to pay that counts," says Chany.

TIP

Consider having a financial safety school — one that is inexpensive enough for you to afford in the event that you can't afford more costly schools to which your college-bound teen has applied.

Filling Out the FAFSA® Form: Free Application for Federal Student Aid

The Free Application for Federal Student Aid — also known as FAFSA® form — is the starting point in applying for financial aid. The name of this statement is kind of misleading because you may assume that you're completing to qualify for student aid through or sponsored by the federal government. While you are, the FAFSA® form information and the analysis of the answers you provide on it are also used by many colleges and universities as a starting point for determining your aid eligibility and ultimately how much a given school will charge your offspring to attend. For a look at the complete FAFSA® form, check out Figure 10-2 at the end of this chapter.

REMEMBER

Many schools also require completing other financial aid forms because they like to gain additional detailed information beyond what the FAFSA® form captures. I cover those other common forms in this chapter as well.

In this section, I highlight the important parts of the FAFSA® form and how to best complete them.

Completing the FAFSA® form online versus on paper

You can complete the FAFSA® form online (https://fafsa.ed.gov) or print and complete a PDF version by hand. With every version, you work on it as you have time — the website enables you to save your work to return for completion later. (There is an app for the FAFSA® form, but I don't recommend using it and entering your personal and financial data through your cellphone.)

There is an important difference between completing the FAFSA® form online versus doing so on paper. The online version information can be sent to up to ten schools versus only four for the printed version. If you're applying to more than that many schools, you can have your FAFSA® form sent to additional schools by jumping through some hoops (see the section, "Sending your FAFSA® form information to more than the 'allowed' number of colleges.")

TIP

I recommend that you go with the online version of the FAFSA® form if at all possible. Like the paper version, you can complete it over time, and the website allows you to save your work and return later. Filling it out by hand means you need to be neat, and if you want to make changes or revisions, you're going to have to complete at least two versions so that your final one is clean and accurate. Also consider that another potential downside to the paper version is that you have to mail it, which means that like any other piece of mail, it could be lost by the U.S. Postal Service. And, finally, the online version enables you to zap your information out to up to ten colleges at a time whereas the paper version only allows sharing the information with up to four colleges at a time.

Sending your FAFSA® form to more than the "allowed" number of colleges

I'm sorry to bog you down in some details so early here in the form completion process, but you should know this before you begin.

According to the U.S. Department of Education, you can list up to ten colleges on your Free Application for Federal Student Aid (FAFSA®) form. Once you receive your Student Aid Report (SAR), which provides you with the info you submitted on your FAFSA® form and summarizes your eligibility for federal student aid, you can make the information available to more than ten colleges through one of the following options. Each option will allow the college to receive an electronic copy of your SAR, and you will also receive an updated SAR.

>> **Option 1:** Click Log In on the home page and log in to your FAFSA® account. You will be given the option to Make FAFSA® Corrections. Remove some of the colleges listed on your FAFSA® form, add the additional school codes, and submit the corrections for processing.

>> **Option 2:** Call the Federal Student Aid Information Center (800-433-3243) and have them add the colleges for you. When you call, you must provide the DRN from your SAR or confirmation page. Refer to the Help page for contact information.

>> **Option 3:** If you have a paper SAR, you can replace the colleges listed on the SAR with other colleges and mail the SAR back to Federal Student Aid. Note that the paper SAR allows you to change up to four colleges — not all ten.

REMEMBER

Important note: If there are ten colleges on your FAFSA® form, any new school codes that you add will replace one or more of the school codes already listed. When this change is made, any college removed from the list will not have automatic access to any new information you provide after you've removed that college. However, the college will still have the data you submitted when you listed that college on your FAFSA® form. You are not deleting your FAFSA® form information from the college's system.

Understanding and dealing with a Federal Student Aid (FSA) ID

If you want to complete, sign, and file your FAFSA® form online, you will need to get what is called an FSA ID, which, ". . . allows students and parents to identify themselves electronically to access Federal Student Aid websites." Per the FAFSA® website,

"An FSA ID is made up of a username and password and can be used to log into the online Free Application for Federal Student Aid (FAFSA®) form. While you aren't required to have an FSA ID to complete and submit a FAFSA® form, it's the fastest way to sign your application and have it processed. It's also the only way to access or correct your information online, or to prefill an online FAFSA® form with information from your previous year's FAFSA® form."

Student is applying for aid

As you begin to complete the FAFSA® form, keep in mind that the questions presume that the student is applying for aid. There is an aspect of this that some people find perplexing and frankly annoying, and dare I say a tad disrespectful, to the people who generally foot most and in some cases all of the college bills — the parents! There also seems to be an assumption that parents are comfortable providing all of their financial details to their teenager in order for them to complete the form.

REMEMBER

The student is the one applying to college and hence the one applying for aid, at least in the minds of those folks running colleges these days. That doesn't mean that students are the ones actually completing these financial aid forms unless they are independent of their parents (for example, a student age 25 or older). I generally think that parents should be the ones completing the forms.

Questions like name, address, social security number, date of birth, and so on in the beginning part of the form refer to the student. Parent information is collected later in the form. Entering parent information in a student section is a common mistake, and when it's an important field like social security number or income, it can cause big problems for your financial aid application. The form could stand some design improvements to address so many people making mistakes like this!

Selective service registration

Many parents and their sons are surprised by the question on the FAFSA® form pertaining to whether the student is registered with United States' selective service, which is the system used to draft young adults into the armed services.

Males 18 years of age and older must be registered in order to be considered for federal aid (which for most people would be loans). You can check a box to initiate and complete that registration process.

Registering doesn't commit a person to serve in the unlikely event that there is ever a future draft.

Interested in work-study consideration?

The FAFSA® form asks if the student is willing to consider "work-study," whereby students are simply given low-paying, on-campus, part-time jobs (working in the dining hall, library, gym, and so on). The time commitment is generally quite minimal and probably no more than ten hours per week, and the schedule is quite flexible so as to not interfere with a student's academic and other campus obligations.

I would recommend saying yes as there's no real downside to saying you're open to this. Students are not in any way committed to follow through on this should it be part of a financial aid award. They can always choose to opt-out of accepting that part of the financial aid package, which simply means your family is on the hook for paying a bit more to make up for that. Your answer to this question has no impact on the grant or other money offered to you elsewhere in the proposed financial aid package.

Federal income tax return questions

A number of FAFSA® form questions ask you to report specific data and line items from your prior year's federal income tax return. You have two options for handling this. First, you can get out your copy of the return (which you should always keep) and look up and record the information yourself.

The second option is to use the *IRS data retrieval tool* to import data from your tax return to answer these questions. You are under no obligation to do it this way. And, I'm well aware that plenty of folks feel that giving the process access to your federal income tax return is an even more invasive approach to financial aid data collection.

In the unlikely event you are quite late in filing and still haven't filed your prior year's federal income tax return, you're just going to have to do your best and estimate.

Income earned from work

Income earned from work is an item you need to report that's not directly on a line of your federal income tax return. (It's possible that a single line item on your tax return — for example for wage income or Schedule C — may correspond to a person's income.) This includes wages paid to you by an employer, business income you may report on Schedule C, and so on. And, the amount should be before contributions you've made to a retirement savings account.

Value of your assets

REMEMBER

As I say many places in this book, under the federal financial aid rules and calculations, retirement account assets are ignored, so don't include their value in this or any other section of the FAFSA® form! Also, your home is not considered an asset under FAFSA® guidelines, so don't include its value here either. (Many colleges will access your home value information through other forms discussed in the remainder of this chapter.)

TIP

If you own financial assets like mutual funds and stocks outside of retirement accounts, you know their value fluctuates, so that does give you some latitude in reporting their current/recent value. Suppose that a recent quarterly statement shows the value of your investments during a recent depressed period. That would be a good date to choose for completing the asked-for data on the form.

TIP

If you own a business or investment real estate, be sure to subtract any debt or other obligations owed on those against a reasonable estimate of those assets' current values. Also, recognize that if you had to sell any of those assets to free up money to pay for college expenses, you would have expenses related to that sale that can easily amount to about 10 percent of the value of that asset.

REMEMBER

Coverdell education savings account balances and 529 plan assets are generally considered a parent's assets for students who are still financially dependent upon their parents. For independent students who don't report parental information on their FAFSA® form, 529 and Coverdell balances owned by the student should be listed as student assets.

Any custodial account balances are listed as a student's assets. As I recommended in Chapter 9, you may want to consider using those assets on your son's or daughter's current needs, as having more money in their name harms their financial aid awards.

Number of college students in household

If you have more than one member of your household who is attending college at least half-time during the same academic year, that generally will improve the financial aid packages offered. This makes sense since the expected family contribution is divided up among the number of colleges attended rather than all going to one college if just one family member were in college.

HOW OWNING A HOME MAY AFFECT YOUR CHILDREN'S QUALIFYING FOR COLLEGE FINANCIAL AID

From a financial aid perspective, the federal financial aid analysis ignores the home as an asset and also ignores the debt you owe on your home (as well as other debt such as on consumer loans) when determining your financial need. The financial aid process only considers debts against assets listed on the forms. This includes real estate loans and margin loans against investment assets.

Financial aid consultant Kal Chany says, ". . . the more selective colleges that elect to use the institutional methodology (which looks at home equity) rather than the federal methodology (which does not) do recognize one kind of debt — mortgages, first and second, on your home." These schools also include at least a portion of the value of your home as an asset. For example, a number of highly selective colleges count the value of your home's equity up to 2.4 times the parents' total annual income. Some schools only count up to 1.2 times the parents' income, while others ignore it completely if a family's income is below a certain threshold. Some colleges actually count all of your home's equity.

The federal financial aid formula provides an *income protection allowance* (IPA); in other words, an estimate of how much of a given family's income is needed to pay for living expenses (such as housing, food, clothing, and so on). The IPA varies based upon the size of the family. For example, a family of four, with one child in college, can supposedly live on $27,250. Chany points out that the IPA, ". . . does not take into account the cost of living in your part of the country."

For families living in or near a higher cost metropolitan area such as Los Angeles, San Francisco, or New York, where the cost of living is quite a bit higher than average, Chany recommends that you provide each college's financial aid office a detailed budget of what it actually costs your family to live.

Because colleges do not recognize debts such as auto loans and credit card debt, if you have sufficient assets available (which do count against your aid) to pay down those loans, doing so will enhance your financial aid award.

In terms of valuing your home, Chany advises that the aid forms are not asking what you could sell your home for if you took a number of months to sell it but rather the price you'd get for it "If you had to sell it in a hurry — at fire-sale prices. . .." Remember that selling costs for a home can easily amount to about 10 percent of the value of the home.

Ultimately, using a home equity loan to help pay for college expenses is worth considering because doing so reduces your equity in the property, which helps future aid awards from colleges that consider home equity an asset. Home equity loans tend to be available at reasonable interest rates — although I would caution that this is not the case for those with less than solid credit scores — and the interest is generally tax deductible.

Getting on Board with the CSS Profile Form

The CSS Profile form and financial needs analysis is overseen by the College Board and is a financial aid form required by many colleges. The CSS Profile form is similar to the FAFSA® form but more detailed. That said, there are plenty of questions common to both forms.

Obviously, for the same question as on the FAFSA® form, you should provide the same and consistent answers on the Profile form. In this section, therefore, I only discuss the different and unique questions on this form compared with the FAFSA® form.

TIP

To access the CSS Profile, head to `https://cssprofile.collegeboard.org/`.

Parent details

In addition to the basic information required about each parent, this section asks you to list the details of your retirement accounts. Colleges generally don't consider these assets when considering financial aid awards, but some schools clearly do; otherwise, they wouldn't request the information.

It's frankly ridiculous, in my humble opinion, that colleges ask for this kind of information. The argument can easily be made that it's none of their business and quite intrusive. After all, this is money earmarked for your future retirement accounts and generally cannot be accessed now for college or other expenses.

Also, the financial aid process fails to ask about vested pension benefits that a person may have earned working for a larger employer or government entity that offers such benefits. The value of such retirement pension benefits can easily be well into the six figures, and in some cases breach the $1-million-dollar mark.

Do colleges have any way to verify the value of your retirement accounts? No, they do not. Colleges can see if you've contributed to retirement accounts in recent years from information on your income tax return if they ask for copies of that document.

Current and future year income

Whenever you have to make an estimate, there are, of course, a range of possible outcomes. For example, how large a raise will you get next year? Will you even get a raise? You may be an optimistic, glass-half-full kind of person. But this isn't the time or place for optimism. You should always present the least optimistic/worst-case scenario here.

Household information

This section has you detail the approximate value of your home as well as the debt owed against it. You are also asked for the purchase price and date.

REMEMBER

As I discuss in the sidebar, "How owning a home may affect your children's qualifying for college financial aid," you should be realistic about valuing your home. The value should be based upon what you believe it would fetch if you needed to sell it quickly. Also, subtract a good 10 percent of that value for selling expenses.

Parent assets

In this section you list bank accounts, stocks, bonds, mutual funds, and so forth outside of retirement accounts. Be sure that these answers are consistent with those provided on the FAFSA® form. Review the advice offered in the earlier section "Value of your assets." (Do not list retirement accounts here as those were to be listed in an earlier section.)

Investment real estate is included in this section as well. This can include if you rent out a portion of your home; if you do, you will detail the portion of it you rent out.

For any asset against which you have debt, be sure to list that debt.

Parent expenses

In this section, you detail medical and dental expenses not paid by insurance. This can include lots of things, including the premiums for insurance including those taken from your paycheck, doctors and dentist office visits, eyeglasses, prescriptions, and so on.

Medical and dental expenses that are IRS approved and can reasonably be included in your totals include:

>> Acupuncture

>> Ambulance

>> Artificial limbs

>> Artificial teeth

>> Birth control treatment

>> Blood sugar test kits for diabetics

>> Breast pumps and lactation supplies

>> Chiropractor

>> Contact lenses and solutions

>> Crutches

>> Dental treatments (including X-rays, cleanings, fillings, sealants, braces, and tooth removals)

>> Doctors' office visits and co-pays

>> Drug addiction treatment

>> Drug prescriptions

>> Eyeglasses (Rx and reading)

>> Fluoride treatments

>> Fertility enhancement (including in-vitro fertilization)

>> Flu shots

>> Guide dogs

>> Hearing aids and batteries

>> Infertility treatment

>> Inpatient alcoholism treatment

- » Insulin

- » Laboratory fees

- » Laser eye surgery

- » Medical alert bracelet

- » Medical records charges

- » Midwife

- » Occlusal guards to prevent teeth grinding

- » Orthodontics

- » Orthotic inserts (custom or off-the-shelf)

- » Over-the-counter medicines and drugs, if prescribed by a doctor

- » Physical therapy

- » Special education services for learning disabilities (recommended by a doctor)

- » Speech therapy

- » Stop-smoking programs (including nicotine gum or patches, if prescribed)

- » Surgery, excluding cosmetic surgery

- » Vaccines

- » Vasectomy

- » Vision exam

- » Walker, cane

- » Wheelchair

Examples of medically related services that may be eligible include:

- » Weight-loss program only if it is a treatment for a specific disease diagnosed by a physician (such as obesity, hypertension, or heart disease)

- » Compression hosiery/socks, antiembolism socks or hose

- » Massage treatment for a specific ailment or diagnosis

- » CPR classes for an adult or child

- » Improvements or special equipment added to a home or other capital expenditures for a physically handicapped person

Checking Off School-Specific Forms

With all the personal and financial data about your life that is collected through the FAFSA® and CSS Profile forms, you might rightfully conclude that that is more than enough for colleges to determine how aid-worthy your family is. And, for most colleges you would be correct.

Unfortunately, however, some schools (mostly those that are more selective) have their own unique financial aid forms that they have you complete if you're applying for aid. There is certainly overlap between these college-specific aid forms and the FAFSA® and CSS Profile forms. So, keep those other completed forms handy as you complete college-specific financial aid forms and be sure that you are giving consistent answers.

While not exhaustive, here is a list that comprises the bulk of the types of questions you will face on college-specific financial aid forms:

>> More detailed questions about your home and debt on the home

>> Detailed questions about your household's monthly living expenses over the past couple of years broken out by category (food, clothing, insurance, and so on)

>> More detailed questions about all of your sources of income

>> Detailed questions about the financial assets you own and income generated by those assets

>> Questions pertaining to cars you own, how much you paid for those cars, and if any debt is owed on them

>> Amount you pay for auto insurance

>> Detailed questions about real estate other than your home that you own

>> Questions about your interest in businesses

>> Questions about your other children's current educational situation and future plans

>> Questions pertaining to specific scholarship categories offered by the college to see if you're eligible or qualify for any of them

Last but not least, some colleges will ask you to provide them with copies of your federal income tax return and/or Schedule C, which small business owners file with their federal income tax return. Typically, you will upload these forms through the College Board's IDOC service.

Yes, this is an intrusive process. And, yes you are turning over all sorts of personal information. But, if you don't, the college or university can refuse to budge on their pricing for your family.

FAFSA®

FREE APPLICATION *for* FEDERAL STUDENT AID

July 1, 2020 – June 30, 2021

Federal Student Aid | *An OFFICE of the U.S. DEPARTMENT of EDUCATION* | PROUD SPONSOR *of the* AMERICAN MIND ♦

Use this form to apply free for federal and state student grants, work-study, and loans.

Or apply free online at fafsa.gov.

Apply by the Deadlines

For federal aid, submit your application as early as possible, but no earlier than October 1, 2019. We must receive your application no later than June 30, 2021. Your college must have your correct, complete information by your last day of enrollment in the 2020-2021 school year.

For state or college aid, the deadline may be as early as October 2019. See the table to the right for state deadlines. You may also need to complete additional forms.

Check with your high school counselor or a financial aid administrator at your college about state and college sources of student aid and deadlines.

If you are filing close to one of these deadlines, we recommend you file either online at **fafsa.gov** or via the myStudentAid mobile app. These are the fastest and easiest ways to apply for aid.

Use Your Tax Return

We recommend that you complete and submit your FAFSA form as soon as possible on or after October 1, 2019. The easiest way to complete or correct your FAFSA form with accurate tax information is by using the IRS Data Retrieval Tool either through **fafsa.gov** or the myStudentAid mobile app. In a few simple steps, most students and parents who filed a 2018 tax return can transfer their tax return information directly into their FAFSA form.

If you (or your parents) have missed the 2018 tax filing deadline of April 2019, and still need to file a 2018 income tax return with the Internal Revenue Service (IRS), you should submit your FAFSA form now using estimated tax information, and then you *must correct* that information *after you file* your return.

Note: Both parents or both the student and spouse may need to report income information on the FAFSA form if they did not file a joint tax return for 2018. For assistance with answering the income information questions in this situation, call 1-800-4-FED-AID (1-800-433-3243).

Fill Out the FAFSA® Form

If you or your family experienced significant changes to your financial situation (such as loss of employment), or other unusual circumstances (such as tuition expenses at an elementary or secondary school or high unreimbursed medical or dental expenses), complete this form to the extent you can and submit it as instructed. Consult with the financial aid office at the college(s) you applied to or plan to attend.

For help in filling out the FAFSA form, go to **StudentAid.gov/completefafsa** or call 1-800-433-3243. TTY users (for the hearing impaired) may call 1-800-730-8913.

Fill the answer fields directly on your screen or print the form and complete it by hand. Your answers will be read electronically; therefore, if you complete the form by hand:

- use black ink and fill in circles completely: Correct ●   Incorrect ⊗ Ⓥ
- print clearly in CAPITAL letters and skip a box between words:

| 1 | 5 | | E | L | M | | S | T | |

- report dollar amounts (such as $12,356.41) like this:

$ | 1 | 2 | 3 | 5 | 6 | no cents

Orange is for student information and purple is for parent information.

Mail Your FAFSA® Form

After you complete this application, make a copy of pages 3 through 8 for your records. Then mail the original of pages 3 through 8 to:

Federal Student Aid Programs, P.O. Box 7650, London, KY 40742-7650.

After your application is processed, you will receive a summary of your information in your *Student Aid Report* (SAR). If you provide an e-mail address, your SAR will be sent by e-mail within three to five days. If you do not provide an e-mail address, your SAR will be mailed to you within three weeks. If you would like to check the status of your application, go to **fafsa.gov** or call 1-800-433-3243.

Let's Get Started!

Now go to page 3 of the FAFSA form and begin filling it out. Refer to the notes on pages 9 and 10 as instructed.

The Federal Student Aid logo and FAFSA are registered trademarks of Federal Student Aid, U.S. Department of Education.

FIGURE 10-2:
The FAFSA® form: Free Application for Federal Student Aid.

Pay attention to any symbols listed after your state deadline.
States and territories not included in the main listing below:
AL*, AS**, AZ*, CO*, FM**, GA*, GU**, HI**, KY^§, MH§**, NC^§, ND^§, NE*, NH**, NM*, OK^§, PR*, PW**, RI**, SD**, UT*§*, VA**, VI**, VT*§*, WA^§, WI* and WY**.

STATE AID DEADLINES

State	Deadline
AK	Alaska Performance Scholarship – June 30, 2020 # $ Alaska Education Grant ^ $
AR	Academic Challenge – June 1, 2020 • * Workforce Grant • Higher Education Opportunity Grant – June 1, 2020 *(date received)*
CA	For many state financial aid programs – March 2, 2020 *(date postmarked)* + * For additional community college Cal Grants – September 2, 2020 *(date postmarked)* + * Contact the California Student Aid Commission or your financial aid administrator for more information.
CT	February 15, 2020 *(date received)* # * *
DC	FAFSA form completed by May 1, 2020 # For DCTAG, complete the DC OneApp and submit supporting documents by May 31, 2020. #
DE	April 15, 2020 *(date received)*
FL	May 15, 2020 *(date processed)*
IA	July 1, 2020 *(date received)* – Earlier priority deadlines may exist for certain programs. *
ID	Opportunity Grant – March 1, 2020 *(date received)* # *
IL	Refer to the Illinois Student Assistance Commission's web site for the Monetary Award Program (MAP) renewal deadline. ^ $
IN	Frank O'Bannon Grant – April 15, 2020 *(date received)* 21st Century Scholarship – April 15, 2020 *(date received)* Adult Student Grant ^ $ – New applicants must submit additional form. Workforce Ready Grant ^
KS	April 1, 2020 *(date received)* # • *
LA	July 1, 2021 (July 1, 2020 recommended)
MA	May 1, 2020 *(date received)* #
MD	March 1, 2020 *(date received)*
ME	May 1, 2020 *(date received)*
MI	March 1, 2020 *(date received)*
MN	30 days after term starts *(date received)*
MO	February 3, 2020 # Applications accepted through April 1, 2020 *(date received)*.
MP	April 30, 2020 *(date received)* # *
MS	June 1, 2020 *(date received)*
MT	December 1, 2019 # • *
NJ	2019-2020 Tuition Aid Grant recipients – April 15, 2020 *(date received)* All other applicants: - Fall and spring terms – September 15, 2020 *(date received)* - Spring term only – February 15, 2021 *(date received)*
NV	Nevada Promise Scholarship – April 1, 2020 * $ Silver State Opportunity Grant ^ $ All other aid • *
NY	June 30, 2021 *(date received)* *
OH	October 1, 2020 *(date received)*
OR	OSAC Private Scholarships – March 1, 2020 * Oregon Promise Grant – Contact state agency. * Oregon Opportunity Grant ^ $
PA	All first-time applicants enrolled in a: community college; business/trade/technical school; hospital school of nursing; designated Pennsylvania Open-Admission institution; or non-transferable two-year program – August 1, 2020 *(date received)* All other applicants – May 1, 2020 *(date received)* *
SC	Tuition Grants – June 30, 2020 *(date received)* SC Commission on Higher Education Need-based Grants ^ $
TN	State Grant – Prior-year recipients receive award if eligible and apply by February 1, 2020. All other awards made to neediest applicants. $ Tennessee Promise – February 1, 2020 *(date received)* State Lottery – Fall term, September 1, 2020 *(date received)*; spring and summer terms, February 1, 2021 *(date received)*
TX	January 15, 2020 # * Private and two-year institutions may have different deadlines. *
WV	PROMISE Scholarship – March 1, 2020. New applicants must submit additional form. Contact your financial aid administrator or state agency. WV Higher Education Grant Program – April 15, 2020

* Additional forms may be required.   ^ As soon as possible after October 1, 2019.
• Check with your financial aid administrator.   # For priority consideration, submit by date specified.
$ Awards made until funds are depleted.   + Applicants encouraged to obtain proof of mailing.

Source: U.S. Department of Education

What is the FAFSA® form?

Why fill out a FAFSA form?

The *Free Application for Federal Student Aid* (FAFSA) is the first step in the financial aid process. You use the FAFSA form to apply for federal student aid, such as grants, work-study, and loans. In addition, most states and colleges use information from the FAFSA form to award nonfederal aid.

Why all the questions?

Most of the questions on the FAFSA form are required to calculate your Expected Family Contribution (EFC). The EFC measures your family's financial strength and is used to determine your eligibility for federal student aid. Your state and the colleges you list may also use some of your responses. They will determine if you may be eligible for school or state aid, in addition to federal aid.

How do I find out what my Expected Family Contribution (EFC) is?

Your EFC will be listed on your *Student Aid Report* (SAR). Your SAR summarizes the information you submitted on your FAFSA form. It is important to review your SAR to make sure all of your information is correct and complete. Make corrections or provide additional information, as necessary.

How much student financial aid will I receive?

Using the information on your FAFSA form and your EFC, the financial aid office at your college will determine the amount of aid you will receive. The college will use your EFC to prepare a financial aid package to help you meet your financial need. Financial need is the difference between the cost of attendance (which can include living expenses), as determined by your college, and your EFC. If you are eligible for a Federal Pell Grant, you may receive it from only one college for the same period of enrollment. If you or your family have unusual circumstances that should be taken into account, contact your college's financial aid office. Some examples of unusual circumstances are: unusual medical or dental expenses or a large change in income from 2018 to this year.

When will I receive the student financial aid?

Any financial aid you are eligible to receive will be paid to you through your college. Typically, your college will first use the aid to pay tuition, fees and room and board (if provided by the college). Any remaining aid is paid to you for your other educational expenses.

How can I have more colleges receive my FAFSA form information?

If you are completing a paper FAFSA form, you can only list four colleges in the school code step. You may add more colleges by doing one of the following:

- After your FAFSA form has been processed, go to **fafsa.gov**, log in to the site, and follow the instructions for correcting your FAFSA form.
- Use the *Student Aid Report* (SAR), which you will receive after your FAFSA form is processed. Your Data Release Number (DRN) verifies your identity and will be listed on the first page of your SAR. You can call 1-800-433-3243 and provide your DRN to a customer service representative, who will add more school codes for you.
- Provide your DRN to the financial aid administrator at the college you want added, and he or she can add their school code to your FAFSA form.

Note: Your FAFSA record can only list up to ten school codes. If there are ten school codes on your record, each new code will need to replace one of the school codes listed.

Where can I receive more information on student financial aid?

The best place for information about student financial aid is the financial aid office at the college you plan to attend. The financial aid administrator can tell you about student aid available from your state, the college itself and other sources.

- You can also visit our web site **StudentAid.gov**.
- For information by phone you can call our Federal Student Aid Information Center at 1-800-433-3243. TTY users (for the hearing impaired) may call 1-800-730-8913.
- You can also check with your high school counselor, your state aid agency or your local library's reference section.

Information about other nonfederal assistance may be available from foundations, faith-based organizations, community organizations and civic groups, as well as organizations related to your field of interest, such as the American Medical Association or American Bar Association. Check with your parents' employers or unions to see if they award scholarships or have tuition assistance plans.

Information on the Privacy Act and use of your Social Security Number

We use the information that you provide on this form to determine if you are eligible to receive federal student financial aid and the amount that you are eligible to receive. Sections 483 and 484 of the Higher Education Act of 1965, as amended, give us the authority to ask you and your parents these questions, and to collect the Social Security Numbers of you and your parents. We use your Social Security Number to verify your identity and retrieve your records, and we may request your Social Security Number again for those purposes.

State and institutional student financial aid programs may also use the information that you provide on this form to determine if you are eligible to receive state and institutional aid and the need that you have for such aid. Therefore, we will disclose the information that you provide on this form to each institution you list in questions 101a - 101h, state agencies in your state of legal residence and the state agencies of the states in which the colleges that you list in questions 101a - 101h are located.

If you are applying solely for federal aid, you must answer all of the following questions that apply to you: 1-9, 14-16, 18, 21-23, 26, 28-29, 32-58, 60-67, 69, 72-100, 102, and 103. If you do not answer these questions, you will not receive federal aid.

Without your consent, we may disclose information that you provide to entities under a published "routine use." Under such a routine use, we may disclose information to third parties that we have authorized to assist us in administering the above programs; to other federal agencies under computer matching programs, such as those with the Internal Revenue Service, Social Security Administration, Selective Service System, Department of Homeland Security, Department of Justice and Veterans Affairs; to your parents or spouse; and to members of Congress if you ask them to help you with student aid questions.

If the federal government, the U.S. Department of Education, or an employee of the U.S. Department of Education is involved in litigation, we may send information to the Department of Justice, or a court or adjudicative body, if the disclosure is related to financial aid and certain conditions are met. In addition, we may send your information to a foreign, federal, state, or local enforcement agency if the information that you submitted indicates a violation or potential violation of law, for which that agency has jurisdiction for investigation or prosecution. Finally, we may send information regarding a claim that is determined to be valid and overdue to a consumer reporting agency. This information includes identifiers from the record; the amount, status and history of the claim; and the program under which the claim arose.

State Certification

By submitting this application, you are giving your state financial aid agency permission to verify any statement on this form and to obtain income tax information for all persons required to report income on this form.

The Paperwork Reduction Act of 1995

According to the Paperwork Reduction Act of 1995, no persons are required to respond to a collection of information unless such collection displays a valid OMB control number. The valid OMB control number for this information collection is 1845-0001. Public reporting burden for this collection of information is estimated to average one and a half hours per response, including time for reviewing instructions, searching existing data sources, gathering and maintaining the data needed, and completing and reviewing the collection of information. The obligation to respond to this collection is voluntary. If you have comments or concerns regarding the status of your individual submission of this form, please contact the Federal Student Aid Information Center, P.O. Box 84, Washington, D.C. 20044 directly. [Note: Please do not return the completed form to this address.]

We may request additional information from you to process your application more efficiently. We will collect this additional information only as needed and on a voluntary basis.

FIGURE 10-2:
(continued)

Page 2

FAFSA®

FREE APPLICATION *for* FEDERAL STUDENT AID

July 1, 2020 – June 30, 2021

Federal **Student Aid**
An OFFICE of the U.S. DEPARTMENT of EDUCATION

PROUD SPONSOR *of*
the AMERICAN MIND ®

Step One (Student): For questions 1-31, leave any questions that do not apply to you (the student) blank. OMB # 1845-0001

Your full name (**exactly as it appears on your Social Security card**) If your name has a suffix, such as Jr. or III, include a space between your last name and suffix.

1. Last name

2. First name

3. Middle initial

Your permanent mailing address

4. Number and street (include apt. number)

5. City (and country if not U.S.)

6. State

7. ZIP code

8. Your Social Security Number **See Notes page 9.**

9. Your date of birth — MONTH DAY YEAR

10. Your telephone number

Your driver's license number and driver's license state (if you have one)

11. Driver's license number

12. Driver's license state

13. Your e-mail address. If you provide your e-mail address, we will communicate with you electronically. For example, when your FAFSA form has been processed, you will be notified by e-mail. Your e-mail address will also be shared with your state and the colleges listed on your FAFSA form to allow them to communicate with you. If you do not have an e-mail address, leave this field blank.

14. Are you a U.S. citizen?
Mark only one.
See Notes page 9.

Yes, I am a U.S. citizen (U.S. national). **Skip to question 16.** ...... ◯ 1

No, but I am an eligible noncitizen. **Fill in question 15.** .... ◯ 2

No, I am not a citizen or eligible noncitizen. **Skip to question 16.** ◯ 3

15. Alien Registration Number

A

16. What is your marital status as of today?
See Notes page 9.

I am single .... ◯ 1   I am separated .... ◯ 3

I am married/remarried ◯ 2   I am divorced or widowed ◯ 4

17. Month and year you were married, remarried, separated, divorced or widowed.
See Notes page 9.

MONTH YEAR

18. What is your state of legal residence?

STATE

19. Did you become a legal resident of this state before January 1, 2015?

Yes ◯ 1

No ◯ 2

20. If the answer to question 19 is "No," give month and year you became a legal resident of that state.

MONTH YEAR

21. Are you male or female?
See Notes page 9.

Male ◯ 1

Female ◯ 2

22. **If female, skip to question 23.** Most male students must register with the Selective Service System to receive federal aid. If you are male, are age 18-25, and have not registered, fill in the circle and we will register you. **See Notes page 9.**

Register me ◯ 1

23. Have you been convicted for the possession or sale of illegal drugs for an offense that occurred while you were receiving federal student aid (such as grants, work-study, or loans)?

No ◯ 1

Answer "No" if you have never received federal student aid or if you have never had a drug conviction for an offense that occurred while receiving federal student aid. If you have a drug conviction for an offense that occurred while you were receiving federal student aid, answer "Yes," but complete and submit this application, and we will mail you a worksheet to help you determine if your conviction affects your eligibility for aid. If you are unsure how to answer this question, call 1-800-433-3243 for help.

Yes ◯ 3

Some states and colleges offer aid based on the level of schooling your parents completed.

24. Highest school completed by Parent 1

Middle school/Jr. high ◯ 1   High school ◯ 2   College or beyond ◯ 3   Other/unknown ◯ 4

25. Highest school completed by Parent 2

Middle school/Jr. high ◯ 1   High school ◯ 2   College or beyond ◯ 3   Other/unknown ◯ 4

26. What will your high school completion status be when you begin college in the 2020-2021 school year?

High school diploma. **Answer question 27.** .... ◯ 1

General Educational Development (GED) certificate or state certificate. **Skip to question 28.** ◯ 2

Homeschooled. **Skip to question 28.** .... ◯ 3

None of the above. **Skip to question 28.** .... ◯ 4

FIGURE 10-2:
(continued)

For Help — StudentAid.gov/completefafsa

Page 3

Step One CONTINUES on Page 4

27. What is the name of the high school where you received or will receive your high school diploma? Enter the complete high school name, and the city and state where the high school is located.

High School Name _____

High School City _____   STATE [ ][ ]

28. Will you have your first bachelor's degree before you begin the 2020-2021 school year?

Yes ◯ 1   No ◯ 2

29. What will your college grade level be when you begin the 2020-2021 school year?

Never attended college and 1st year undergraduate .... ◯ 0

Attended college before and 1st year undergraduate .... ◯ 1

2nd year undergraduate/sophomore .... ◯ 2

3rd year undergraduate/junior .... ◯ 3

4th year undergraduate/senior .... ◯ 4

5th year/other undergraduate .... ◯ 5

1st year college graduate/professional (MBA, MD, PhD, etc.) .... ◯ 6

Continuing graduate/professional or beyond (MBA, MD, PhD, etc.) .. ◯ 7

30. What college degree or certificate will you be working on when you begin the 2020-2021 school year?

1st bachelor's degree .... ◯ 1

2nd bachelor's degree .... ◯ 2

Associate degree (occupational or technical program) .... ◯ 3

Associate degree (general education or transfer program)................. ◯ 4

Certificate or diploma (occupational, technical or education program of less than two years)... ◯ 5

Certificate or diploma (occupational, technical or education program of two or more years) .... ◯ 6

Teaching credential (nondegree program)........................ ◯ 7

College graduate or professional degree (MBA, MD, PhD, etc.) .... ◯ 8

Other/undecided .... ◯ 9

31. Are you interested in being considered for work-study?   Yes ◯ 1   No ◯ 2   Don't know ◯ 3

Step Two (Student): Answer questions 32–57 about yourself (the student). If you were never married, or are separated, divorced or widowed and are not remarried, answer only about yourself. If you are married or remarried as of today, include information about your spouse.

32. For 2018, have you (the student) completed your IRS income tax return or another tax return listed in question 33?

I have already completed my return .... ◯ 1

I will file but have not yet completed my return .... ◯ 2

I'm not going to file. **Skip to question 38.** ◯ 3

33. What income tax return did you file or will you file for 2018?

IRS 1040 .... ◯ 1

A foreign tax return, IRS 1040NR or 1040NR-EZ. **See Notes page 9.** .... ◯ 3

A tax return with Puerto Rico, another U.S. territory, or Freely Associated State. **See Notes page 9.** ...... ◯ 4

34. For 2018, what is or will be your tax filing status according to your tax return?

Single .... ◯ 1

Head of household................... ◯ 4

Married—filed joint return .... ◯ 2

Married—filed separate return .... ◯ 3

Qualifying widow(er)................. ◯ 5

Don't know .... ◯ 6

35. Did (or will) you file a Schedule 1 with your 2018 tax return? Answer **"No"** if you did not file a Schedule 1 or only filed a Schedule 1 to report an Alaska Permanent Fund dividend or one of the other exceptions listed in the **Notes on page 9.**   Yes ◯ 2   No ◯ 1   Don't know ◯ 3

For questions 36–44, if the answer is zero or the question does not apply to you, enter 0. Report whole dollar amounts with no cents.

36. What was your (and spouse's) adjusted gross income for 2018? Adjusted gross income is on IRS Form 1040—line 7. $ [ ][ ][ ][ ][ ][ ]

37. Enter your (and spouse's) income tax for 2018. Income tax amount is the total of IRS Form 1040—line 13 minus Schedule 2—line 46. If negative, enter a zero here. $ [ ][ ][ ][ ][ ][ ]

Questions 38 and 39 ask about earnings (wages, salaries, tips, etc.) in 2018. Answer the questions whether or not a tax return was filed. This information may be on the W-2 forms or on the tax return selected in question 33: IRS Form 1040—line 1 + Schedule 1—lines 12 + 18 + Schedule K-1 (IRS Form 1065)—Box 14 (Code A). If any individual earning item is negative, do not include that item in your calculation.

38. How much did you earn from working in 2018? $ [ ][ ][ ][ ][ ][ ]

39. How much did your spouse earn from working in 2018? $ [ ][ ][ ][ ][ ][ ]

40. As of today, what is your (and spouse's) total current balance of cash, savings, and checking accounts? **Don't include** student financial aid. $ [ ][ ][ ][ ][ ][ ]

41. As of today, what is the net worth of your (and spouse's) investments, including real estate? **Don't include** the home you live in. **See Notes page 9.** $ [ ][ ][ ][ ][ ][ ]

42. As of today, what is the net worth of your (and spouse's) current businesses and/or investment farms? **Don't include** a family farm or family business with 100 or fewer full-time or full-time equivalent employees. **See Notes page 9.** $ [ ][ ][ ][ ][ ][ ]

FIGURE 10-2:
(continued)

CHAPTER 10 Filling Out the Common Financial Aid Forms to Your Best Advantage   **163**

43. Student's 2018 Additional Financial Information (Enter the combined amounts for you and your spouse.)

a. Education credits (American Opportunity Tax Credit and Lifetime Learning Tax Credit) from IRS Form 1040 Schedule 3—line 50. $ ☐☐☐☐☐☐

b. Child support paid because of divorce or separation or as a result of a legal requirement. **Don't include** support for children in your household, as reported in question 93. $ ☐☐☐☐☐☐

c. Taxable earnings from need-based employment programs, such as Federal Work-Study and need-based employment portions of fellowships and assistantships. $ ☐☐☐☐☐☐

d. Taxable college grant and scholarship aid **reported to the IRS as income**. Includes AmeriCorps benefits (awards, living allowances and interest accrual payments), as well as grant and scholarship portions of fellowships and assistantships. $ ☐☐☐☐☐☐

e. Combat pay or special combat pay. Only enter the amount that was taxable and included in your adjusted gross income. **Don't include** untaxed combat pay. $ ☐☐☐☐☐☐

f. Earnings from work under a cooperative education program offered by a college. $ ☐☐☐☐☐☐

44. Student's 2018 Untaxed Income (Enter the combined amounts for you and your spouse.)

a. Payments to tax-deferred pension and retirement savings plans (paid directly or withheld from earnings), including, but not limited to, amounts reported on the W-2 forms in Boxes 12a through 12d, codes D, E, F, G, H and S. **Don't include** amounts reported in code DD (employer contributions toward employee health benefits). $ ☐☐☐☐☐☐

b. IRA deductions and payments to self-employed SEP, SIMPLE, Keogh and other qualified plans from IRS Form 1040 Schedule 1—total of lines 28 + 32. $ ☐☐☐☐☐☐

c. Child support received for any of your children. **Don't include** foster care or adoption payments. $ ☐☐☐☐☐☐

d. Tax exempt interest income from IRS Form 1040—line 2a. $ ☐☐☐☐☐☐

e. Untaxed portions of IRA distributions and pensions from IRS Form 1040—line 4a minus line 4b. **Exclude rollovers.** If negative, enter a zero here. $ ☐☐☐☐☐☐

f. Housing, food and other living allowances paid to members of the military, clergy and others (including cash payments and cash value of benefits). **Don't include** the value of on-base military housing or the value of a basic military allowance for housing. $ ☐☐☐☐☐☐

g. Veterans noneducation benefits, such as Disability, Death Pension, or Dependency & Indemnity Compensation (DIC) and/or VA Educational Work-Study allowances. $ ☐☐☐☐☐☐

h. Other untaxed income not reported in items 44a through 44g, such as workers' compensation, disability benefits, untaxed foreign income, etc. Also include the untaxed portions of health savings accounts from IRS Form 1040 Schedule 1—line 25. **Don't include** extended foster care benefits, student aid, earned income credit, additional child tax credit, welfare payments, untaxed Social Security benefits, Supplemental Security Income, Workforce Innovation and Opportunity Act educational benefits, on-base military housing or a military housing allowance, combat pay, benefits from flexible spending arrangements (e.g., cafeteria plans), foreign income exclusion or credit for federal tax on special fuels. $ ☐☐☐☐☐☐

i. Money received, or paid on your behalf (e.g., bills), not reported elsewhere on this form. This includes money that you received from a parent or other person whose financial information is not reported on this form and that is not part of a legal child support agreement. **See Notes page 9.** $ ☐☐☐☐☐☐

Step Three (Student): Answer the questions in this step to determine if you will need to provide parental information. Once you answer **"Yes" to any** of the questions in this step, skip Step Four and go to Step Five on page 8.

45. Were you born before January 1, 1997? .... Yes ○₁ No ○₂

46. As of today, are you married? (Also answer "Yes" if you are separated but not divorced.) .... Yes ○₁ No ○₂

47. At the beginning of the 2020-2021 school year, will you be working on a master's or doctorate program (such as an MA, MBA, MD, JD, PhD, EdD, graduate certificate, etc.)?.. Yes ○₁ No ○₂

48. Are you currently serving on active duty in the U.S. Armed Forces for purposes other than training? **See Notes page 9.** .... Yes ○₁ No ○₂

49. Are you a veteran of the U.S. Armed Forces? **See Notes page 9.**.. Yes ○₁ No ○₂

50. Do you now have or will you have children who will receive more than half of their support from you between July 1, 2020 and June 30, 2021?.. Yes ○₁ No ○₂

51. Do you have dependents (other than your children or spouse) who live with you and who receive more than half of their support from you, now and through June 30, 2021?... Yes ○₁ No ○₂

52. At any time since you turned age 13, were both your parents deceased, were you in foster care or were you a dependent or ward of the court? **See Notes page 10.**.. Yes ○₁ No ○₂

53. As determined by a court in your state of legal residence, are you or were you an emancipated minor? **See Notes page 10.** .. Yes ○₁ No ○₂

54. Does someone other than your parent or stepparent have legal guardianship of you, as determined by a court in your state of legal residence? **See Notes page 10.** .... Yes ○₁ No ○₂

55. At any time on or after July 1, 2019, did your high school or school district homeless liaison determine that you were an unaccompanied youth who was homeless or were self-supporting and at risk of being homeless? **See Notes page 10.** Yes ○₁ No ○₂

56. At any time on or after July 1, 2019, did the director of an emergency shelter or transitional housing program funded by the U.S. Department of Housing and Urban Development determine that you were an unaccompanied youth who was homeless or were self-supporting and at risk of being homeless? **See Notes page 10.** .... Yes ○₁ No ○₂

57. At any time on or after July 1, 2019, did the director of a runaway or homeless youth basic center or transitional living program determine that you were an unaccompanied youth who was homeless or were self-supporting and at risk of being homeless? **See Notes page 10.** .... Yes ○₁ No ○₂

FIGURE 10-2:
(continued)

If you (the student) answered "No" to every question in Step Three, go to Step Four.
If you answered "Yes" to any question in Step Three, skip Step Four and go to Step Five on page 8.
(Health professions and law school students: Your college may require you to complete Step Four even if you answered "Yes" to any Step Three question.)
If you believe that you are unable to provide parental information, see Notes page 10.

Step Four (Parent): Complete this step if you (the student) answered "No" to all questions in Step Three.

Answer all the questions in Step Four even if you do not live with your legal parents (biological, adoptive, or as determined by the state [for example, if the parent is listed on the birth certificate]). Grandparents, foster parents, legal guardians, widowed stepparents, aunts, uncles, and siblings are not considered parents on this form unless they have legally adopted you. If your legal parents are married to each other, or are not married to each other and **live together**, answer the questions about both of them. If your parent was never married or is remarried, divorced, separated or widowed, **see StudentAid.gov/fafsa-parent** and/or **Notes page 10** for additional instructions.

58. As of today, what is the marital status of your parents?

Never married...................... ○ 2   Married or remarried.............. ○ 1

Unmarried and both legal parents living together.............................. ○ 5   Divorced or separated............. ○ 3

Widowed.......................... ○ 4

59. Month and year they were married, remarried, separated, divorced or widowed.

MONTH   YEAR

What are the Social Security Numbers, names and dates of birth of the parents reporting information on this form? If your parent does not have a Social Security Number, you must enter 000-00-0000. Don't enter an Individual Taxpayer Identification Number (ITIN) in the Social Security Number field. If the name includes a suffix, such as Jr. or III, include a space between the last name and suffix. Enter two digits for each day and month (e.g., for May 31, enter 05 31).

Questions 60-63 are for Parent 1 (father/mother/stepparent)

60. SOCIAL SECURITY NUMBER   **61.** LAST NAME, AND   **62.** FIRST INITIAL   **63.** DATE OF BIRTH

Questions 64-67 are for Parent 2 (father/mother/stepparent)

64. SOCIAL SECURITY NUMBER   **65.** LAST NAME, AND   **66.** FIRST INITIAL   **67.** DATE OF BIRTH

68. Your parents' e-mail address. If you provide your parents' e-mail address, we will let them know your FAFSA form has been processed. This e-mail address will also be shared with your state and the colleges listed on your FAFSA form to allow them to electronically communicate with your parents.

69. What is your parents' state of legal residence?   STATE

70. Did your parents become legal residents of this state before January 1, 2015?   Yes ○ 1   No ○ 2

71. If the answer to question 70 is "No," give the month and year legal residency began for the parent who has lived in the state the longest.   MONTH   YEAR

72. How many people are in your parents' household?
Include:
- yourself, even if you don't live with your parents,
- your parents,
- your parents' other children (even if they do not live with your parents) if (a) your parents will provide more than half of their support between July 1, 2020 and June 30, 2021, or (b) the children could answer "No" to every question in Step 5 of this form, and
- other people if they now live with your parents, your parents provide more than half of their support and your parents will continue to provide more than half of their support between July 1, 2020 and June 30, 2021.

73. How many people in your parents' household (from question 72) will be college students between July 1, 2020 and June 30, 2021? Always count yourself as a college student. Do not include your parents. Do not include siblings who are in U.S. military service academies. You may include others only if they will attend, at least half-time in 2020-2021, a program that leads to a college degree or certificate.

At any time during 2018 or 2019, did you, your parents, or anyone in your parents' household (from question 72) receive benefits from any of the federal programs listed? Mark all that apply. Answering these questions will NOT reduce eligibility for student aid or these programs. TANF has different names in many states. Call 1-800-433-3243 to find out the name of your state's program. If you, your parents, or anyone in your household receives any of these benefits after filing the FAFSA form but before December 31, 2019, you must update your response by logging in to **fafsa.gov** and selecting "Make FAFSA Corrections."

74. Medicaid or Supplemental Security Income (SSI) ○

75. Supplemental Nutrition Assistance Program (SNAP) ○

76. Free or Reduced Price School Lunch ○

77. Temporary Assistance for Needy Families (TANF) ○

78. Special Supplemental Nutrition Program for Women, Infants, and Children (WIC) ○

If your answer to question 58 was "Unmarried and both legal parents living together," contact 1-800-433-3243 for assistance with answering questions 79-92.

79. For 2018, have your parents completed their IRS income tax return or another tax return listed in question 80?

My parents have already completed their return. ○ 1

My parents will file but have not yet completed their return................................... ○ 2

My parents are not going to file. **Skip to question 86**............................ ○ 3

80. What income tax return did your parents file or will they file for 2018?

IRS 1040 .... ○ 1

A foreign tax return, IRS 1040NR or IRS 1040NR-EZ. **See Notes page 9.** .... ○ 3

A tax return with Puerto Rico, another U.S. territory or Freely Associated State. **See Notes page 9.** .... ○ 4

81. For 2018, what is or will be your parents' tax filing status according to their tax return?

Single .... ○ 1
Head of household................... ○ 4
Married—filed joint return .... ○ 2
Married—filed separate return ...... ○ 3
Qualifying widow(er)................. ○ 5
Don't know .... ○ 6

82. Did (or will) your parents file a Schedule 1 with their 2018 tax return? Answer "**No**" if they did not file a Schedule 1 or only filed a Schedule 1 to report an Alaska Permanent Fund dividend or one of the other exceptions listed in the **Notes on page 9.**   Yes ○ 2   No ○ 1   Don't know ○ 3

83. As of today, is either of your parents a dislocated worker? **See Notes page 10.**   Yes ○ 1   No ○ 2   Don't know ○ 3

FIGURE 10-2: (continued)

For questions 84–92, if the answer is zero or the question does not apply, enter 0. Report whole dollar amounts with no cents.

84. What was your parents' adjusted gross income for 2018? Adjusted gross income is on IRS Form 1040—line 7. $ ☐☐☐☐☐☐☐

85. Enter your parents' income tax for 2018. Income tax amount is the total of IRS Form 1040—line 13 minus Schedule 2—line 46. If negative, enter a zero here. $ ☐☐☐☐☐☐☐

Questions 86 and 87 ask about earnings (wages, salaries, tips, etc.) in 2018. Answer the questions whether or not a tax return was filed. This information may be on the W-2 forms or on the tax return selected in question 80: IRS Form 1040—line 1 + Schedule 1—lines 12 + 18 + Schedule K-1 (IRS Form 1065)—Box 14 (Code A). If any individual earning item is negative, do not include that item in your calculation. Report the information for the parent listed in questions 60-63 in question 86 and the information for the parent listed in questions 64-67 in question 87.

86. How much did Parent 1 (father/mother/stepparent) earn from working in 2018? $ ☐☐☐☐☐☐☐

87. How much did Parent 2 (father/mother/stepparent) earn from working in 2018? $ ☐☐☐☐☐☐☐

88. As of today, what is your parents' total current balance of cash, savings, and checking accounts? **Don't include** student financial aid. $ ☐☐☐☐☐☐☐

89. As of today, what is the net worth of your parents' investments, including real estate? **Don't include** the home in which your parents live. **See Notes page 9.** $ ☐☐☐☐☐☐☐

90. As of today, what is the net worth of your parents' current businesses and/or investment farms? **Don't include** a family farm or family business with 100 or fewer full-time or full-time equivalent employees. **See Notes page 9.** $ ☐☐☐☐☐☐☐

91. Parents' 2018 Additional Financial Information (Enter the amounts for your parent[s].)

   a. Education credits (American Opportunity Tax Credit and Lifetime Learning Tax Credit) from IRS Form 1040 Schedule 3—line 50. $ ☐☐☐☐☐☐☐

   b. Child support paid because of divorce or separation or as a result of a legal requirement. **Don't include** support for children in your parents' household, as reported in question 72. $ ☐☐☐☐☐☐☐

   c. Your parents' taxable earnings from need-based employment programs, such as Federal Work-Study and need-based employment portions of fellowships and assistantships. $ ☐☐☐☐☐☐☐

   d. Your parents' taxable college grant and scholarship aid **reported to the IRS as income.** Includes AmeriCorps benefits (awards, living allowances and interest accrual payments), as well as grant and scholarship portions of fellowships and assistantships. $ ☐☐☐☐☐☐☐

   e. Combat pay or special combat pay. Only enter the amount that was taxable and included in your parents' adjusted gross income. **Don't include** untaxed combat pay. $ ☐☐☐☐☐☐☐

   f. Earnings from work under a cooperative education program offered by a college. $ ☐☐☐☐☐☐☐

92. Parents' 2018 Untaxed Income (Enter the amounts for your parent[s].)

   a. Payments to tax-deferred pension and retirement savings plans (paid directly or withheld from earnings), including, but not limited to, amounts reported on the W-2 forms in Boxes 12a through 12d, codes D, E, F, G, H and S. **Don't include** amounts reported in code DD (employer contributions toward employee health benefits). $ ☐☐☐☐☐☐☐

   b. IRA deductions and payments to self-employed SEP, SIMPLE, Keogh and other qualified plans from IRS Form 1040 Schedule 1—total of lines 28 + 32. $ ☐☐☐☐☐☐☐

   c. Child support received for any of your parents' children. **Don't include** foster care or adoption payments. $ ☐☐☐☐☐☐☐

   d. Tax exempt interest income from IRS Form 1040—line 2a. $ ☐☐☐☐☐☐☐

   e. Untaxed portions of IRA distributions and pensions from IRS Form 1040—line 4a minus line 4b. **Exclude rollovers.** If negative, enter a zero here. $ ☐☐☐☐☐☐☐

   f. Housing, food and other living allowances paid to members of the military, clergy and others (including cash payments and cash value of benefits). **Don't include** the value of on-base military housing or the value of a basic military allowance for housing. $ ☐☐☐☐☐☐☐

   g. Veterans noneducation benefits, such as Disability, Death Pension, or Dependency & Indemnity Compensation (DIC) and/or VA Educational Work-Study allowances. $ ☐☐☐☐☐☐☐

   h. Other untaxed income not reported in items 92a through 92g, such as workers' compensation, disability benefits, untaxed foreign income, etc. Also include the untaxed portions of health savings accounts from IRS Form 1040 Schedule 1—line 25. **Don't include** extended foster care benefits, student aid, earned income credit, additional child tax credit, welfare payments, untaxed Social Security benefits, Supplemental Security Income, Workforce Innovation and Opportunity Act educational benefits, on-base military housing or a military housing allowance, combat pay, benefits from flexible spending arrangements (e.g., cafeteria plans), foreign income exclusion or credit for federal tax on special fuels. $ ☐☐☐☐☐☐☐

FIGURE 10-2: (continued)

Step Five (Student): Complete this step only if you (the student) answered "Yes" to any questions in Step Three.

93. How many people are in your household?
Include:
- yourself (and your spouse),
- your children, if you will provide more than half of their support between July 1, 2020 and June 30, 2021, even if they do not live with you, and
- other people if they now live with you, you provide more than half of their support and you will continue to provide more than half of their support between July 1, 2020 and June 30, 2021.

94. How many people in your (and your spouse's) household (from question 93) will be college students between July 1, 2020 and June 30, 2021? Always count yourself as a college student. Do not include family members who are in U.S. military service academies. Include others only if they will attend, at least half-time in 2020-2021, a program that leads to a college degree or certificate.

At any time during 2018 or 2019, did you (or your spouse) or anyone in your household (from question 93) receive benefits from any of the federal programs listed? Mark all that apply. Answering these questions will NOT reduce eligibility for student aid or these programs. TANF has different names in many states. Call 1-800-433-3243 to find out the name of your state's program. If you (or your spouse) or anyone in your household receives any of these benefits after filing the FAFSA form but before December 31, 2019, you must update your response by logging in to **fafsa.gov** and selecting "Make FAFSA Corrections."

95. Medicaid or Supplemental Security Income (SSI) ◯

96. Supplemental Nutrition Assistance Program (SNAP) ◯

97. Free or Reduced Price School Lunch ◯

98. Temporary Assistance for Needy Families (TANF) ◯

99. Special Supplemental Nutrition Program for Women, Infants, and Children (WIC) ◯

100. As of today, are you (or your spouse) a dislocated worker? **See Notes page 10.**   Yes ◯ 1   No ◯ 2   Don't know ◯ 3

Step Six (Student): Indicate which colleges you want to receive your FAFSA information.

Enter the six-digit federal school code and your housing plans for each college or school you want to receive your FAFSA information. You can find the school codes at **fafsa.gov/schoolsearch** or by calling 1-800-433-3243. If you cannot obtain a code, write in the complete name, address, city and state of the college. If you want more schools to receive your FAFSA information, read **What is the FAFSA form?** on page 2. All of the information you included on your FAFSA form, *with the exception of the list of colleges*, will be sent to each of the colleges you listed. In addition, all of your FAFSA information, *including the list of colleges*, will be sent to your state grant agency. For federal student aid purposes, it does not matter in what order you list your selected schools. However, the order in which you list schools may affect your eligibility for state aid. Consult your state agency or **StudentAid.gov/order** for details.

	1ST FEDERAL SCHOOL CODE		NAME OF COLLEGE / ADDRESS AND CITY	STATE	HOUSING PLANS	
101.a		OR			101.b on campus ◯ 1 / with parent ◯ 2 / off campus ◯ 3	
101.c	2ND FEDERAL SCHOOL CODE	OR	NAME OF COLLEGE / ADDRESS AND CITY	STATE	101.d on campus ◯ 1 / with parent ◯ 2 / off campus ◯ 3	
101.e	3RD FEDERAL SCHOOL CODE	OR	NAME OF COLLEGE / ADDRESS AND CITY	STATE	101.f on campus ◯ 1 / with parent ◯ 2 / off campus ◯ 3	
101.g	4TH FEDERAL SCHOOL CODE	OR	NAME OF COLLEGE / ADDRESS AND CITY	STATE	101.h on campus ◯ 1 / with parent ◯ 2 / off campus ◯ 3	

Step Seven (Student and Parent): Read, sign and date.

If you are the student, by signing this application you certify that you (1) will use federal and/or state student financial aid only to pay the cost of attending an institution of higher education, (2) are not in default on a federal student loan or have made satisfactory arrangements to repay it, (3) do not owe money back on a federal student grant or have made satisfactory arrangements to repay it, (4) will notify your college if you default on a federal student loan and (5) will not receive a Federal Pell Grant from more than one college for the same period of time.

If you are the parent or the student, by signing this application you certify that all of the information you provided is true and complete to the best of your knowledge and you agree, if asked, to provide information that will verify the accuracy of your completed form. This information may include U.S. or state income tax forms that you filed or are required to file. Also, you certify that you understand that **the Secretary of Education has the authority to verify information reported on this application with the Internal Revenue Service and other federal agencies.** If you electronically sign any document related to the federal student aid programs using an FSA ID (username and password) and/or any other credential, you certify that you are the person identified by that username and password and/or other credential, and have not disclosed that username and password and/or other credential to anyone else. If you purposely give false or misleading information, you may be fined up to $20,000, sent to prison, or both.

102. Date this form was completed
MONTH   DAY   2019 ◯   2020 ◯   2021 ◯

103. Student (Sign below)
1

Parent (A parent from Step Four sign below.)
2

If a fee was paid to someone for advice or for completing this form, that person must complete this section.

Preparer's name, firm and address

104. Preparer's Social Security Number (or 105)

105. Employer ID number (or 104)

106. Preparer's signature and date
1

COLLEGE USE ONLY   FEDERAL SCHOOL CODE
D/O ◯ 1   Homeless Youth Determination ◯ 4

FAA Signature
1

DATA ENTRY USE ONLY: ◯ P   ◯ *   ◯ L   ◯ E

FIGURE 10-2: (continued)

Notes for question 8 (page 3)

Enter your Social Security Number (SSN) as it appears on your Social Security card. If you are a resident of one of the Freely Associated States (i.e., the Republic of Palau, the Republic of the Marshall Islands, or the Federated States of Micronesia) and were issued an identification number beginning with "666" when submitting a FAFSA form previously, enter that number here. If you are a first-time applicant from one of the Freely Associated States, enter "666" in the first three boxes of the Social Security Number field and leave the remaining six positions blank, and we will create an identification number to be used for federal student aid purposes. Do not enter an Individual Taxpayer Identification Number (ITIN) in the Social Security Number field.

Notes for questions 14 and 15 (page 3)

If you are an eligible noncitizen, write in your eight- or nine-digit Alien Registration Number. Generally, you are an eligible noncitizen if you are (1) a permanent U.S. resident with a Permanent Resident Card (I-551); (2) a conditional permanent resident with a Conditional Green Card (I-551C); (3) the holder of an Arrival-Departure Record (I-94) from the Department of Homeland Security showing any one of the following designations: "Refugee," "Asylum Granted," "Parolee" (I-94 confirms that you were paroled for a minimum of one year and status has not expired), T-Visa holder (T-1, T-2, T-3, etc.) or "Cuban-Haitian Entrant;" or (4) the holder of a valid certification or eligibility letter from the Department of Health and Human Services showing a designation of "Victim of human trafficking."

If you are in the U.S. and have been granted Deferred Action for Childhood Arrivals (DACA), an F1 or F2 student visa, a J1 or J2 exchange visitor visa, or a G series visa (pertaining to international organizations), select "No, I am not a citizen or eligible noncitizen." You will not be eligible for federal student aid. If you have a Social Security Number but are not a citizen or an eligible noncitizen, including if you have been granted DACA, you should still complete the FAFSA form because you may be eligible for state or college aid.

Notes for questions 16 and 17 (page 3)

Report your marital status as of the date you sign your FAFSA form. If your marital status changes after you sign your FAFSA form, check with the **financial aid office at the college.**

Notes for questions 21 and 22 (page 3)

To be eligible for federal student aid, male citizens and male immigrants residing in the U.S. aged 18 through 25 are required to register with the Selective Service System, with limited exceptions. The Selective Service System and the registration requirement applies to any person assigned the sex of male at birth (see **www.sss.gov/Registration-Info/Who-Registration**). The Selective Service System and the registration requirement for males preserves America's ability to provide resources in an emergency to the U.S. Armed Forces. For more information about the Selective Service System, visit **sss.gov.** Forms are available at your local U.S. Post Office.

Notes for questions 33 (page 4)
and 80 (page 6)

If you filed or will file a foreign tax return, IRS 1040NR or IRS 1040NR-EZ, or a tax return with Puerto Rico, another U.S. territory (e.g., Guam, American Samoa, the U.S. Virgin Islands, Swain's Island or the Northern Marianas Islands) or one of the Freely Associated States, use the information from that return to fill out this form. If you filed a foreign return, convert all monetary units to U.S. dollars, using the published exchange rate in effect for the date nearest to today's date. To view the daily exchange rates, go to **federalreserve.gov/releases/h10/current.**

Notes for questions 35 (page 4)
and 82 (page 6)

Answer "**No**" if you (and if married, your spouse) did not file a Schedule 1.

Answer "**No**" if you (and if married, your spouse) did or will file a Schedule 1 to report **only one or more** of the following items:

1. Capital gain (line 13 – may not be a negative value)
2. Unemployment compensation (line 19)
3. Other income to report an Alaska Permanent Fund dividend (line 21 – may not be a negative value)
4. Educator expenses (line 23)
5. IRA deduction (line 32)
6. Student loan interest deduction (line 33)

Answer "**Yes**" if you (or if married, your spouse) filed or will file a Schedule 1 and reported additional income or adjustments to income on any lines **other than or in addition to** the six exceptions listed above.

If you do not know if you filed or will file a Schedule 1, select "**Don't know.**"

Notes for questions 41 and 42 (page 4), 44i (page 5),
and 89 and 90 (page 7)

Net worth means the current value, as of today, of investments, businesses, and/or investment farms, minus debts related to those same investments, businesses, and/or investment farms. When calculating net worth, use 0 for investments or properties with a negative value.

Investments include real estate (do not include the home in which you live), rental property (includes a unit within a family home that has its own entrance, kitchen, and bath rented to someone other than a family member), trust funds, UGMA and UTMA accounts, money market funds, mutual funds, certificates of deposit, stocks, stock options, bonds, other securities, installment and land sale contracts (including mortgages held), commodities, etc.

Investments also include qualified educational benefits or education savings accounts (e.g., Coverdell savings accounts, 529 college savings plans and the refund value of 529 prepaid tuition plans). For a student who does not report parental information, the accounts owned by the student (and/or the student's spouse) are reported as student investments in question 41. For a student who must report parental information, the accounts are reported as parental investments in question 89, including all accounts owned by the student and all accounts owned by the parents for any member of the household.

Money received, or paid on your behalf, also includes distributions to you (the student beneficiary) from a 529 plan that is owned by someone other than you or your parents (such as your grandparents, aunts, uncles, and non-custodial parents). You must include these distribution amounts in question 44i.

Investments do not include the home you live in, the value of life insurance, ABLE accounts, retirement plans (401[k] plans, pension funds, annuities, non-education IRAs, Keogh plans, etc.) or cash, savings and checking accounts already reported in questions 40 and 88.

Investments also do not include UGMA and UTMA accounts for which you are the custodian, but not the owner.

Investment value means the current balance or market value of these investments as of today. Investment debt means only those debts that are related to the investments.

Business and/or investment farm value includes the market value of land, buildings, machinery, equipment, inventory, etc. Business and/or investment farm debt means only those debts for which the business or investment farm was used as collateral.

Business value does not include the value of a small business if your family owns and controls more than 50 percent of the business and the business has 100 or fewer full-time or full-time equivalent employees. For small business value, your family includes (1) persons directly related to you, such as a parent, sister or cousin, or (2) persons who are or were related to you by marriage, such as a spouse, stepparent or sister-in-law.

Investment farm value does not include the value of a family farm that you (your spouse and/or your parents) live on and operate.

Notes for question 48 (page 5)

Answer "**Yes**" if you are currently serving in the U.S. Armed Forces or are a National Guard or Reserves enlistee who is on active duty for other than state or training purposes.

Answer "**No**" if you are a National Guard or Reserves enlistee who is on active duty for state or training purposes.

Notes for question 49 (page 5)

Answer "**Yes**" (you are a veteran) if you (1) have engaged in active duty (including basic training) in the U.S. Armed Forces, or are a National Guard or Reserves enlistee who was called to active duty for other than state or training purposes, or were a cadet or midshipman at one of the service academies, **and** (2) were released under a condition other than dishonorable. Also answer "**Yes**" if you are not a veteran now but will be one by June 30, 2021.

Answer "**No**" (you are not a veteran) if you (1) have never engaged in active duty (including basic training) in the U.S. Armed Forces, (2) are currently an ROTC student or a cadet or midshipman at a service academy, (3) are a National Guard or Reserves enlistee activated only for state or training purposes, or (4) were engaged in active duty in the U.S. Armed Forces but released under dishonorable conditions.

Also answer "**No**" if you are currently serving in the U.S. Armed Forces and will continue to serve through June 30, 2021.

FIGURE 10-2:
(continued)

Notes continue on Page 10.

Notes for question 52 (page 5)

Answer **"Yes"** if at any time since you turned age 13:

- You had no living parent, even if you are now adopted; or
- You were in foster care, even if you are no longer in foster care today; or
- You were a dependent or ward of the court, even if you are no longer a dependent or ward of the court today. For federal student aid purposes, someone who is incarcerated is not considered a ward of the court.

If you are not sure if you were in foster care, check with your state child welfare agency. You can find that agency's contact information at **childwelfare.gov/nfcad**.

The financial aid administrator at your school may require you to provide proof that you were in foster care or a dependent or ward of the court.

Notes for questions 53 and 54 (page 5)

The definition of legal guardianship does not include your parents, even if they were appointed by a court to be your guardians. You are also not considered a legal guardian of yourself.

Answer **"Yes"** if you can provide a copy of a court's decision that as of today you are an emancipated minor or are in legal guardianship. Also answer **"Yes"** if you can provide a copy of a court's decision that you were an emancipated minor or were in legal guardianship immediately before you reached the age of being an adult in your state. The court must be located in your state of legal residence at the time the court's decision was issued.

Answer **"No"** if you are still a minor and the court decision is no longer in effect or the court decision was not in effect at the time you became an adult. Also answer **"No"** and contact your school if custody was awarded by the courts and the court papers say "custody" (not "guardianship").

The financial aid administrator at your college may require you to provide proof that you were an emancipated minor or in legal guardianship.

Notes for questions 55–57 (page 5)

Answer **"Yes"** if you received a determination at any time on or after July 1, 2019, that you were an unaccompanied youth who was homeless or at risk of being homeless.

- **"Homeless"** means lacking fixed, regular and adequate housing. You may be homeless if you are living in shelters, parks, motels, hotels, public spaces, camping grounds, cars, abandoned buildings, or temporarily living with other people because you have nowhere else to go. Also, if you are living in any of these situations and fleeing an abusive parent, you may be considered homeless even if your parent would otherwise provide a place to live.

- **"Unaccompanied"** means you are not living in the physical custody of your parent or guardian.

Answer **"No"** if you are not homeless or at risk of being homeless, or do not have a determination. However, even if you answer **"No"** to each of questions 55, 56, and 57, you should contact the financial aid administrator at the college you plan to attend if you are either (1) homeless and unaccompanied or (2) at risk of being homeless, unaccompanied, and providing for your own living expenses - as your college financial aid office can determine that you are "homeless" and are not required to provide parental information.

The financial aid administrator at your college may require you to provide a copy of the determination if you answered **"Yes"** to any of these questions.

Notes for students unable to provide parental information on pages 6 and 7

Under very limited circumstances (for example, your parents are incarcerated; you have left home due to an abusive family environment; or you do not know where your parents are and are unable to contact them), you may be able to submit your FAFSA form without parental information. **If you are unable to provide parental information**, skip Steps Four and Five, and go to Step Six. Once you submit your FAFSA form without parental data, **you must follow up with the financial aid office at the college you plan to attend**, in order to complete your FAFSA form.

Notes for Step Four, questions 58–92 (pages 6 and 7)

Review all instructions below to determine who is considered a parent on this form:

- If your parent was never married and does not live with your other legal parent, or if your parent is widowed and not remarried, answer the questions about that parent.
- If your legal parents (biological, adoptive, or as determined by the state [for example, if the parent is listed on the birth certificate]) are not married to each other and **live together**, select "Unmarried and both legal parents living together" and provide information about both of them regardless of their gender. Do not include any person who is not married to your parent and who is not a legal or biological parent. Contact 1-800-433-3243 for assistance in completing questions 79–92, or visit **StudentAid.gov/fafsa-parent**.
- If your legal parents are married, select "Married or remarried." If your legal parents are divorced but living together, select "Unmarried and both legal parents living together." If your legal parents are separated but living together, select "Married or remarried," not "Divorced or separated."
- If your parents are divorced or separated, answer the questions about the parent you lived with more during the past 12 months. (If you did not live with one parent more than the other, give answers about the parent who provided more financial support during the past 12 months or during the most recent year that you actually received support from a parent.) **If this parent is remarried as of today, answer the questions about that parent and your stepparent.**
- If your widowed parent is remarried as of today, answer the questions about that parent and your stepparent.

Notes for questions 83 (page 6) and 100 (page 8)

In general, a person may be considered a dislocated worker if he or she:

- is receiving unemployment benefits due to being laid off or losing a job and is unlikely to return to a previous occupation;
- has been laid off or received a lay-off notice from a job;
- was self-employed but is now unemployed due to economic conditions or natural disaster; or
- is the spouse of an active duty member of the Armed Forces and has experienced a loss of employment because of relocating due to permanent change in duty station; or
- is the spouse of an active duty member of the Armed Forces and is unemployed or underemployed, and is experiencing difficulty in obtaining or upgrading employment; or
- is a displaced homemaker. A displaced homemaker is generally a person who previously provided unpaid services to the family (e.g., a stay-at-home mom or dad), is no longer supported by the spouse, is unemployed or underemployed, and is having trouble finding or upgrading employment.

Except for the spouse of an active duty member of the Armed Forces, if a person quits work, generally he or she is not considered a dislocated worker even if, for example, the person is receiving unemployment benefits.

Answer **"Yes"** to question 83 if your parent is a dislocated worker. Answer **"Yes"** to question 100 if you or your spouse is a dislocated worker.

Answer **"No"** to question 83 if your parent is not a dislocated worker. Answer **"No"** to question 100 if neither you nor your spouse is a dislocated worker.

Answer **"Don't know"** to question 83 if you are not sure whether your parent is a dislocated worker. Answer **"Don't know"** to question 100 if you are not sure whether you or your spouse is a dislocated worker. You can contact your financial aid office for assistance in answering these questions.

The financial aid administrator at your college may require you to provide proof that your parent is a dislocated worker, if you answered **"Yes"** to question 83, or that you or your spouse is a dislocated worker, if you answered **"Yes"** to question 100.

FIGURE 10-2:
(continued)

Page 10

Chapter **11**

Tricks and Tips for Finding Scholarships and Borrowing Money

Traditional colleges are expensive — at least seemingly so on the surface when you look at their full sticker prices. To afford them, most families need some help.

The assistance that colleges may offer is in the form of financial aid. They can reduce the sticker price through grants and scholarships. You may also be offered loans to help finance what you can't afford to pay out of pocket now or to simply enable you to spread the payments out over time.

This chapter helps by highlighting how and where you can find money to make college more affordable.

Gaining Grants and Scholarships

There's no doubt about it — the best financial aid of all is the kind that you don't have to pay back. Grants and scholarships directly and immediately reduce the cost for your son or daughter to attend a college. They aren't loans and therefore never have to be paid back.

Many, including the colleges themselves, talk about schools "giving away" money, which I think is misleading terminology. What they're actually doing is offering you a less inflated tuition price by discounting their full sticker price, which most people don't pay. Remember — the average price that families pay at private four-year colleges is typically about half of the full price.

College and university grants and scholarships

The vast majority of grant and scholarship money, especially for private colleges, comes from the institution itself. It may be based upon demonstrated financial need (which is typically called a grant) or may be based upon merit (which is usually called a scholarship). So-called institutional grants (from the college/ university) comprise a whopping 28 percent of all undergraduate financial aid. (The portion is substantially higher at four-year private colleges.)

In Chapter 4, I discuss in detail the common merit-based awards for strong academics or other talents, such as playing a varsity sport at certain colleges and universities.

Need-based grants are the result of the schools analyzing your financial aid documents such as the FAFSA® form, the CSS Profile form, as well as the school's own particular forms. See Chapter 10 for how to best complete these forms. Put the necessary time and thought into filling out these forms because that is where most families find the biggest return on their invested time and energy.

Federal and state government grants

TIP

In addition to grants and scholarships available through schools, there are grants available through the federal and state governments. As a percentage of total undergraduate financial aid, federal Pell grants amount to about 15 percent of all aid, federal veterans' benefits another 6 percent, and state grants amount to another 7 percent. Most government grant money ends up going to students from lower- and middle-income families attending state (public) colleges and universities.

If you qualify, which you can only know if you complete and submit the FAFSA® form, you will be notified if you are awarded federal government grants (for information on filling out this form, see Chapter 10). Grants available through state government programs may require a separate application, although some states use the FAFSA® form.

If you'd like to find out more about state-based grants, see the list of state education departments at www2.ed.gov/about/contacts/state/index.html. Also check out the links you can find for each state at The National Association of Student Financial Aid Administrators compilation of State Financial Aid Programs (NASFAA): www.nasfaa.org/State_Financial_Aid_Programs

"Outside" grants and scholarships

Private organizations (including employers, banks, credit unions, foundations, and community groups) also offer grants and scholarships that are "outside" of what colleges and universities offer. These private and employer grants account for about 7 percent of all undergraduate financial aid. So, in comparison to school-based grants and scholarships, the total dollars at stake are a lot less.

WARNING

Unfortunately, outside grants and scholarships sometimes reduce school-based grants and scholarships. This is not always the case, but I raise this issue here because your best efforts are generally going to be made at the college level with regards to getting grants and scholarships. Of course, if you get nothing there and you really want your son or daughter to attend that school, by all means, go for outside money.

Looking at larger award sources first

Most private scholarships are quite small in comparison to the cost of college, so don't burn a lot of time searching for those. A number of resources and strategies can help you focus and maximize your efforts, which I get to in a moment.

INVESTIGATE

Substantial private scholarships are available. Here are some examples:

>> The Coca-Cola Scholars Program Scholarship (www.coca-colascholars foundation.org) is primarily focused upon academic merit.

>> "The Coolidge Scholarship is an annually awarded, full-ride, presidential scholarship that covers a student's tuition, room, board, and expenses for four years of undergraduate study. The Coolidge may be used by recipients at any accredited American college or university. Anyone of any background, pursuing any academic discipline of study, may apply to this non-partisan, need-blind, program." Find out more at: https://coolidgescholars.org/.

>> The Gates Millennium Scholars program (`https://gmsp.org/`) seeks "to promote academic excellence and to provide an opportunity for outstanding minority students with significant financial need to reach their highest potential."

>> The Jack Kent Cooke Foundation College Scholarship Program (`www.jkcf.org/our-scholarships/college-scholarship-program`) is based upon a student being from a low-income family and having academic potential.

>> QuestBridge's National College Match program (`www.questbridge.org`) targets high-achieving students from low-income families who are the first in their family to attend college.

Enlisting scholarship search websites

There are many national scholarships which are listed on database search websites. The advantage of using these free websites is that after you take a few minutes to enter personal information, they will match you to scholarships that you may want to consider. Websites to look at include:

>> **Cappex.com:** `www.cappex.com`

>> **Chegg:** `www.chegg.com/scholarships`

>> **College Board's Scholarship Search:** `https://bigfuture.collegeboard.org/scholarship-search`

>> **Fastweb:** `www.fastweb.com`

>> **Scholarships.com:** `www.scholarships.com`

>> **Unigo.com:** `www.unigo.com`

WARNING

Now, there are some downsides to beware of with these types of websites. And the biggest concern has to do with the fact that you aren't getting something for nothing when you divulge personal information to such websites. These websites appear to be free, but in fact your information and data is being sold to colleges and other companies interested in reaching teenagers and young adults to sell them other stuff. Also recognize that you will hear from plenty of colleges that you and your family may not really be interested in and that are hungry for more students.

I strongly recommend that parents set up a separate email to field and deal with the junk email deluge that awaits when you use these scholarship search websites. You can then simply close down or delete said account when its usefulness passes.

One other website in this field worth considering is MyScholly https://
myscholly.com/. After a free trial period, this site charges $44.99 per year for
access. In addition to being able to search for scholarships, the membership also
includes Scholly Editor, which is their "AI-powered personal writing assistant
that instantly proofreads and improves any piece of writing" and Scholly Math,
which is their "AI-powered math solver that instantly interprets and solves any
math problem, providing clear, step-by-step instructions."

The U.S. Department of Labor also has a scholarship finder tool called CareerOne-
Stop at www.careeronestop.org/Toolkit/Training/find-scholarships.aspx.

Another resource to consider is the College Affordability Guide (www.
collegeaffordabilityguide.org). This website offers state- and college-
specific suggestions for average and lower-income students.

A final resource you may find useful is "101 College Grants You've Never
Heard Of," which you can find at: www.collegescholarships.org/grants/101-
grants.htm.

Searching for small dollars locally

You can also search for private scholarships locally. Organizations such as the
local Chamber of Commerce, churches and other houses of worship, Kiwanis, and
Rotary may have a small amount of money to dole out annually for college-bound
students from the local area. Typical awards are small — in the range of hundreds
of dollars to perhaps a couple thousand.

This is one area in which high school guidance counselors may be informed and
helpful. Your college-bound student can ask his high school guidance counselor
for suggestions.

Borrowing for College

Many financial aid packages include student loans. Whether they do or not, they
also generally involve a chunk of money that the family is expected to pay —
typically listed on a line that says something like "Contribution from Parents" or
"Parental Contribution" and "Contribution from Student" or "Student Summer
Savings."

The financial aid process and the colleges expect parents and their offspring to use
their assets and a portion of current earnings from work to pay these amounts. In

reality, some families end up borrowing money to cover a portion of their expected contributions. They may not need to do that, and whether they do may depend upon their comfort in using some of their assets to pay for college.

Tapping assets versus borrowing

So, should you tap into assets to pay for college costs? If the alternative to using some of your assets is to borrow more, most people will find themselves better off financially if they borrow less.

The answer depends upon a number of factors including:

>> **Tax consequences of tapping assets:** If you hold stocks or mutual funds that have appreciated in value, you may owe capital gains tax if you sell and realize that profit. (Please do not consider using retirement account assets — you'll generally have to pay current federal and state income taxes on withdrawals as well as possible early withdrawal penalties unless you've reached age 59½.)

>> **Expected future rate of return versus the cost of borrowing money:** Do you believe that you can earn more per year on average continuing to invest your money than the cost of borrowing for college now? For that to happen, you have to take a fair amount of risk with your investments and invest in more growth-oriented vehicles. (You may be able to have some tax deductions for student loan interest — up to $2,500 per year — but remember that you have to pay income tax on your investment income and profits when realized. See Chapter 13 for more details.)

Borrowing against your home equity and other assets

If you're a homeowner, you may be able to borrow against the equity (market value less the outstanding mortgage loan) in your property. This option is useful because you can borrow against your home at a reasonable interest rate, and the interest is generally tax-deductible subject to IRS limits (typically on up to $750,000 of mortgage debt under the Tax Cuts and Jobs Act tax bill that took effect in 2018). This is true for first mortgages and for home equity loans used to buy, build, or improve your home.

Some company retirement plans — for example, 401(k)s — allow borrowing as well. Parents are allowed to make penalty-free withdrawals from individual retirement accounts if the funds are used for college expenses.

WARNING

Although you won't be charged an early-withdrawal penalty, the IRS (and most states) will treat the amount withdrawn as taxable income. On top of that, the financial aid office will look at your beefed-up income and assume that you don't need as much financial aid. Because of these negative ramifications, funding college costs in this fashion should only be done as an absolute last resort.

Borrowing against cash value life insurance balances

Some people with kids have life insurance plans that accumulate a cash balance. Such plans may be called whole life, universal life, and so on. They combine traditional life insurance protection with an investment savings–like account.

I don't generally recommend that parents needing life insurance get these kinds of plans. Term life insurance gives you much more bang for your buck. If you want to save money in a tax-sheltered account, you can earn much better long-term returns and generally enjoy better tax benefits in most retirement savings accounts like a 401(k), IRA, or SEP-IRA.

If you own a life insurance plan with a cash balance, you can borrow against that cash balance to come up with extra cash for college costs. Alternatively, you can cash in the policy and simply get the cash out of it. If you need life insurance coverage, be sure to secure a new term life policy before you cash in your current policy.

Using federal government loan programs

WARNING

Thanks to changes implemented as part of the 2010 healthcare bill, federal student loans are no longer originated by banks. Thus, banks have no incentive to help educate prospective borrowers about those programs and instead push private loans, which they can originate. Private loans tend to be riskier as they carry variable interest rates, generally require a co-signer, and have higher fees. Rates on these loans are driven by your credit risk (and FICO score).

Federal government educational loans have fixed interest rates. Most programs add a couple percent (or more) to the current interest rates on ten-year Treasury Notes. Thus, current rates on federally approved educational loans for undergraduate students are in the vicinity of rates charged on fixed-rate mortgages (parents' loan rates are a little higher). In recent years, those rates have been around 4.5 percent. You can see the historic rates at https://studentaid.ed.gov/sa/types/loans/interest-rates#older-rates.

ENLISTING YOUR KID'S HELP

Your child can work and save money during high school and college. In fact, if your child qualifies for financial aid, she is often expected to contribute a certain amount to education costs from savings and employment during the school year or summer breaks. Besides giving your child a stake in her own future, this training encourages sound personal financial management.

Most kids working summer or part-time jobs won't be earning so much that it undermines their potential financial aid awards. While the calculations can get complicated and depend upon the specific college in question and what financial forms and methodology they employ, generally speaking we can say that upperclassmen can earn up to about $7,000 per year without impacting their awards. For freshman only, the income limit at some private schools that utilize an institutional methodology is about $5,200.

A number of loan programs, such as the Direct Parent Loans for Undergraduate Students (PLUS), are available even when your family is not deemed financially needy. These loans are at a much higher interest rate — 2.5 percent higher in fact compared to the student loans.

Only "subsidized" loans, on which the federal government pays the interest that accumulates while the student is still in school, are limited to students deemed financially needy. Note that six months after graduation, the student becomes responsible for paying all interest going forward.

Most loan programs limit the amount that you can borrow per year, as well as the total you can borrow for a student's higher educational years. If you need more money than your limits allow, PLUS loans can fill the gap: Parents can borrow the full amount needed after other financial aid is factored in.

Parents must go through a credit qualification process. Unlike privately funded college loans, you can't qualify for a federal loan if you have negative credit (recent bankruptcy, more than three debts over three months past due, and so on). For more information from the federal government about these student loan programs, call the Federal Student Aid Information Center at 800-433-3243 or visit its website at http://studentaid.ed.gov.

Chapter **12**

Reviewing Financial Aid Offers and Appealing Them

E veryone wants to be accepted! And, while not everyone gets into every school they want, hopefully, your son or daughter will have at least one acceptance offer and ideally multiple offers. Regardless of the number, you should spend time researching those colleges that have offered your kid a spot.

Also, if you've applied for financial aid, you should review those packages as well and possibly appeal them. This chapter explains what additional research you may benefit from doing on your top colleges as well as how to make sense of financial aid offers.

Getting Word on College Acceptances and Doing More Research

I remember going to the mailbox daily around the time that college admissions decisions were due to come in. Today's applicants often can find out online at a specified time.

Some schools will actually call applicants if there's good news to share. And some will even send out the old-fashioned decision letter in the mail.

No matter how your student hears the decisions from the colleges to which she's applied, I strongly recommend that she postpone making any final decisions until she's conducted some more due diligence. This should always be the case if they have multiple offers of admission. However, even if your child has just one admission offer, I don't think she should take that offer simply because it's the only one that she has.

REMEMBER

Most students and parents have a ranking of colleges and universities in their minds, and that ranking often parallels broad public perceptions of supposed college quality and reputations. Your kid is signing up to spend four academic years at a college, and it's likely going to cost your family a load of money. So, take your time and do some more digging and research! Don't simply default into a particular college because of its supposed ranking. What matters is how the school fits your particular teenager!

Open house/Acceptance day

Many colleges have something along the lines of an "open house" or "acceptance day." It's usually not a full day — more like a half day or six hours or so.

Typically, an administrator or two will speak. Students may meet in groups to discuss academics or other campus happenings. Most colleges include a campus tour. Usually, a meal will be served.

These types of days are orchestrated and filled with lots of good feelings. After all, everyone invited has been admitted, and the college wants to put its best foot forward to seal the deal. (Some colleges hold open houses for any interested prospective students.)

TIP

While it's fine to attend these feel-good days, please don't limit your additional due diligence at a particular college to what it chooses to share with you. You should research areas, topics, and people that you care about. Interested in engineering or pre-med? How about a business degree? Then, do lots of digging in those areas.

Overnight visits

Staying overnight on campus can certainly yield more insights about campus life than simply visiting for part of a day. Perhaps you know someone at the college from your own high school or neighboring towns. Alternatively, many schools, through their admissions office, will help arrange an overnight visit for interested students, especially if you've received an offer of admission.

INVESTIGATE

By staying overnight, it should be easier to attend some classes, which I strongly encourage prospective students to do. You can also partake of a couple of dining hall meals and have plenty of time to interact with numerous current students.

Try to ask probing questions. And, don't just ask people to pontificate about all that they love about the college and being a college student. Ask them questions like the following:

» What most surprised you once you got to this college and had spent several months here that you didn't know before arriving?

» What most gets on your nerves or concerns you about being a student here? What types of students seem to be unhappy here?

» If you had to do it over again, what other colleges do you wish you had taken a harder look at and why?

» Are you happy with the types of majors and courses that are at your disposal on campus? What are your longer-term plans post college?

Talk to more people!

TIP

To more fully research and investigate particular colleges, you don't have to limit yourself to people you encounter during a campus visit or stay. You can find lots of posted comments from current and past students on websites listed in Chapter 11.

Also, your child should ask his high school guidance counselor for names of students from his high school who have attended particular colleges over the past five to ten years. Friends of your family may be able to connect you with prior graduates also.

Yes, this takes time and energy. But, you should want to make a more informed decision. Many students who desire to transfer after one or two years at a college could have made a better decision if they had done more homework and due diligence before committing.

Almost without exception, those who are disenchanted with their chosen college after just one year discovered far too many things they didn't like about the college after they arrived. While it's not possible to know everything before committing, you can reduce the number of surprises by speaking with more people and doing more research in general about a particular college before committing to attend.

(Really) review the course catalog and majors

Let's face it, when a student is in college, the bulk of her time is spent taking classes and doing homework for those classes. Given that fact, it may make sense for prospective students to spend a lot of time reviewing the course offerings and graduation requirements at colleges they are considering.

What major(s) look appealing? How about individual courses? Colleges have all sorts of quirky and specific course requirements to complete for graduation. The broader graduation requirements can greatly limit the courses that one can take outside of his major.

As an example, I can tell you of a young man who was interested in being an undergraduate business major. He was considering about eight or nine different colleges but was able to greatly whittle that list down once he examined the over-all graduation requirements as well as the requirements for completing a business major. Upon close inspection, he found that a number of colleges forced him to take too many classes that he believed he wasn't interested in taking. Now, you could argue that since he's your typical 18-year-old, he may not really know what he would be interested in until he actually tried something. Using that logic, how-ever, would suggest that your kid's reactions and your reactions to specifics at a given college should never matter.

Taking a Long, Hard Look at the Bottom-Line Price

Financial aid packages comprise three main components: grants and scholar-ships, federal work-study, and student loans. Here's how these components play out:

>> **Grants** are free money and the best aid you can get because unlike a loan, you don't repay a grant, which can come from state or local government funding or colleges. They are also tax-free. The same holds true for

scholarships, the lion's share of which comes from colleges themselves and may have certain conditions attached (such as academic performance or sport's team participation).

>> **Work-study** is a federally funded program to pay for part-time student jobs. Colleges can also expect a student to contribute a certain amount of money from summer work.

>> Some federal government **student loans** are interest free during the time that the student is in school and at modest interest rates thereafter. The rest start accumulating interest charges from the moment they are taken out.

Asking for a better price

When a school makes a financial aid offer, it is not cast in stone and may well be negotiable, depending in part upon the financial condition of the college and how badly they want a particular student. Some schools leave some "bargaining room." Less selective schools that have to work harder to fill their entering classes may be more amenable to offering more if pressed.

TIP

Don't use the term "negotiating" with colleges and their financial aid offices and personnel. Technically speaking, that's what you're actually going to be doing, but negotiating is generally viewed as a dirty business-type word that colleges don't generally care for. To get a better price, you will "appeal" the financial aid award.

There are two main reasons to consider appealing financial aid awards/pricing decisions that you receive from particular colleges. The first reason is that the offer seems paltry compared with your expectations or what a similar school has offered. A second common reason to appeal is something has changed in your situation that makes you less able to shell out as much money for college as when you originally completed the financial aid documents.

TIP

In preparing your appeal and maximizing your chances of success (getting a lower price from the college), I recommend the following:

>> Put your appeal in writing and be sure to document anything that has changed for the negative since you originally completed the financial aid documents. Examples of items to highlight would be unexpected expenses (such as healthcare costs), reduced work hours and pay, and so forth. This is one case where your "bad news" could be "good news" for getting a better price!

>> Consider calling the financial aid office, and ask to speak with the aid officer assigned to your family. A primary reason to call would be to express general concern about the high cost of attendance given the offer and ask the financial aid officer if there were specific aspects of your situation that led to the relatively low offer. You may learn, for example, that a school's low financial aid offer may be driven by a relatively high value they assigned to your home, which may be something you could address specifically in your appeal. (I have seen cases where financial aid offices have taken home values off of home valuations websites, which may be too high by 20 percent or more.) Be sure to express that the college is your son's or daughter's first choice and be careful not to say too much in the phone call. Use it to primarily listen and hear why you got the financial aid offer that you did.

>> If any of the offers include merit money and your son or daughter's academic numbers have improved since applying, update the school(s). The updated and better numbers may lead to more merit money.

>> Always make your appeals *before* making a deposit for the college. You probably will have less leverage with a school once they know you've made this initial commitment.

Reviewing the admission and financial aid offers

Ideally, you'd like your son or daughter to have multiple offers to choose among. Of course, that doesn't always happen. Gaining admission to selective colleges is challenging in and of itself. Also, students who apply and are accepted through so-called "Early Decision" are in theory bound to attend that specific college.

Asking for more when you have just one offer

You may rightfully feel that you have no leverage to ask for better pricing when you have a single, solitary offer. This can happen when there's one offer of admission scattered among a bunch of rejections from other colleges. This also happens when your son or daughter has applied Early Decision and gotten an offer of admission from such an application.

You are not stuck with and forced to accept a price/financial aid package that seems subpar and unattractive to you. And, yes, I feel this way in the case of an Early Decision offer of admission. You absolutely, positively have the right to expect a better price/financial aid package as a condition of attendance.

Look at Early Decision offers this way. By applying to a college or university Early Decision, you're telling them that they are your first choice and you will accept their offer if they make one. To see the financial danger and unfairness in this, imagine you found a home for sale and you directed your agent to tell the seller that the home is the one that you want and you will buy it if they are willing to sell to you. Something's missing, however — the price! And, that's a mighty important detail! Just as you wouldn't agree to buy a home without specifying and negotiating a price, I don't think you should agree unconditionally for your son or daughter to agree to attend a given college without knowing the final price you will pay!

Here's an example to illustrate what can go wrong with the lack of leverage that an Early Decision candidate has and how to successfully fight back. Mary had two older siblings who were later in their college careers and who were each paying about half the full price at costly private colleges. Mary applied Early Decision to an expensive private college and was admitted and offered zero aid! This is amazing to consider given that she would be the third in her family in college at the same time and her older siblings were paying nowhere near the full cost.

Mary's family pushed back on this poor offer, and in speaking with the financial aid office, discovered among other things that they had used a value for their home (taken apparently from a home valuation website) that was a good 25 to 30 percent above actual market value. The officer also admitted that they could do "more" to factor in the older siblings being in college. In the end, after a couple of rounds of back and forth, the school's final offer was to award grant money that sliced about one-third off the cost of attendance. So, clearly, it was well worthwhile for this family to speak up.

Many people in this situation say nothing. And, their reward for being obedient sheep is to pay far more than is necessary. Remember that colleges know they kind of have your son or daughter (and you) in a disadvantageous situation if they know by applying Early Decision that your child is effectively committing to attend the school should admission be offered.

You always have other choices. There's nothing that mandates that your son or daughter has to accept the one and only offer he or she has. Your child could take a year and do something different, like working, and apply to colleges again next year. Or, you could explore together the alternatives to college discussed in Part 3.

Dealing with multiple offers

As a general rule, you should have more leverage to improve financial aid awards if you have multiple offers of admission. That way, you can compare and contrast and potentially have at least one of them improve.

TIP

When you speak with or communicate with a particular college about how their offer stacks up against others that you've received, you should expect them to highlight differences between the colleges in question.

If your child's first-choice school hasn't made the best offer among those received, by all means, be in touch with the top school and see what they can do to improve their offer. Communicate that they are the number-one choice but that their financial aid offer has been beaten by other colleges. You should generally expect that the school will expect to see documentation of this situation, so don't try to make something up and expect them to accept your vague and unsupported statements.

5

The Part of Tens

Make use of education tax credits and deductions.

Complete college in a timely fashion.

Manage money as a young adult.

Minimize the cost of student loans.

Chapter **13**

(Almost) Ten Education Tax Breaks and Rules You Should Know About

The U.S. tax laws are unnecessarily complicated and extensive. But, it's worth taking the time to understand how to make them work for you. And, the good news is that I've slogged through the details, so that you don't have to, and I highlight what you need to know.

The tax rules and regulations include numerous breaks for parents of college students and some for young adults as well who have previously incurred college costs and taken out some college loans. Those who are knowledgeable about the tax laws and associated strategies can save themselves a lot of tax dollars. This chapter highlights ten things you should know related to educational expenses that can legally and permanently reduce the income taxes that you pay.

Contributing to Retirement Accounts

As a parent working and earning money, one of the financially smartest things you can generally do (unless you pay low federal income taxes), is to contribute to a retirement savings plan. Besides reducing your current and future federal (and state) income taxes, funding retirement plans helps you build up a nest egg, so you don't have to work for the rest of your life. Also, for purposes of the financial aid system, your retirement accounts are generally the best places your assets to reside.

As you're earning it, you can exclude money from your taxable income by tucking it away in employer-based retirement plans, such as 401(k) or 403(b) accounts, or self-employed retirement plans, such as SEP-IRAs. If your combined federal and state marginal tax rate is, say, 30 percent and you contribute $1,000 to one of these plans, you reduce your federal and state taxes by $300. Also, some employer plans provide free matching money. And when your money is inside a retirement account, it can compound and grow without taxation.

WARNING

Many people miss this great opportunity to reduce their income taxes because they *spend* all (or too much) of their current employment income and, therefore, have nothing (or little) left to put into a retirement account. If you're in this predicament, you first need to reduce your spending before you can contribute money to a retirement plan.

If your employer doesn't offer the option of saving money through a retirement plan, lobby the benefits and human resources departments. If they resist, you may want to add this to your list of reasons for considering another employer. Many employers offer this valuable benefit, but some don't. Some company decision-makers either don't understand the value of these accounts or feel that they're too costly to set up and administer.

If your employer doesn't offer a retirement savings plan, individual retirement account (IRA) contributions may or may not be tax-deductible, depending on your circumstances. See Chapter 2 for more on retirement accounts.

Checking to See if You Qualify for the Saver's Tax Credit

TIP

Married couples filing jointly with adjusted gross incomes (AGIs) of less than $65,000 and single taxpayers with an adjusted gross income of less than $32,500 can earn a federal income tax credit (claimed on Form 8880) for retirement account contributions. Unlike a deduction, a *tax credit* directly reduces your income tax bill by the amount of the credit.

This saver's income tax credit, which is detailed in Table 13-1, is a percentage of the first $2,000 contributed (or $4,000 on a joint return). The credit is not available to those under the age of 18, full-time students, or people who are claimed as dependents on someone else's tax return.

TABLE 13-1   **Special Tax Credit for Retirement Plan Contributions**

Singles Adjusted Gross Income	Married-Filing-Jointly Adjusted Gross Income	Tax Credit for Retirement Account Contributions
$0–$19,500	$0–$39,000	50%
$19,500–$21,250	$39,000–$42,500	20%
$21,250–$32,500	$42,500–$65,000	10%

Understanding the Tax Benefits of 529 Plans

Money invested in section 529 plans is sheltered from taxation and is not taxed upon withdrawal as long as the money is used to pay for eligible education expenses. Some states also provide small tax incentives to fund these accounts.

Subject to eligibility requirements, 529 plans allow you to sock away upwards of $200,000. Please be aware, however, that funding such accounts may reduce your potential financial aid. See Chapter 9 for details on these accounts and a discussion of the factors you should weigh before deciding whether you should contribute to one.

Considering Coverdell Education Savings Accounts (ESAs)

As I discuss in Chapter 9, Coverdell Education Savings Accounts (ESAs) are similar to 529 plan accounts. The contribution limits, however, are dramatically lower — up to just $2,000 per year per child. Money in ESAs grows without taxation and isn't taxed when withdrawn if used for qualified educational expenses, which includes college as well as K–12 education.

Higher income earners lose the ability to fund these accounts. The single taxpayers' phase-out range is from $95,000 to $110,000 of income. The range is $190,000 to $220,000 for all other taxpayers.

Utilizing the American Opportunity Tax Credit

The American Opportunity (AO) tax credit provides up to $2,500 per student per year of college that families incur at least $4,000 of educational expenses. Up to $1,000 of this credit is refundable. Use of this credit is limited for each child for up to four years of undergraduate expenses.

There are income limitations for using this credit. Single taxpayers' phase out of being able to take this credit at modified adjusted gross incomes (MAGIs) of $80,000 to $90,000. Other taxpayers' phase-out is from $160,000 to $180,000.

When parents claim this credit for one of their children for a particular tax year, they may not claim the next credit — the Lifetime Learning credit. Each tax year, for a particular child, you may only take one or the other of these credits.

Taking Advantage of the Lifetime Learning Credit

Like the American Opportunity tax credit, the Lifetime Learning (LL) credit also was designed to provide tax relief to low- and moderate-income earners facing higher education costs. The LL credit may be up to 20 percent of the first $10,000 of qualified educational expenses — up to $2,000 per taxpayer.

For parents filing tax returns, only one of these credits may be claimed for each child per tax year, and parents are subject to the same income limitations. Single taxpayers' phase-out being able to take this credit at modified adjusted gross incomes (MAGIs) of $59,000 to $69,000. Other taxpayers' phase-out is from $118,000 to $138,000.

Understanding the Retirement Account Withdrawal Penalty Waiver

Normally, when you withdraw money from a retirement account early (the year in which you turn 59½), you pay a 10 percent federal income tax penalty and whatever penalty your state assesses. You also owe current federal and state income tax on the taxable amount withdrawn.

If withdrawn retirement account money is used to pay for higher education expenses, the penalty is waived. That's a good thing and perhaps worth considering.

WARNING

However, taking money from retirement accounts to pay for college costs is generally not advised. For starters, you're tapping money you've earmarked for your nonworking future years. Second, despite the penalty for early withdrawal being waived, the taxable amount withdrawn will show up on your federal and state income tax returns and you will owe federal and state income tax. Your higher reported income will harm your financial aid chances.

Finishing on Time without High Income Earning Years

When students continually take breaks from college, especially due to the financial stress of full-time attendance and the associated costs, the likelihood of not finishing rises. Also, when a student is working enough to be making $10,000, $15,000, $20,000 or more in a tax year, that really begins to affect the financial aid/pricing that the school assesses the family.

TIP

If a student's interest in college courses has noticeably dropped in the first or second year, it's worth examining why and doing so with an open mind. Given the high cost of attendance and the fact that increasing numbers of lower cost and potentially more effective alternatives exist, consider the alternatives to high-cost colleges.

Taking the Student Loan Interest Deduction

You may take up to a $2,500 deduction for student loan interest that you pay on IRS Form 1040 for college costs as long as your modified adjusted gross income (AGI) is less than or equal to $70,000 for single taxpayers and $140,000 for married couples filing jointly. Your deduction is phased out if your AGI is between $70,000 and $85,000 for single taxpayers and between $140,000 and $170,000 for married couples filing jointly.

This deduction is not an itemized deduction, so anyone can take it on Form 1040 as a so-called "adjustment to income." Each of your lenders should be able to provide you with a yearly summary that shows how much you paid in interest for the tax year. If you paid $600 or more in interest to a single lender, that lender is required to provide you with Form 1098-E, which documents the interest you paid for the year.

Chapter **14**

Ten Tips for Getting Your College Degree Quicker

At the traditional length of four years, completing a four-year college education is both time consuming and costly. And as I discuss in Chapter 1, too many students don't complete their college degrees or take a longer time to do so. Private nonprofit colleges have an overall six-year graduation rate of just 66 percent; public colleges graduate about 59 percent, and for-profit colleges graduate only 21 percent of their first-time, full-time students within six years.

So, if some or all of your kids are going to go for a four-year college degree, it's imperative that you and they have a clear and well-thought-out plan for getting the job done efficiently and cost effectively. This chapter highlights ten tips for doing just that.

Communicating Is Key

These are big decisions. College is tremendously expensive and takes a good deal of time. And, it's hard to really know what you're getting until the student is there and well into the experience.

Of course, you should expect that parents and aspiring college students aren't going to think the same thoughts or have the same concerns and priorities when it comes to selecting colleges. Take your time and be open to your kid's thoughts, ideas, and concerns. And be patient explaining your thoughts, ideas, and concerns.

TIP

Be candid with your kids about your financial constraints but be careful in using those concerns to steer your kids too much to what you want for them. Yes, you should lead and guide. You're the parent and have decades of experience as an adult in the real world, which your teenagers lack. And, yes, you should sometimes say no because sometimes kids get goofy and unrealistic ideas in their heads. Remember to continue the dialogue with them to find some common ground.

Keeping All Your Options Open

As I emphasize throughout the rest of this book, especially in Part 3, be sure you and your children explore all the reasonable post–high school options that help prepare them to work and have a career. A four-year college degree isn't the only way to do that. Among families and students that end up the most unhappy with college are those who too quickly zeroed in on that option without having good reasons or having considered alternatives.

Pay attention to the warning signs in the early semesters of attendance at college. If your student is unmotivated, uninspired, and having a hard time staying focused on school, it may be a sign that you need to evaluate and consider other options.

Planning Ahead Financially

A common mistake that some families make when addressing the cost of college is that in the beginning, they are thinking about the first-year expenses and meeting those. It's imperative, however, that you consider the whole four-year cost and how those expenses will be paid.

Students who stop out for a semester, a year, or more are at far greater risk of failing to complete their college degree. Often, these breaks in attendance are caused by strained family finances and the student feeling pressured to work and earn money to meet current living costs and potential future college costs. By coming up with a strong financial plan, you can minimize these issues from arising. See Chapter 9 for more details.

Picking Colleges with High Graduation Rates

Colleges calculate and report their graduation rates, typically over four and six years. In Chapter 1, I list the colleges with the highest such rates so you can start with those as a point of comparison.

Colleges with higher graduation rates are generally better choices. For starters, high graduation rates show that the college is doing the necessary things to ensure that students can complete their degrees in a reasonable amount of time. Higher graduation rates also indicate a motivated student population that is demonstrating that they can complete the degree requirements in a timely fashion.

REMEMBER

I'm not suggesting that you immediately rule out colleges with graduation rates that are merely good but not exceptional. A school that takes more risks on accepting a more financially diverse student body, for example, will tend to have a somewhat lower graduation rate. If a particular college seems to check all the right boxes but has a lower graduation rate, inquire as to why that is.

Selecting Colleges that Offer Your Desired Courses and Majors

Especially at larger colleges and universities, and those that are public, it may take longer to complete all required courses for the simple reason that there are so many students competing for limited spaces in some courses. So, be sure to ask lots of questions when you're considering such schools so that you have an informed perspective on the realities of getting into and completing certain courses and majors.

Also, be aware that changing majors can lead to problems graduating within four years at some colleges, again with more issues at the larger public schools.

Choosing Schools with Affordable Housing

Besides having trouble getting their desired courses in a timely fashion, another challenge for some college students getting through college efficiently is being able to find and retain affordable housing. This can be especially problematic in high cost of living areas where there aren't a lot of rentals available at reasonable prices.

WARNING

I can tell you from the personal experience of having toured dozens of college and university campuses that too many schools gloss over and fail to disclose their lack of housing. At numerous schools, housing may only be guaranteed, for example, for the first two years. If you look at the attendance numbers for a college and then compare them with the number of students living on campus, you can get to the bottom of the campus housing situation.

Getting College Credit in High School

Some colleges will give you course credits for college-level classes — for example, advanced placement (AP) courses — that you have completed and done well on the AP exam taken at your high school. At most colleges, on the AP exam grading scale of 1 to 5, with 5 being the highest and best score possible, scores from 3 to 5 are considered passing grades. More selective colleges, however, may only consider a 4 or 5 score acceptable.

Especially at the most selective colleges, the credits won't typically help you to graduate earlier or sooner. For example, if a student did well in AP calculus or statistics, such colleges will then place that student into a higher-level introductory course so that at a minimum, they aren't taking the same course in college that they recently took in high school.

Some colleges do offer credits for high school AP and equivalent courses that may be used toward meeting graduation requirements. So, investigate that option as you survey colleges to consider, because knocking a semester or full year off your kid's college attendance plans can save your family quite a bit of money.

Making Use of Advisors and Deans

Many college administrators enjoy working with students — that's part of the reason they were attracted to a job on a college campus. (The flip side, unfortunately, as you may experience, is they are generally less enthusiastic about hearing from parents despite the fact that you're the ones paying the bills!)

Part of what students (and their families) are paying for are all the advisors and deans who can help in many situations. So, when it comes to issues with course scheduling, planning for majors, graduating in a timely fashion, and not breaking the bank, administrators often can help and enjoy doing so. Remember — your student has to ask!

Try your best to have your student contact the administrator on their own. If they repeatedly refuse to do so, then I think it's fair game for you to contact someone to raise the issue and solicit help for your student.

Having Students Work during College

As I explain in Chapter 11, upperclassmen can earn up to about $7,000 per calendar (tax) year without impacting their financial aid awards. (For freshman, the income limit at some private schools that utilize an institutional methodology is about $5,200.)

So, during the summer and while working part-time during some of the school year, students can help pitch in and earn some money toward their college costs and living expenses. Ideally, they would earn up to the levels allowed without affecting financial aid awards.

Avoiding Stopping School to Work

Stopping for a semester or going to college part-time may sound financially appealing when you consider all the income a student can earn. However, that doesn't consider the entire picture. What about the impact that the higher income will have on the pricing/financial aid package the college offers?

Also, working more and going to college less will inevitably lead to a four-year college experience stretching out to five, six, or even seven years. Part-time jobs during college generally pay much less than full-time, post-college jobs.

Chapter **15**

Ten Important Money Management Steps for Young Adults

Hopefully the day will soon arrive when your offspring will have completed their college degree or other desired training. And, even better, your now young adult will also hopefully find a job and become financially independent of you!

Congratulations to you for when this day arrives. While you should feel proud and satisfied, don't rest just yet. Make sure that you set your kids turned young adults out into the real world with the important knowledge regarding managing their money and making the most of the money that they earn.

This chapter highlights ten important things that your young adult offspring should know. So, I've written this chapter for and directed to your kids. Ask them to read it!

Getting Financially Fit, Now!

Moving to a full-time (first) job is a big deal and a big change for most young adults. Embrace getting your feet on the ground financially speaking!

Probably the most important thing you can do is to keep your living expenses down and subdued so that you can live within your paycheck and hopefully save some money regularly (more on that in a moment).

Some say to live like a college student! Most people are happy during college despite living in small living quarters and not wasting a lot of money on clothing, furniture, and so on. Maybe you even saved money then by taking care of your own food preparation. But, if you got most or all of your meals in a dining hall, know that having someone else make all your meals is usually pretty costly!

Don't procrastinate getting on top of your personal finances. You may overspend and accumulate high-cost debts, fail to save toward goals and things you care about, lack proper insurance coverage, or take other unnecessary risks. Early preparation can save you from these pitfalls. Learn as soon as possible how to live within your means, save and invest regularly, legally minimize your taxes, and so forth.

Adapting and Adjusting Along the Way

Changes require change. Over the years, your life will inevitably evolve and change. Even once your financial house is in order, a life change — such as moving to a new area, switching careers, getting married, buying a home, starting a business, and so forth — should prompt you to review your personal financial strategies. Life changes affect your income, spending, insurance needs, and ability to take financial risk.

Making the most of changes and transitions requires managing stress and your emotions. Life changes often are accompanied by stress and other emotional upheavals. Don't make snap decisions during these changes. Take the time to become fully informed and recognize and acknowledge your feelings and financial considerations. Educating yourself is key.

Cancelling Consumer Credit

The use and abuse of consumer credit can cause long-term financial pain and hardship. To get off on the right financial foot, young workers need to shun the habit of making purchases on credit cards that they can't pay for in full when the monthly bill is due.

If you keep a credit card, be certain that you can pay each month's bill in full and on time. Setting up for automatic electronic payment from your bank/investment account can help you accomplish that.

I have no problem with your using "reward cards" to earn benefits from your credit card transactions. Just be sure that you're not spending/buying more to get more rewards!

Here's the simple solution to not run up outstanding credit card balances if you have had or may have that tendency: Don't carry a credit card. If you need the convenience of making purchases with a piece of plastic, get a debit card. Just be aware that debit cards quickly deduct transacted amounts within a day or two from the connected bank checking account in contrast with a credit card, which sends you a monthly statement and has you pay once per month.

Reviewing Your Budget and Spending Plans

Even before getting your first full-time job and moving into your apartment, how about putting together a preliminary budget/spending plan? This will take some research, especially with regards to apartment rental costs. Go out and look at actual apartments. And take one of your parents with you. You may not always agree with them, but they have decades of experience in the real world including making housing decisions. They can help you avoid common mistakes.

Your parents, who have been paying bills for decades, can clue you into the cost of the other things in your prospective budget. You could also speak with older siblings and friends.

In addition to housing costs, here are some other important expenses to consider and understand:

>> **Income and other taxes:** Employers quote you the gross (before-tax) salary or wage they will pay you. What matters, though, is your take-home pay after taxes. Social security taxes will lop 7.65 percent right off the top, and you will pay federal income taxes as well as state income taxes in most but not all

states. The IRS website (www.irs.gov/individuals/tax-withholding-estimator) and your state's website have tools that enable you to estimate the tax withholding that you will face.

>> **Transportation:** If you expect to have a car, you can figure your insurance costs by contacting insurers and getting quotes for a car you may be considering. Gasoline and maintenance costs will add to those expenses — your folks can help you estimate those too. If you're going to take public transit or use taxis/ride-share services on occasion, be realistic when you estimate those costs.

>> **Personal insurance:** You need to have health insurance and should also have long-term disability insurance. Your employer may offer them both and can tell you what your cost for these will be. That's another reason you should always take the time to understand your employer's benefits. You don't need life insurance unless others are financially dependent upon you.

>> **Food:** Some employers offer subsidized meals so that may help. Estimate what you will spend for food that you buy in grocery stores and for meals out or delivered. If you're a bar hopper with your friends — which is a costly habit — include those expected expenses as well.

>> **Clothing:** Again, be realistic here!

>> **Entertainment:** This can include cable and streaming services, sporting events, concerts, comedy clubs, or whatever else you enjoy that costs money.

>> **Cell phone and internet service:** Be sure to shop around as prices vary quite a bit and there's lots of competition these days.

Also, if you have student loans, you should understand when you will be required to begin repayment and what those monthly payments will be. For more on dealing with student loans, please see Chapter 16.

Striving to Regularly Save and Invest

Ideally, you should start saving and investing money from your first paycheck. Try saving 5 percent of every paycheck and then eventually increase your saving to 10 percent. If you're having trouble saving money, track your spending and make cutbacks as needed.

You may want to first accumulate an emergency/rainy day fund and then direct some savings into a retirement account that offers you some tax benefits. Some employers even match a portion of contributions.

You may not want to save in a retirement account if you have some other shorter-term goal in mind, like accumulating down-payment money for a home purchase or saving money to someday start your own small business. Thinking about a home purchase or retirement is usually not in the active thought patterns of first-time job seekers. Regardless, saving money as you're earning is a great habit and widens your options over time!

Ensuring that You're Properly Insured

When you're young and healthy, imagining yourself feeling otherwise is hard for most people to do. Many twenty-somethings give little thought to the potential for healthcare expenses. But because accidents and unexpected illnesses can strike at any age, forgoing coverage can be financially devastating. You don't want to again become financially dependent upon your folks, do you?

Check your employer's benefit package to see whether it includes long-term disability insurance coverage. Smaller employers are more likely not to offer it. When you're in your first full-time job with more-limited benefits, buying disability coverage, which replaces income lost due to a long-term disability, is wise if you're not covered through your employer.

Continuing Your Education

After you get out in the workforce, you (like many other people) may realize how little you learned in formal higher education that can actually be used in the real world and, conversely, how much you need to learn that school never taught you. Lucky for you that some companies provide training and make entry-level hires often for "aptitude and attitude," not specific skills.

Read, learn, and continue to grow. Continuing education, and the increasing numbers of alternatives to college (discussed in Part 3), can help you advance in your career and enjoy the world around you.

Always Being Prepared for a Job Change

During your adult life, you'll almost surely change jobs — perhaps several times a decade. I hope that most of the time you'll be changing by your own choice. But let's face it: Job security is not what it used to be. Downsizing has impacted even the most talented workers, and more industries are subjected to global competition.

No matter how happy you are in your current job, knowing that your world won't fall apart if you're not working tomorrow can give you an added sense of security and encourage openness to possibility. So, structure your finances to afford an income dip.

Spending less than you earn always makes good financial sense, but if you're approaching a possible job change, spending less is even more important, particularly if you're entering a new field or starting your own company and you expect a short-term income dip. Many people view a lifestyle of thriftiness as restrictive, but ultimately those thrifty habits can give you more freedom to do what you want to do. Be sure to keep an emergency reserve fund — three month's worth of living expenses is a good start.

Evaluating the Total Cost of Relocating

At some point in your career, you may have the option of relocating. But don't call the moving company until you understand the financial consequences of such a move. You shouldn't simply compare salaries between the two jobs.

Benefits matter too, and benefits can be worth quite a bit. You also need to compare the cost of living between the two areas: housing, commuting, state income taxes and other taxes, food, utilities, and all the other major expenditure categories.

Ensuring Compatibility when Picking a Partner

Think you're ready to tie the knot with the one you love? In addition to the emotional and moral commitments that you and your spouse will make to one another, you're probably going to be merging many of your financial decisions and resources. Even if you're largely in agreement about your financial goals and strategies, managing your finances in partnership with another person is far different than managing your money on your own.

Many couples never talk about their goals and plans before marriage and failing to do so breaks up some marriages. Finances are just one of numerous issues you should discuss. Ensuring that you know what you're getting yourself into is a good way to minimize your chances for heartache. Ministers, priests, and rabbis sometimes offer premarital counseling to help bring issues and differences to the surface.

Chapter **16**

Ten Things to Know About Student Loans

Student loans may seem simple. Unfortunately, appearances can be deceiving.

There are numerous types of federal student loans and repayment plan options and lots of private loans. Repayment options and forgiveness of some loan balances are not widely or well understood.

So, in this chapter I discuss staying on top of those loans and repaying them on time and at as low a cost as possible for you, the borrower.

Keeping Track of Your Loans

During the years of college, you'll get bombarded with various financial aid forms and financial aid award letters and notices. If you take out student loans, you should also begin to receive various notices about those.

Students, of course, are likely to be changing addresses, especially post-graduation. Parents and families may move as well when residency for local schooling options is no longer required or retirement beckons. So, be sure that you keep all of your student lenders (and servicers) informed and updated regarding your correct mailing addresses.

Especially if you've taken loans from numerous sources (for example, federal government–sponsored and private), total up the amount of debt accumulated. Debt surprises are rarely good! And be sure you are tracking all of your student loans as they may well be represented by multiple lenders and/or servicers by the time that college degree is earned.

Understanding What Cosigners Means for Responsibility

If parents have cosigned student loans with their son or daughter, everyone who has cosigned is legally responsible for the repayment of those loans. Of course, different families will have different expectations as to who actually will make the repayments. In many families, it's a joint effort and project whereas in other families, the parents elect to carry the full burden. And, in some families, the son or daughter is expected to make all payments.

TIP

At a minimum, families should have candid discussions about expectations and plans for repaying the student loans they've taken out. And, putting an agreement in writing is a fine idea to ensure that everyone is clear on the plan and so that there's some accountability. That's not to say that a written plan can never change; with discussion and agreement, your plan can be modified.

Knowing the Loan Terms

Whenever you take out a federal government student loan, you will sign a federal student loan promissory note that spells out all the terms and conditions of the loan. You can see an example of that in Figure 16-1 and at: https://studentaid.gov/app/subUnsubHTMLPreview.action.

During the years of college, you should have received in the mail periodic updates on the outstanding student loans to which you have committed. For federal student loans, there are nonprofit processing companies (see the following list) that will keep you updated on your loans.

OMB No. 1845-0007
Form Approved
Exp. Date 04/30/2019

Master Promissory Note
Direct Subsidized Loans and Direct Unsubsidized Loans
William D. Ford Federal Direct Loan Program

WARNING: Any person who knowingly makes a false statement or misrepresentation on this form or any accompanying document is subject to penalties that may include fines, imprisonment, or both, under the U.S. Criminal Code and 20 U.S.C. 1097.

BEFORE YOU BEGIN

Before you begin, read the **Instructions** on page 14 of this Master Promissory Note.

BORROWER INFORMATION

1. Name and Permanent Address (see Instructions)

2. Social Security Number

3. Date of Birth (mm-dd-yyyy)

4. Driver's License State and Number

5. Email Address (optional)

6. Area Code/Telephone Number

REFERENCE INFORMATION

List two persons with different U.S. addresses who have known you for at least three years. The first reference should be a parent or legal guardian.

7. First Name: _____ Middle Initial: ____ Last Name: _____

Permanent Address (Street, City, State, Zip Code):

Email Address (optional): _____

Area Code/Telephone Number: (_____) _____ - _____

Relationship to You: _____

8. First Name: _____ Middle Initial: ____ Last Name: _____

Permanent Address (Street, City, State, Zip Code):

Email Address (optional): _____

Area Code/Telephone Number: (_____) _____ - _____

Relationship to You: _____

SCHOOL INFORMATION - TO BE COMPLETED BY THE SCHOOL

9. School Name and Address

10. School Code/Branch

11. Identification No.

Borrower's Name: _____ Social Security Number: __ __ __ - __ __ - __ __ __ __

BORROWER REQUEST, CERTIFICATIONS, AUTHORIZATIONS, AND UNDERSTANDINGS

12. This is a Master Promissory Note (MPN) for one or more Federal Direct Stafford/Ford (Direct Subsidized) Loans and/or Federal Direct Unsubsidized Stafford/Ford (Direct Unsubsidized) Loans. I request a total amount of Direct Subsidized Loans and/or Direct Unsubsidized Loans under this MPN not to exceed the allowable maximums under the Act ("the Act" is defined in the MPN Terms and Conditions section of this MPN under Governing Law). My school will notify me of the loan type and loan amount that I am eligible to borrow. Within certain timeframes, I may cancel a loan or request a lower amount by contacting my school, or by refusing to accept or returning all or a portion of a loan disbursement that is made to me. The Borrower's Rights and Responsibilities Statement that accompanies this MPN and the disclosure statements that will be provided to me contain additional information about my right to cancel a loan or request a lower amount.

FIGURE 16-1:
Sample federal government student loan promissory note.

13. Under penalty of perjury, I certify that:

A. The information I have provided on this MPN and as updated by me from time to time is true, complete, and correct to the best of my knowledge and belief and is provided in good faith.

B. I will use the money I receive from any loan made under this MPN only to pay for my authorized educational expenses for attendance at the school that determined I was eligible to receive the loan. I will immediately repay any loan money that cannot be attributed to educational expenses for attendance on at least a half-time basis at that school.

C. If I owe an overpayment on a Federal Perkins Loan, Federal Pell Grant, Federal Supplemental Educational Opportunity Grant (FSEOG), Academic Competitiveness Grant (ACG), National Science and Mathematics Access to Retain Talent (SMART) Grant, or Leveraging Educational Assistance Partnership Grant, I have made satisfactory arrangements to repay the amount owed.

D. If I am in default on any loan I received under the Federal Perkins Loan Program (including National Direct Student Loans), the William D. Ford Federal Direct Loan (Direct Loan) Program, or the Federal Family Education Loan (FFEL) Program, I have made satisfactory repayment arrangements with the loan holder to repay the amount owed.

E. If I have been convicted of, or if I have pled nolo contendere (no contest) or guilty to, a crime involving fraud in obtaining funds under a program authorized under Title IV of the Higher Education Act of 1965, as amended (HEA), I have fully repaid the funds to the U.S. Department of Education (ED) or to the loan holder in the case of a Title IV federal student loan. The Title IV, HEA programs include the Federal Pell Grant, FSEOG, ACG, SMART Grant, Leveraging Educational Assistance Partnership Grant, Teacher Education Assistance for College and Higher Education (TEACH) Grant, Federal Work-Study (FWS), Federal Perkins Loan, Direct Loan, and FFEL programs.

14. For each Direct Subsidized Loan and Direct Unsubsidized Loan I receive under this MPN:

A. I authorize my school to certify my eligibility for the loan.

B. I authorize my school to credit my loan money to my student account at the school, and to pay to ED any refund that may be due up to the full loan amount.

C. I authorize ED and its agents and contractors to investigate my credit record and report information about my loan status to persons and organizations permitted by law to receive that information.

D. I authorize ED to defer repayment of principal on my loan while I am enrolled at least half-time at an eligible school, unless I notify ED differently.

E. I authorize my schools, ED, and their agents and contractors to release information about my loan to the references I provide and to my immediate family members unless I submit written directions otherwise.

F. I authorize my schools, ED, and their agents and contractors to share information about my loan with each other.

G. I authorize my schools, ED, and their agents and contractors to contact me regarding my loan request or my loan, including repayment of my loan, at any cellular telephone number I provide now or in the future using automated dialing equipment or artificial or prerecorded voice or text messages.

15. I understand that:

A. ED will give me the opportunity to pay the interest that accrues on each loan made under this MPN during grace, in-school, deferment (including in-school deferment), forbearance, and other periods as provided under the Act. If I do not pay the interest that accrues during these periods, ED may add unpaid interest that accrues on each loan made under this MPN to the principal balance of that loan (this is called "capitalization") at the end of the grace, deferment, forbearance, or other period. Capitalization will increase the principal balance on my loan and the total amount of interest I must pay.

B. ED has the authority to verify information reported on this MPN with other federal agencies.

PROMISE TO PAY

16. I promise to pay to ED all loan amounts disbursed under the terms of this MPN, plus interest and other charges and fees that may become due as provided in this MPN. **I understand that more than one loan may be made to me under this MPN.** I understand that by accepting any disbursement issued at any time under this MPN, I agree to repay the loan associated with that disbursement.

17. If I do not make a payment on a loan made under this MPN when it is due, I will also pay reasonable collection costs, including but not limited to attorney fees, court costs, and other fees.

18. I will not sign this MPN before reading the entire MPN, even if I am told not to read it, or told that I am not required to read it. I am entitled to an exact copy of this MPN and the Borrower's Rights and Responsibilities Statement.

19. My signature certifies that I have read, understand, and agree to the terms and conditions of this MPN, including the Borrower Request, Certifications, Authorizations, and Understandings, the MPN Terms and Conditions, the Notice About Subsequent Loans Made Under this MPN, and the Borrower's Rights and Responsibilities Statement.

I UNDERSTAND THAT I MAY RECEIVE ONE OR MORE LOANS UNDER THIS MPN, AND THAT I MUST REPAY ALL LOANS THAT I RECEIVE UNDER THIS MPN.

20. **Borrower's Signature** _____

21. **Today's Date (mm-dd-yyyy)** __ __ - __ __ - __ __ __ __

FIGURE 16-1:
(continued)

Borrower's Name: _____   Social Security Number: _____   Identification Number: _____

Source: U.S. Department of Education

Table 16-1 offers a list of the loan processors that the U.S. Department of Education uses.

TABLE 16-1

Loan Processors

Loan Servicer	Contact
CornerStone	1-800-663-1662
FedLoan Servicing (PHEAA)	1-800-699-2908
Granite State – GSMR	1-888-556-0022
Great Lakes Educational Loan Services, Inc.	1-800-236-4300
HESC/Edfinancial	1-855-337-6884
MOHELA	1-888-866-4352
Navient	1-800-722-1300
Nelnet	1-888-486-4722
OSLA Servicing	1-866-264-9762
ECSI	1-866-313-3797

REMEMBER

Generally, six months after graduation, federal student loan payments begin. You will definitely be hearing from the loan processor(s) for your loans around and continuously after that time.

Private loans work differently and have different terms and conditions, which hopefully you took the time to understand before you took those out.

Using the Auto-Pay Feature to Save Money

When your student loan repayments begin, I recommend that you set them up for automatic payment. This feature drafts the money from your bank account monthly on or before the payment due date.

In addition to ensuring that you don't have late payments or missed payments, most loan servicers or lenders will knock 0.25 percent or so off of the effective interest rate you're paying for using auto payment. Some private lenders may reduce the rate a tad more than that.

One potential downside to putting your student loan repayments on auto-payment would be if it ever leads to your bank checking account being overdrawn. So, be sure you're keeping a close eye on your account balance so that nasty surprise doesn't occur.

Understanding Loan Forgiveness Conditions

There are a number of conditions under which a portion or all of government student loans can be discharged or forgiven. Most commonly this occurs because the student-borrower is working in a field of public service. However, this may also occur when the student-borrower suffers adverse health conditions.

Borrowers who are working in education, government, military, certain nonprofit organizations (not labor unions or partisan political organizations), law enforcement, or public health may be eligible for the Public Service Loan Forgiveness program. To be eligible, borrowers must have completed 120 monthly (that's 10 years' worth) on-time payments. Borrowers must also be working full-time in public service and be paying their loans back under an income-driven repayment plan. For more information, please visit: https://studentaid.gov/manage-loans/forgiveness-cancellation/public-service.

Unfortunately, the other conditions under which student loan balances can be discharged are less pleasant to consider. This can happen if the student-borrower suffers a long-term disability or passes away. To find out more about those and other circumstances under which discharge can occur, please visit https://studentaid.gov/manage-loans/forgiveness-cancellation.

Knowing Your Federal Loan Repayment Options

Believe it or not, there are currently eight different repayment plans/options for your federal student loans. I give you a brief overview here so that you're aware of the range of what's currently available and what may benefit and work for you.

A number of the repayment plans are sensitive to and based upon the student's income relative to the amount of student loans he has outstanding. The repayment schedule, however, is not tailored to the local cost of living (strangely, there's only an adjustment for students in Alaska and Hawaii). So, students turned workers who are living in high-cost urban areas like New York City, Chicago, Boston, Washington, San Francisco, and so on don't get any special breaks. Your salary may be a bit higher working for employers in those high-cost areas, which actually undermines your chances and ability to qualify for income-based repayment plans.

Here, then, is a quick overview of the repayment plan options for so-called direct and federal family education student loans:

>> **Standard repayment:** Your payment amount is fixed and allows the loans to be repaid in up to ten years. This plan works well for students who have a modest debt outstanding relative to their incomes and for whom the monthly payment amount fits within their budgets from the beginning of their working years after college.

>> **Graduated repayment:** All borrowers may use this plan, which begins your payments at a reduced level compared with the standard repayment plan and then bumps them up every two years or so. This plan, which leads to some-what higher total interest charges compared with the ten-year plan, still ensures the loans are paid off within ten years.

>> **Extended repayment:** Students who have more than $30,000 in eligible loans outstanding may repay them on a fixed payment or graduated repayment basis over a period of up to 25 years. Thus, total interest paid will be significantly higher than under the ten-year repayment plans.

>> **Revised pay as you earn repayment (REPAYE):** Under this plan, your monthly payments are annually set at 10 percent of your *discretionary income,* which is the difference between your annual income and 150 percent of the poverty guideline for your family size and state of residence. Payments are recalculated each year and based upon your updated income and family size (if you're married, your spouse's income and student loans are considered as well). Any undergraduate outstanding student loan balance will be forgiven if you haven't repaid your loan in full after 20 years.

>> **Pay as you earn repayment (PAYE):** For this plan, you must have a high debt relative to your income. Your monthly payment will never be more than the ten-year standard plan amount. The details of the annual payment reset are the same as under the REPAYE option.

>> **Income-based repayment (IBR):** This option is similar to PAYE except for the following differences. Your monthly payments will be either 10 or 15 percent of discretionary income, depending on when you received your first loans, but never more than you would have paid under the ten-year standard repayment plan. Any outstanding balance on your loan will be forgiven if you haven't repaid your loan in full after 20 years or 25 years, depending on when you received your first loans.

>> **Income-contingent repayment (ICR):** Your monthly payment will be the lesser of 20 percent of discretionary income or the amount you would pay on a repayment plan with a fixed payment over 12 years, adjusted according to your income. For this plan, discretionary income is the difference between your annual income and 100 percent of the poverty guideline for your family size and state of residence. Any outstanding balance will be forgiven if you haven't repaid your loan in full after 25 years.

>> **Income-sensitive repayment:** Your monthly payment is based on your annual income, but your loan will be paid in full within 15 years.

One more important detail: You aren't locked into a payment plan once you choose it. You can switch among the various repayment plan options as you are qualified to do so. It is possible but harder to negotiate a different repayment plan for private student loans.

There may be additional requirements to qualify for some of the repayment plans discussed in this section. For more information on federal student loan repayment options, visit https://studentaid.gov/manage-loans/repayment/plans.

Cautiously Considering Refinance Possibilities

The interest on each student loan, both federal and private, varies based upon when it is originated. Therefore, it is possible that by the time a student graduates and begins repayment, interest rates on newer, comparable loans may be lower. When that situation occurs, it may be possible to refinance some of your student loans with a private lender (see my short list later in this section) at a lower interest rate than you are currently paying on those loans.

TIP

When contemplating a refinance, always compare the interest rate being offered on a new loan to the rate you are paying on your existing student loans. If the rate is lower on a new loan that would provide you with funds to pay off some of your existing student loans, then you should consider refinancing. You also need to weigh and factor in any additional fees and charges — loan application fees, credit report fee, and so on — for a new loan you're considering.

There's a simple way any lender can make a refinance appear attractive that you should never fall for. They will show you how a refinance can lower your monthly payments — but that can always be done by offering you longer-term loans. Your total payments and total interest paid will be higher if you fall for this trick.

WARNING

Beware the hucksters out there pitching you to refinance your student loans or rub out problems like your late payments if you fork over a hefty up-front fee to them. As I explain in the next section, if you're behind in your payments, there are no-cost steps that you can take to address that with lenders and possibly get some relief.

You need excellent credit to be able to refinance student loans and do so at an attractive interest rate. One way to boost the creditworthiness of a young borrower with a limited credit history is to have parents cosign the loans. This, of course, puts the parents in a place of responsibility for the loans. If you'd like to look around, start with some of the proven players in this space like CommonBond, Credible, Earnest, and SoFi.

Asking for Relief

Hard times can happen, often without warning. Employers sometimes have to lay off workers. Or perhaps you have some significant unexpected expenses and you're having a hard time making your required monthly loan payments. There is some good news herein: You may qualify for some relief from making your federal student loan payments until you can afford to do so again.

There are two ways in which you may qualify for what is called "forbearance" of your federal student loans. There are two types of forbearance: general and mandatory. The following explanation, courtesy of `https://studentaid.gov`, details how it works.

With *general forbearance,* your federal student loan servicer decides whether to grant a request for forbearance. For this reason, a general forbearance is sometimes called a *discretionary forbearance.* You can request a general forbearance if you are temporarily unable to make your scheduled monthly loan payments for the following reasons:

>> Financial difficulties

>> Medical expenses

>> Change in employment

>> Other reasons acceptable to your loan servicer

General forbearances are available for Direct Loans, Federal Family Education (FFEL) Loan program, and Perkins Loans. For loans made under all three programs, a general forbearance may be granted for no more than 12 months at a time. If you're still experiencing a hardship when your current forbearance expires, you may request another general forbearance. However, there is a cumulative limit on general forbearances of three years.

If you meet the eligibility requirements for a *mandatory forbearance*, your loan servicer is required to grant the forbearance. (*Note:* The mandatory forbearances discussed in the following list apply only to Direct Loans and FFEL Program loans unless otherwise noted.) You may be eligible for a mandatory forbearance in the following circumstances:

>> **AmeriCorps:** You are serving in an AmeriCorps position for which you received a national service award.

>> **Department of Defense Student Loan Repayment Program:** You qualify for partial repayment of your loans under the U.S. Department of Defense Student Loan Repayment Program.

>> **Medical or dental internship or residency:** You are serving in a medical or dental internship or residency program, and you meet specific requirements.

>> **National Guard duty:** You are a member of the National Guard and have been activated by a governor, but you are not eligible for a military deferment.

>> **Student loan debt burden:** The total amount you owe each month for all the federal student loans you received is 20 percent or more of your total monthly gross income, for up to three years. (*Note:* This mandatory forbearance type applies to Direct Loans, FFEL Program loans, and Perkins Loans.)

>> **Teacher loan forgiveness:** You are performing teaching service that would qualify you for teacher loan forgiveness.

Mandatory forbearances may be granted for no more than 12 months at a time. If you continue to meet the eligibility requirements for the forbearance when your current forbearance period expires, you may request another mandatory forbearance.

REMEMBER

You *must* continue making payments on your student loan(s) until you have been notified that your request for forbearance has been granted. If you stop paying and your forbearance is not approved, your loan(s) will become delinquent and you may go into default.

Making Use of the Student Loan Interest Deduction

You may take up to a $2,500 federal income tax deduction for each tax (calender) year for student loan interest that you pay on IRS Form 1040 for college costs as long as your modified adjusted gross income (AGI) is less than or equal to $70,000 for single taxpayers and $140,000 for married couples filing jointly. This tax deduction is phased out if your AGI is between $70,000 and $85,000 for single taxpayers and between $140,000 and $170,000 for married couples filing jointly. (These AGI amounts are for tax year 2020.)

This deduction is not an itemized deduction, so anyone can take it on her Form 1040 as an "adjustment to income." Each of your lenders should be able to provide you with a yearly summary that shows how much you paid in interest for the tax year. If you paid $600 or more in interest to a single lender, that lender is required to provide you with Form 1098-E, which documents the interest you paid for the year. Otherwise, ask your lender or loan servicer what you paid in interest for the year in question.

Pausing Your Loans with a Return to Higher Education

Getting a college degree may not be the end of a person's higher education. Returning to school at least half-time enables those who have subsidized federal government student loans to hit the pause button on those loans. Remember that with subsidized federal student loans, interest does not accumulate, and no loan payments are due while the student is in school (again, at least half-time).

Private student loans and nonsubsidized federal student loans are, of course, a different matter. The interest keeps accumulating on those even if a former college graduate returns to school at least half-time. And, with some private student loans, you won't be able to defer making payments and will need to make payments regardless of your student status.

Index

W

Wells Fargo, apprenticeship program at, 119

Wintour, Anna (fashion designer), 14

Wolff, Rick (radio show host and author)

Coaching Kids For Dummies, 32

on discovering facts about scholarships, 34

Parenting Young Athletes the Ripken Way: Ensuring the Best Experience for Your Kids in Any S port, 33

work. *See* employment; job market

work-money connection, developing of, 46–49

work-study, 132, 152, 182, 183

Y

Yale University, Office of Career Strategy, 103

Yellowbrick, online program at, 121

Z

Zinmeister, Karl (author)

Almanac of American Philanthropy, 70

About the Author

Eric Tyson is a syndicated personal finance writer, lecturer, and counselor. He is dedicated to teaching people to manage their personal finances better. Eric is a former management consultant at Bain & Company to Fortune 500 financial service firms. Over the past three decades, he has successfully invested in securities as well as in real estate, started and managed several growing businesses, and earned a bachelor's degree in economics at Yale and an MBA at the Stanford Graduate School of Business.

An accomplished freelance personal finance writer, Eric is the author of four other national bestsellers in the *For Dummies* series, including *Personal Finance For Dummies, Investing For Dummies, Home Buying For Dummies,* and *Real Estate Investing For Dummies* (which he coauthored). Eric was an award-winning journalist for *The San Francisco Chronicle/Examiner.* His work has been featured and praised in hundreds of national and local publications, including *Kiplinger's, The Wall Street Journal, Money, Los Angeles Times, Chicago Tribune,* and on NBC's *Today Show,* Fox News, PBS's *Nightly Business Report,* Fox Business, CNBC, CNN, *The Oprah Winfrey Show,* ABC, Bloomberg Business Radio, CBS National Radio, and National Public Radio.

Eric has counseled thousands of clients on a variety of personal finance, investment, and real estate quandaries and questions and is a much sought-after speaker.

You can visit him on the web at www.erictyson.com.

Author's Acknowledgments

Numerous people at Wiley helped to make this book possible. They include senior acquisitions editor Tracy Boggier, development editor Linda Brandon, and copy editor Christine Pingleton! Thanks also to everyone else at Wiley who contributed to getting this book done and done right.

Thank you also to our brilliant technical reviewer, Shannon Vasconcelos of Bright Horizons, who helped ensure the completeness and accuracy of the content.

Publisher's Acknowledgments

Senior Acquisitions Editor: Tracy Boggier

Development Editor: Linda Brandon

Copy Editor: Christine Pingleton

Technical Editor: Shannon Vasconcelos, Director of College Finance for Bright Horizons College Coach

Production Editor: Siddique Shaik

Cover Image: © 3dfoto/Getty Images

Take dummies with you everywhere you go!

Whether you are excited about e-books, want more from the web, must have your mobile apps, or are swept up in social media, dummies makes everything easier.

Find us online!

dummies.com

Leverage the power

Dummies is the global leader in the reference category and one of the most trusted and highly regarded brands in the world. No longer just focused on books, customers now have access to the dummies content they need in the format they want. Together we'll craft a solution that engages your customers, stands out from the competition, and helps you meet your goals.

Advertising & Sponsorships

Connect with an engaged audience on a powerful multimedia site, and position your message alongside expert how-to content. Dummies.com is a one-stop shop for free, online information and know-how curated by a team of experts.

- Targeted ads
- Video
- Email Marketing
- Microsites
- Sweepstakes sponsorship

20 **MILLION** PAGE VIEWS **EVERY SINGLE MONTH**

15 MILLION **UNIQUE** VISITORS PER MONTH

43% OF ALL VISITORS ACCESS THE SITE **VIA THEIR MOBILE DEVICES**

700,000 NEWSLETTER SUBSCRIPTIONS **TO THE INBOXES OF** *300,000* UNIQUE **INDIVIDUALS EVERY WEEK**

# of dummies

PERSONAL ENRICHMENT

Staying Sharp
9781119187790
USA $26.00
CAN $31.99
UK £19.99

Facebook
9781119179030
USA $21.99
CAN $25.99
UK £16.99

Guitar
9781119293354
USA $24.99
CAN $29.99
UK £17.99

Investing
9781119293347
USA $22.99
CAN $27.99
UK £16.99

Beekeeping
9781119310068
USA $22.99
CAN $27.99
UK £16.99

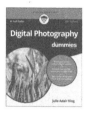
Digital Photography
9781119235606
USA $24.99
CAN $29.99
UK £17.99

Meditation
9781119251163
USA $24.99
CAN $29.99
UK £17.99

Pregnancy
9781119235491
USA $26.99
CAN $31.99
UK £19.99

Samsung Galaxy S7
9781119279952
USA $24.99
CAN $29.99
UK £17.99

iPhone
9781119283133
USA $24.99
CAN $29.99
UK £17.99

Crocheting
9781119287117
USA $24.99
CAN $29.99
UK £16.99

Nutrition
9781119130246
USA $22.99
CAN $27.99
UK £16.99

PROFESSIONAL DEVELOPMENT

Windows 10
9781119311041
USA $24.99
CAN $29.99
UK £17.99

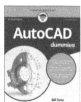
AutoCAD
9781119255796
USA $39.99
CAN $47.99
UK £27.99

Excel 2016
9781119293439
USA $26.99
CAN $31.99
UK £19.99

QuickBooks 2017
9781119281467
USA $26.99
CAN $31.99
UK £19.99

macOS Sierra
9781119280651
USA $29.99
CAN $35.99
UK £21.99

LinkedIn
9781119251132
USA $24.99
CAN $29.99
UK £17.99

Windows 10
9781119310563
USA $34.00
CAN $41.99
UK £24.99

SharePoint 2016
9781119181705
USA $29.99
CAN $35.99
UK £21.99

Fundamental Analysis
9781119263593
USA $26.99
CAN $31.99
UK £19.99

Networking
9781119257769
USA $29.99
CAN $35.99
UK £21.99

Office 2016
9781119293477
USA $26.99
CAN $31.99
UK £19.99

Office 365
9781119265313
USA $24.99
CAN $29.99
UK £17.99

Salesforce.com
9781119239314
USA $29.99
CAN $35.99
UK £21.99

Coding
9781119293323
USA $29.99
CAN $35.99
UK £21.99

dummies.com

dummies®
A Wiley Brand

Learning Made Easy

ACADEMIC

9781119293576
USA $19.99
CAN $23.99
UK £15.99

9781119293637
USA $19.99
CAN $23.99
UK £15.99

9781119293491
USA $19.99
CAN $23.99
UK £15.99

9781119293460
USA $19.99
CAN $23.99
UK £15.99

9781119293590
USA $19.99
CAN $23.99
UK £15.99

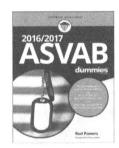

9781119215844
USA $26.99
CAN $31.99
UK £19.99

9781119293378
USA $22.99
CAN $27.99
UK £16.99

9781119293521
USA $19.99
CAN $23.99
UK £15.99

9781119239178
USA $18.99
CAN $22.99
UK £14.99

9781119263883
USA $26.99
CAN $31.99
UK £19.99

Available Everywhere Books Are Sold

Small books for big imaginations

9781119177173
USA $9.99
CAN $9.99
UK £8.99

9781119177272
USA $9.99
CAN $9.99
UK £8.99

9781119177241
USA $9.99
CAN $9.99
UK £8.99

9781119177210
USA $9.99
CAN $9.99
UK £8.99

9781119262657
USA $9.99
CAN $9.99
UK £6.99

9781119291336
USA $9.99
CAN $9.99
UK £6.99

9781119233527
USA $9.99
CAN $9.99
UK £6.99

9781119291220
USA $9.99
CAN $9.99
UK £6.99

9781119177302
USA $9.99
CAN $9.99
UK £8.99

Unleash Their Creativity

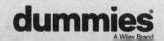